Lifestyle Gardening

This book is dedicated to
Joshua Coventry

COMHAIRLE CHONTAE CHORCAI
LIBRARY SERVICE RULES

1. Readers must return this book on or before the last date shown below.
2. Books are loaned for fourteen days and if kept beyond this time a fine will be charged.

Life

g

35 Longfield Road
Crookes
Sheffield
S10 1QW
England
www.karenplatt.co.uk

First Black Tulip Publishing edition in April 2007

British Library Cataloguing in Publication data.

Platt, Karen
ISBN: 978-0-9545764-6-2

Printed and bound in Singapore

Front cover image: © Hadrian Garden Design

Title Page: Lytes Cary Manor
Half Title Page: RHS Wisley
Page 3 Imperial Garden, Tokyo
This page: Japanese Tea Garden, San Francisco

Other titles by Karen Platt
- Black Magic and Purple Passion
- Gold Fever
- Silver Lining
- Seed Sowing and Growing Success
- Plant Synonyms

For future releases please visit
www.karenplatt.co.uk

See also a complete range of lifestyle products on the
website, from furniture to photographs and cards

The International Black Plant Society founded by Karen
Platt exists to promote black plants. To join, visit
www.blackplants.co.uk

Contents

Introduction

What is lifestyle gardening? The term defines gardening to suit your needs and the pressures of modern living, taking into account your surroundings and thinking about the planet.

Gardening is about choices. If you are led by design, influenced by needs, environment, practicality and function, the garden will reflect your lifestyle. Merge your home and garden whether you elect to be traditional, to embrace the old and the new, or to be ultra-modern.

Today we are faced with more choice than ever and it is important to plan the garden thereby avoiding a bitty look of things gathered over the years without rhyme or reason. Although there is much more available to us, much is of a muchness. Sameness is not sanity but a kind of madness in which imagination and creativity do not exist. Gardens should be personal, imaginative and practical. They should be inspiring; raise the spirit and touch the soul as well as offering a refuge from the demands of modern life. The garden should express the personality of its owner in a given time and place.

Some bemoan the loss of a leading style in late 20th century gardens; a century that also saw an unprecedented number of garden restorations. Gardens change slowly and with them our ideas of design and purpose change too. Of course, there is nothing wrong with tradition; ideas are borrowed from the past, reshaped, reformed and brought to life again in modern interpretation. Every original idea has a root in the past. The 21st century is an exciting time to garden, with no leading style; we can each follow our own ideas and set our own goals. New ground is being broken all the time.

This book is for all who love gardens, plants and design wherever they garden. It includes the principles of garden design in simple steps combined with the individuality of garden style and the spirit of great gardens from around the world.

It provides inspirational ideas, professional tips, options and solutions and guidance to create a unique and personal space.

This book is for all those starting a garden from scratch or altering an existing garden space for whatever reason. It enables you to design your own garden or discuss it knowledgeably with a garden designer. At some point in our lives, downsizing home and garden often becomes a necessity; our lifestyles alter. At a certain age, or through illness, we become less able to cope. I myself have had three lifestyle changes; my garden evolving each time.

This book helps you decide what you want in terms of style or mood. Plentiful examples of gardens small and large offer inspiration. It is a design and style source book that looks at all aspects of garden design and the materials you need to create an harmonious garden.

Writing this book has been a pleasure, explaining the spirit and core of gardens I love and my involvement with plants and design and above all my love of nature. I trust that you will derive as much pleasure from reading the book and that it helps you to find a satisfactory solution to your own garden.

An oasis of calm is necessary to my being, a reflection of my soul - this I find in a garden. I urge you to garden like a poet.

Dale Chihuly glass sculpture

Using this book

My aim is to help you find a unique solution. Look at your garden afresh and imagine a lifestyle garden. Experiment with new ways to make your garden a low maintenance, easy-to-use outdoor space

The book is divided into five sections: planning, inspiration, designing, garden elements and the future of gardening. Each section will help you discover exactly what it is you want from your garden and the resources section will help you achieve the look.

In section one the distinction between formal and informal style is outlined. Examine your reasons for creating a garden as you are presented with options and solutions.

There is much inspiration found in section two. Each style from medieval through to the 21st century is described with its own unique elements in both hard and softscaping explained.

In section three garden design is discussed enabling you to follow the key principles and understand the process.

In section four each garden element is defined so that you can make choices to design the garden as a whole, with each of your chosen elements bringing unity. In this section you wil find over 200 easy to maintain plants.

In the final section I talk about the future of gardening and how to bring your garden into the 21st century and live in harmony with nature.

The text is amplified by abundant illustrations of gardens from the U.K and around the world that typify each style. Lastly is the source book. I urge you to visit as many open gardens as you can. In addition thcrc is a list of suppliers to help you source elements for the garden.

Note: I have coined the phrases hardscaping and softscaping, I prefer that to hard and soft landscaping.

Herbaceous border at RHS Wisley

Inspiration and ideas can be found at the flower shows and in gardens around the world. Above a design from Philip Nash at the RHS Chelsea Flower Show.
Next page: A Garden of Contrasts by Dizzy Shoemark at RHS Wisley

Planning

Options

Let's take a look at options, choices and solutions to create your ideal garden. Before you design there are multiple considerations to take into account - the site, style, your needs and the purpose of the garden. Assess the space and decide exactly what you want. Look at what has gone before, what is happening now, where is gardening going?

Reasons to create a garden
Gardens are multi-faceted having many reasons for being. Many see them as pure enjoyment and something beautiful to gaze upon. Whatever the reason, make sure you use that outdoor space.

We all need extra room and fresh air. On the face of it, reason enough to create a garden. But for many of us, it goes skin deep, deeper than that, it comes from the soul, this yearning. I cannot imagine living without a garden of some sort; for me gardening seems to be inborn. An outdoor room is essential. I remember being struck by this idea on my first visit to Spain, where owing to the climate people live outdoors much more. I have known garden writers and workers in the industry who do not have a garden. I have known people with beautiful gardens who never get their own hands dirty. I know many plant enthusiasts; I myself have a collection of black plants. Yet a garden is so much more than just plants. Follow your dream; use that space to create a place that enhances your lifestyle. There is immense satisfaction to be derived from creating a garden.

As a reflection of your personality the garden is a place to explore your own creativity. Let your imagination run loose injecting a little magic into the garden. At **Whitehurst's Garden** there is a wonderful, ornate spiral staircase that leads to a walk through the treetops. The Treehouse at **Alnwick Castle Garden** is magical. Explore your inner self. Get creative.

Gardens mean many things to many people. Created for survival, to grow food, for religious reasons, as status symbols or to shock and simply for recreational purposes - the garden wears many hats. Gardens have existed since time immemorial with different types evolving the world over in response to their surroundings and the different needs of their creators.

If we listen to market forecasters, gardening is perhaps no longer the buzzword. I personally feel that is false. Gardening has changed; the market has changed. Who wants to toil in the soil? Few want to spend back-breaking hours in the garden. The emphasis has shifted; the doing was the enjoyment, now the relaxation is the enjoyment. People are taking a pride in their outdoor space.

Chartered surveyors and estate agents (realtors) purport that a well-designed garden is considered to add to the value of a property by as much as at least 5 % the total value of the house. Property owners now realize that they can have an extra outdoor room to enjoy that is also a worthwhile investment. Many rented houses in England have decent-sized back gardens; use that space to enhance your lifestyle.

The physical and mental benefits of gardening have been promoted since early times. It is simply great to be outdoors. For some a walk around a garden is uplifting, for others getting their hands dirty is akin to cleansing the soul. The garden is a place to paint, study or simply chill.

From a practical point of view, plants can be used to encourage wildlife into the garden. Plants can control soil erosion and fight atmospheric and noise pollution. They can provide you with shade or food. Scented plants have pleasing aromas, relaxing, uplifting or calming.

All gardens, large or small, have a reason for being, a purpose and this is the starting point of a design. Discover what you really want. Make a list of what you want to use your garden for, and what you need in it. You might be creating a garden from scratch on a new plot, transforming your existing garden or wish to make the garden less demanding on your time. It might simply be the desire for something different, a new garden that reflects the new you. You might have to live without some of the things on your wish list, but at least you will not miss anything out if you think it through carefully and write it down. At this stage, take a good look at your garden from all viewpoints - an empty space with a view. Visualize your new space. Before we look at how to create a garden, I cannot emphasize enough how important it is to make plans, to thoroughly prepare and to learn all about gardening that you possibly can. Focus on the space you are going to transform.

Your space

Look at your space as a reason to create a unique garden that says something about you, reflects the inner you. In this space you can be yourself

The most loved gardens in the world, considered the crème de la crème, are those that have a sense of belonging. They fit into their space utilizing a given area perfectly by connecting with the surroundings and usually, but not always, with the home around which they are built. When the garden is right, it just clicks. The Italian gardens built on terraces, the French Baroque gardens, the English landscape gardens and the Japanese style are all examples of gardens that are perfectly adapted to their surroundings. They look best in their original settings; transferred to another time and place, something is lost.

Individuality is diminishing as we find the same old stores with the same old goods on offer. Look inwards at your own personality to create a personal space just for you.

The garden is your oyster, dream on. The limitation of the plot is what most people talk about, however, let's employ positive thinking and turn that on its head. Limitation is a daunting word. All negative aspects have a positive side.

Whatever the shape and size, plan and maximize the potential space by thinking ahead. Is the space overlooked and is privacy a factor? What can you get from your space? Think about how to divide it up to get the most from your garden. Section off the service areas and then decide what you want. Take care not to divide the plot into equal parts but to make areas of differing sizes rendering the space much more intriguing. Fluidity is important. There is no need to use every bit of space; empty areas can balance busy areas. Retain simplicity and strive for an uncluttered look. Spaces can be enclosed or open. They can exhibit a flow of materials or a change in pattern.

What you choose sets the tone of the garden with its distinctive style. Make sure you tick the right boxes and can live with it. Some things look good for a few hours, others for a lifetime. Remember, you cannot have everything, unless your garden is vast and there are no limits. Include the necessities first, the luxuries if the budget allows for them. Denial is good for the soul.

Function

The garden is multi-functional; its function may alter with the years as your needs and personality change

For most this is an easy decision. You know exactly what you want. What best suits your needs; it might be a place to relax, entertain, dream, play, talk or work. What is your idea of a garden? Think of each individual that will use the garden and their needs. When will you use the garden, weekends only or in the evenings? Are you at home most of the time or do you spend much time away from home? What makes you happy? Will children be happy with a sandpit or tree house or do you really need a football field in the back yard? Will you actively garden – growing vegetables and plants or do you just want minimal evergreens to look neat? Will you sit, dine or want to lie down and sunbathe?

Treat the garden as a simple space like any room of the house and decide its function to reach a solution. Once you know what you want to do in the garden and how you want to use the space, you can move forward.

Think carefully about how you allot space by first exploring all possibilities. Reflect on your lifestyle not the restrictions of the plot or your budget. Live with the space and get to know it intimately. How does it look in winter? Where would you take advantage of, or refuge from summer sun? Once you know the site thoroughly, you can use it to its full potential.

You don't have to conform but be definite about what you want to create. There are plenty of choices. You can still have your plants and eat them or at least enjoy them. This is very much about fitting in what you want where it looks good. Modern lifestyles leave little time for relaxation and your garden, carefully planned, can provide the ultimate space to chill out.

Once you have the answers, then it is time to look at the costs involved. Explore alternatives applicable to your budget. If one idea turns out too expensive, look at different materials. Moving earth and stonework are the most costly aspect. Calculate the work involved and be realistic about how much work you wish to do, initially and in maintenance. First, let's look at some options.

The mood

Capture your own mood and that of the surroundings and create a sense of belonging, a sense of place

Interior design is far more controlled than garden design. In the latter you can control the hardscaping but to get the softscaping effect you want from plants requires much more skill. Gardening is the manipulation of nature, in such a way as to appear natural. Use it to express a mood; reflect your character by creating an atmosphere. The successful garden consists of the interplay of many elements some of which you will find easier to control and use than others. Create a mood by using different components of the garden to make one whole. Use a palette board to ensure harmony of materials not only with regard to colour, but also texture. Colour is a chief factor in setting mood and if you have not already read them, my books on garden colour are extremely useful. Colour is found in all aspects of the garden not just the plants. It has the power to warm up a space or cool it down, so too wood is considered warm and metal cool. In this way colour and materials work in harmony. Chosen materials can also affect the look of a garden in terms of modern or otherwise.

It is so easy for gardens to become dull, a square of grass and a few bedding plants; roses planted alone; unimaginative planting and plants that do not really work together. Follow your intuition and your chosen style or theme, tying everything together.

Be bold, exciting and stylish. You can conjure an aura of mystery with a secret or magical garden. A calming oasis to de-stress, the ultimate in relaxation with almost the same powers as a vacation to rest the soul and mind. Such gardens are uncluttered and feed the soul as much as the eye. The garden can be a showpiece to impress your friends or a space where you shut yourself off from the world - a refuge. The garden is capable of arousing the senses or lull them to sleep. It can be outrageous, as the mood takes you. It can be dynamic, lively and energetic for the partygoer as an entertaining space. Enliven the garden with strings of bright lights, bright colour and unusual furniture. It can be a quiet zone, a space to breathe, with seating, cushions, soft candlelight. The garden can be anything you want.

Style solutions

The very essence of your style is what makes you tick, what helps you relax, what do you relate to?

You might not find the solution in a pre-arranged style. This is all about expressing yourself. Gardens are a personal reflection of the owner's character. Style is a very personal matter and although there might be unwritten rules, which vary from gardener to gardener and from designer to designer, basically it's what you want that matters. In striving for a workable garden, one that pleases the heart and the eye, it is best to stick to just one representation, especially in a small town garden. This is why the town garden has become the domain of contemporary style. In a larger garden, one can get away with different styles by splitting the garden into rooms. It helps to bring the garden together if you have one vision that you follow through, as long as you express the style in an individual way. As a general rule, it's difficult to mix styles, so you have to decide at the beginning. A cottage style border and tropical bonanza look at odds together. Yet sometimes it is hard to forego a favourite feature or beloved plant. No room for soft-hearted sentimental feelings, be strict, elements that do not fit, have to go.

Gardens are an outdoor room, an extension of the home. This is not a new idea; even the Egyptians planned garden and home as one. The operative words are harmony and balance. Today, we have so much more choice in materials not to mention plants. The garden can of course contrast with the house, but it is more natural for it to be an extension of the house itself and match the architecture. A modernist garden would look at odds with a 16th century cottage yet contemporary style can work with many buildings from the past. The house can often suggest the style of garden. A 1920's house is a must for an Arts and Crafts style garden.

Garden themes must be followed through to be effective and can dictate the type of plants, furniture and style - formal or otherwise of the garden. A Gothic garden uses arches, gothic furniture and dark plants to complete the effect. Styles often suggest the plants that can be used. According to the limitation of your soil, aspect and palette the vast choice of plants is gradually narrowed down.

Formal or Informal

Which style suits you? This section is all about choices and solutions. Read through each style until you find the one that best fits your needs and suits the style of your home. If you have a period property this is easily achieved by matching dates. You are then faced with the choice of slavishly copying a traditional style or trying to inject a little bit of yourself into it and coming up with a unique solution for your garden. Modern properties have a much wider choice as there is no overriding, predominant style so choose something that suits their character. If the plot itself or the architecture of the house does not immediately suggest a style to you, consider your options carefully. The house might determine the building materials to be used. Opt for a style that fits in with the surroundings and satisfies your needs. Keep clippings from magazines and follow an idea through. Remember that once you have made your decision all parts of the garden and all its elements must adhere to one style.

To simplify your ideas into a cohesive, working plan use the style key elements for each garden style, the inspiration and resources at the end of the book.

Below: Hadrian Garden Design

The initial choice in style is either formal or informal although each embraces a much wider range of options. Many gardens actually contain elements from both styles. The classic formal style is mathematically precise, symmetrical and possesses a beauty all of its own. The flamboyance of informal gardens appeals to the romantic or even unruly side of our nature, though the style is not in itself wild. Pioneered by great English designers like William Robinson or Gertrude Jekyll, the cottage garden has endured. Whereas formal gardens can appeal to those who do not really like plants, especially in its modern forms of minimalism, the cottage garden, crammed with plants is definitely for the plant lover. The informal style is not always cottage-garden, but emulates its principles.

The Natural style mimics nature and is a fluid style often with native or wild plants. Until the beginning of the 20th century, formal style ruled. In the 20's and 30's, the Bauhaus movement was formed in Germany. Bauhaus designers broke the formal mould and stretched the boundaries. Outside space became a 'room'. The Minimalist movement has its roots in Modernism, but often without the aesthetics. It's 'the room stripped bare' look, often cold and clinical. Deconstructivist gardens are often not recognized as gardens at all; here plants have a secondary role if any.

Formal gardens

Entering a yew enclosure, surrounded by green texture, one feels as if the whole world is a garden

Being orderly, manicured and clean looking, formal gardens suit extremely tidy people. Simple they may look, yet on a large scale, it takes devotion and much hard work to keep those straight lines clipped to perfection. The advent of power tools for hedge cutting has lessened the daunting task especially in a small garden. Yet topiary still requires clipping by hand.

In the formal garden, the entrance is usually central affording balance and symmetry. Straight lines of symmetry bisect one another to create divisions or even garden rooms. It is easiest to create this sort of garden in long rectangular spaces, often with a change of level - a sunken garden or terrace. A flat surface is adaptable as is a hillside. Due north or due south gardens are ideal, if the garden lies east-west then part of the garden will always be in shade which affects the plants that can be grown successfully. In this situation, it is better to employ an asymmetrical design, working from corner to corner, diagonally across the plot.

Planting is restrained with evergreens forming the backbone of quiet, green elegance exuded by formal gardens. Closely clipped hedging defines the symmetrical layout, which often contains nothing more than topiary. Dense plants are clipped into fantastic miniature or giant forms; geometric shapes rule. Vertical elements in topiary or stone include cones, spheres and pyramids that are regularly spaced providing rhythm in shape and colour. Balance, repetition and proportion is supreme. Plants are normally laid out in a line, often with just one plant species used. Pyramids, cones or lollipop topiaries may be used at the four corners of a square, or where two paths cross.

Whilst providing continuity, for a real plantsperson, it is often not enough to satisfy plant lust. Yet one has to admire the structure and geometry, the exquisite shapes, straight lines relieved by topiary, stilt hedges, a solid hedge with a window offering a glimpse of what lies beyond. The style is dignified; the structured evergreens easily pass the test of winter.

Interesting silhouettes are found in crenellated yew hedges and topiary balls or spirals. Terraces or steps are often lined with cypress evoking an Italianate air. Other features include sunken areas, wide stone or marble steps, grottoes and fountains.

Crisp geometrical surfacing with clean lines and angles are found in the formal garden. Enhance outlines with edging and kerbs in contrasting materials. Allowing plants to tumble and adorn the walls introduces an element of luxurious planting to soften the plain stone, brick or wood, which forms the backbone of the hardscaping. Natural stone suits the formal garden, whether smooth or textured. Paths are often made with setts or brick, in a straight or horizontal pattern or gravel.

Long walks usually end with a focal point in the form of a well-placed statue or urn. Long allées guide the eye to that all-important piece of sculpture. Think of the great gardens of the Renaissance and Baroque with classical statues of gods and goddesses at every turn. In a period garden opt for classical ornament leading the eye along a row of statues or one sculpture used as a focal point. In the modern garden such grandiose ornament is dispensed with in favour of something more contemporary that is still at one with the formal garden.

Once the province of grand houses, the classical garden led to garden rooms and formality has been transformed in contemporary gardens. Few can aspire to that most appropriate background for the classical formal garden as it looks best in a landscape park setting. There has to be a vista; it looks entirely wrong with a view of the neighbour's garage. The formal garden of the past, to show off one's riches, is defunct nowadays. Although one can replicate the past, it is not always satisfactory to do so. Adaptation and creativity are much preferred. The modern formal garden works in an enclosed space. The principles translate well to small spaces and can be successful in the town garden as exemplified in much contemporary style. Many feel secure and safe with formal style. To match minimalist buildings, the formal garden often consists of no more than a few species simply repeated in straight lines. Enclose the garden with high walls or allow a view of the surrounding landscape.

The modern formal garden and its exponents embrace the style whilst having a firm eye on the future. Their designs are distinctive, influenced by but not stuck in the past. Wirtz and Caruncho have different approaches but both work with nature bringing the landscape closer to the garden. A designer who understands the past, the history and essence of the place, can break new ground when working with nature. Wirtz designed the **Alnwick Garden**. An important feature of the Wirtz design team is a strong unifying green backbone.

The structure and backbone of the formal garden has survived to grace many modern gardens often with the embellishment of quiet perennials. To bring the formal garden up-to-date, especially in smaller gardens, try repeat plants such as lollipop topiaries. Modern formality embraces plants with architectural form. Formal gardens are essentially green, but one can modernize and introduce colour in the enclosed formal garden. Try golden-leaved *Taxus* (yew), blue-leaved *Juniperus* or dramatic *Fagus sylvatica Purpurea Group*, purple beech hedges turning rich caramel or variegated box. Be aware that to alter the colour of the plants in a classical Italian garden would detract from the overall effect and the suggestions here are best used in a modern garden.

Informal gardens

If the symmetry and rigidity of the formal garden is not for you, try a looser, informal style. Freer of spirit, with relaxed planting, the informal garden has one foot firmly in the cottage garden style. It is a riot of colour provided by foliage and flowers in sweeping curves without symmetry but with balance and movement. Even plants thought of as static have movement when planted in a serpentine line. Perennials form the basis of planting and mixed borders are fine. Colours can be jumbled or themed. Empty gaps are quickly filled with potted plants or brightly-coloured annuals. Planting is fluid and abundant with certain plants adding structure such as *Melianthus, Phormium* (New Zealand flax) or tall grasses such as *Stipa gigantea* (golden oats). This relaxed effect is often the most time-consuming method. Interest is maintained over a long season and there is much work to be done. The effects are stunning but this is gardening for real garden lovers who want to get their hands dirty on a regular basis. The informal garden contains structures made from natural materials. Although it is a loose style, it is often enclosed within a formal framework.

It is ideal for plots that are irregular in shape or on uneven plots of land. In the town or city, it would be necessary to disguise the boundaries whereas in the countryside, the informal garden can blend into the landscape. The smaller town garden struggles with the size of borders needed for a full-blown effect and has to make do with smaller, scaled-down borders and is better with raised beds. Try smaller perennials and add height with climbers. The informal garden evokes a relaxed atmosphere where you can forget your worries and enjoy the beauty of plants.

Mellow stone such as York stone suits the informal garden. Elaborate patterns with setts or cobbles are often featured in ultra contemporary gardens to offset the starkness of materials and lack of planting. Styling can link seamlessly with buildings, the flooring being similar to that of the walls of the building. Wood fits in nicely or wrought iron furniture.

At Veddw in Wales, the formal hedging is imbued with character, undulating and green

Combination gardens

Many gardens fall between the two styles, borrowing the informal approach to planting within a more formal structure so that total anarchy does not reign. Many modern gardens have geometry in hardscaping and informal plantings. This adaptation is ideal for the gardener who loves fresh air and relaxation, but hates the idea of getting the shears, secateurs or lawnmower out every week. It particularly suits small, town gardens. For the busy gardener, contemporary formality offers an ordered space in which you can relax. Many gardens, such as that at **Plas Newydd** and **Bodnant** in Wales, adopt a formal scheme close to the house, with an informal area further away, at the bottom of the garden. **Hinton Ampner,** nr Alresford, Hants is a superb mix of the two styles, with a formal layout enhanced by informal planting and using magnificent vistas of the surrounding countryside.

A balance between the styles, neither too formal nor informal is often best. I recently visited a garden open to the public on a garden tour, an unscheduled stop. When the tour guide asked my opinion of it, I stated that it was too informal. He replied that he had never heard that criticism, and that he had frequently heard the opposite that gardens were often too formal. Formality appeals to the person who wants to control nature to a certain extent, but the other side of the coin is a garden without any structure and plants plonked anyhow. To my trained eye, the garden had no rhyme or reason. There were no lines, no focal points and no order. The owner had fallen into the trap of buying plants willy-nilly and sticking them anywhere. The garden had obviously not been planned. The informal style is most attractive but still requires skill in the selection and placement of plants.

Top: The formal layout at Sissinghurst by Sir Harold Nicholson is a masterpiece of structure, luxuriantly planted in Vita Sackville-West's informal style
Bottom: The formal topiary at Castle Howard contrasts with the one colour Antirrhinum (snapdragon) infilling and the Delphinium border in the background
Next page: A Japanese inspired planting, Keukenhof

Inspiration

Sources of Inspiration

If you have no ideas on garden design and wish to use a garden designer, you will find that their first task is to tap into your lifestyle, asking questions about you and your life. However, if you are happy to dabble, you need a starting point. You have already considered your reasons for wanting a garden but you need a springboard to get the ideas flowing.

Inspiration can be found in everything and anything. Your starting point is to see all the possibilities. A garden is a means of expression. My own garden is a small but useful place to explore plants, their behaviour and relationship to one another, hardiness and so on.

Some professionals use mood boards; others create mini scale models like architects. If you are unsure, these will help you focus on what works for you. Mood boards are a collection of ideas exploring different themes. Building a model allows you to get the feel for the space. Pin all the ideas associated with a design or a proposal for a planted area on a large board. Consider a design file or book to keep everything together. In this way, you can contrast and compare styles and ideas, materials and suppliers. Send for brochures for flooring, fencing, seeds, plants and enjoy the process.

Inspiration from the RHS Chelsea Flower Show

Flower shows

Although I have designed show gardens in the USA and two exhibits at the Chelsea Flower Show for the International Black Plant Society, one has to admit that shows are a false arena often displaying totally impractical designs. Stick a huge orange paper elephant in a Thai tropical garden and win a gold medal. My inspiration for the two show gardens in San Francisco and Seattle was taken from circles. One judge suggested that since the theme was black plants, I could have had a burnt out car or melted hairdryers; which begged the question exactly what have they to do with gardening? The English shows are more grounded but show gardens are just that, use them as inspiration not as actual gardens you can copy. Show gardens are created to win an award, to shock, to show expensive innovations. They are a good place to see contemporary style in action. Chelsea is still the cream of the crop but shows occur the world over.

Without visiting flower shows or festivals, the gardener has many other sources to offer inspiration. Take nature – I love green hills, blue skies, trees, lakes, big flowers and big leaves. The objects and shapes in nature are all you need to get you going; to trigger a train of thought. Think out of the box. Whilst your inspiration might well come from something garden-related, it could equally be non-garden related. View things from different angles, play games of association and see where the inspiration leads. Be open to new ideas. Try not to rush this process.

You may be an avid gardener with definite ideas or perhaps you have never owned a garden before. Get into the habit of carrying a notebook and jotting down ideas. Jot down all ideas you associate with the initial theme. Use cut-outs from magazines, sketches and words to develop each theme. Look out for all aspects of the garden not just plant ideas. Concentrate on the things you find tricky, like the change in level or a shady corner and collect all you can to build a complete picture in your mind of what is possible. Explore the idea fully and decide how to proceed. It is much easier with the advent of the internet to search for materials related to your concept.

Use your site to inspire you. A slope lends itself to terraces or decking, dramatic waterfalls or steps whilst a flat site is suitable for a formal garden. An odd shape is easily adapted to an informal style.

Developing a Style

Themes can arise from a particular country such as an American prairie garden, an English wildflower garden, an Italianate garden or a style connected to a feature such as a rock or water garden although the latter is usually just one part of the whole. The style might be suggested by a collection of plants, for example *Primula auricula,* that you might wish to house in an Auricula theatre which in turn might lead you to develop a Victorian garden. Think about your lifestyle and the kind of garden you need to create. Visit as many gardens as possible. Once you have made your decision, do not veer from your chosen course.

The Japanese garden

You might wish to create a Japanese garden as many have done already. You could start by looking at what has been done and then make a list with or without photographs of the key elements involved, deciding which ones you would like to include.

Let's take a closer look at creating a Japanese garden. Japanese gardens are a true art form, designed to be viewed from certain vantage points. Bound by tradition and religion, everything has a meaning. Miniature trees and flowers represent truth; stone is the strength of nature and bamboo screens and soft mosses represent delicacy. Japanese gardens evoke tranquility being havens of peace for contemplation. As such they are at odds with the Western view of the garden as an outdoor room and a place to play and entertain. The plantings are simple but very effective. Chosen plants are limited and their positioning creates harmony within the allotted space. Simplicity, clean lines, balance and placement of objects are paramount. Practice restraint. Texture is important as is the choice of plants. Materials are limited too; this brings the garden together as a whole natural landscape. In traditional gardens, every element is imbued with its own significance and symbolism. In the West, we cannot emulate the philosophical or religious meaning yet many people opt for the Japanese style to create a harmonious, peaceful atmosphere. The predominant colour is green with Japanese maples providing some colour with their fabulous foliage in plum or gold, not to mention their autumn colours.

The formal Japanese garden is not like formal Western gardens. It does not use symmetry as in the West. Yet, the Japanese style is one of the most favoured styles with many interpretations found outside Japan. Anyone who has visited several of these gardens outside Japan, soon realizes that they vary a great deal, some more true to the style than others. There is nothing wrong with interpretation, but there is nothing like the real thing, baby. See as many gardens as you can in anyway possible, in person, through books or the Internet, magazine articles or photos. Some elements of the garden can be adapted to small spaces, but to fit in all areas would take a large garden. It is possible to create a Japanese-style garden in a small space.

There are many elements associated with this style. Gardens rely on the skill of the designer to arrange components so that in a very limited space the illusion of a grand, natural landscape is achieved. Gardens are much more at one with nature than the forced style of the Western garden. Crisp lines are usually not in evidence; instead zig-zag paths offer a sequence of views. The focal point is not mere ornament but the representation of the natural world. Japanese gardens are not divided up into rooms being one complete unit. Often they are entirely enclosed and not at one with the outside world, the exception to this is *shakkei*, the principle of borrowed scenery. Plants are usually common evergreens as gardens are meant for solitude and meditation. They are restrained not showy. Pines are trained and pruned to maintain the required size. Shrubs are pruned into rounded forms. The gardens evoke the beauty of the natural world, the very essence of nature. Mounds of earth become mountains whilst ponds represent oceans.

There are different types of Japanese garden – the 'hill garden' known as *tsukiyama* and the 'waterless stream garden' or 'dry garden' known as '*karesansui*'. The hill garden features a hill representing a mountain, pond and stream, shrubs and plants. It is viewed from vantage points along a path. In Kyoto both **Tenryuji** and **Salhoji Temples** are good examples of the hill garden which was most popular during the Edo Period. A popular type of hill garden is the tortoise and crane garden, featuring two favoured animals representing long life and happiness, on separate islands.

In the dry garden, rocks and sand are the main elements. The sand raked into furrows represents the sea and its movements, the rocks its waterfalls. The gardens are associated with Zen Buddhism that began in China. Plants are of very little importance and often not represented at all. The garden is often viewed from a single seated perspective, like looking at a painting. The first one created in Japan is credited to the **Kenchoji Temple** in Kamakura. Also in Kyoto, **Ryoanji** and **Daitokuji Temples** are excellent examples of dry gardens. In the 14th century the introduction of the tea ceremony, the *chaniwa* with a garden attached to the tea house, came into being. Stepping stones led to the tea house, the garden often no more than a path. This type of garden also features stone lanterns and stone water basins, *tsukabai*, where guests would cleanse their hands before taking part in the tea ceremony. Stone basins are often coin-shaped. The tea gardens are not usually open to the public.

Japanese garden elements

A bamboo boundary encloses the garden in a natural material. A symbolic gateway leads into the garden. The Japanese garden is usually inward-looking, a complete representation of nature without the interference of the outside world. A zigzag path leads from the gateway, never taking a straight line, to avoid evil spirits entering the garden.

Within the garden, the tea house represents a place of quiet contemplation far away from the intrusion of the world. Stepping stones are associated with the path to the tea house. Lanterns made from stone, often hand-carved, granite or iron are found on the way to the tea house. They may be low or tall. Their function is ceremonial. Another building often constructed is the pavilion providing one of the many places offering a set view, usually with a viewing platform.

Structures consist of one or more bridges used as viewing points. Like the path, a zig-zag bridge prevents evil spirits from crossing. The drum-shaped bridge is a curious feature. Small sculptures or shrines represent deities such as Buddha or spirits.

Right: The Zen garden at the Japanese Tea Garden, San Francisco
Previous page: Kyoto Japanese Garden, London

Rocks are used to create natural sculpture, they symbolize calm, timelessness and stability. They represent strength, endurance and character, the anchor of the garden. Their placement is crucial. Each rock has its own character, tone and value and is chosen with immense care , as a symbol of security.

Used in the dry garden, the sand or gravel is raked daily into a special design. It symbolizes water

Natural looking streams or waterfalls with no muddy banks have clear, pure water. Water is used to symbolize the passage of time, renewal and continuity. The waterfall expresses the mountain valley, soothing music to quiet the soul. Koi are often found in ponds symbolizing life, strength and perseverance. Bamboo water features, such as the deer scarer are also included.

A benched seating area is most often found in modern gardens. Simple, straight granite or wood benches offer viewing points, a quiet spot for contemplation.

Wind chimes or rain chains are hung from pavilions, they add sound to the garden. They might look simply decorative but were used to collect rainwater for use by the household.

Materials used in the Japanese garden include, wood, bamboo, stone and gravel. Nothing jars, everything fits in a natural style.

Above and bottom right: The Japanese Tea Garden, San Francisco
Top right: The Japanese Garden, Pine Lodge, Cornwall
Bottom left: The Japanese Garden, Tatton Park, Chesire

Japanese garden plants

Serene green is the colour of the Japanese garden. The art of Japanese gardening where plants are concerned is your skill in pruning. Shrubs are neat rounded forms, pines in particular take great skill to achieve the correct form. Foliage is of chief importance, with flowers taking a subsidiary role. Secondary colour comes from maple leaves, bark and some flowers. Plant texture is also provided by bark, and by grasses and moss. Plants are used to express emotions with trees trained to represent the wind. A part of the garden may be dedicated to the art of bonsai. Ferns and mosses also take their place in the garden enhancing the look. Often seen in Japanese gardens in the West, the flowering cherry is not a traditional Japanese garden plant.

Acer

Although many Japanese maples used in the garden are green, the golden **A. shiraswanum** 'Aureum' and several red-leaved cultivars are often found in the predominantly green landscape. The **Dissectum Group** offers lacy foliage, exquisitely fine with a pendulous habit, forming a dome shape. They grow happily in containers, where they will not reach the 3m (10ft) they would in open ground. Even green maples offer autumn colours setting the garden aflame with a flamboyant show in what is otherwise a restrained atmosphere. Trees or shrubs are pruned often and lightly. All *Acers* are best in filtered light out of cold winds. 6m (20ft). Z5.

Camellia

A stunning show of bright pink to red or white blooms to cheer the mid-winter garden along with evergreen, glossy leaves. *Camellias* enjoy a sheltered position in dappled shade so they are happy beneath the light canopy of trees. A west-facing aspect is ideal in well-drained neutral to acid soil. On chalky soils grow camellias in pots of ericaceous compost. Plants are not tolerant of drought. After flowering, prune to keep in shape, before any growth begins. Flowers can be single, semi-double or double. Their growth rate is rather slow, about 30cm (1ft) a year 2m (8ft) in 10 years. **C. 'Carolyn Willams'** is a showy pink with flattish flowers. **C. 'Caerhays'** is a double purplish pink. There is a National Collection of plants at Mount Edgcumbe, see the Period Gardens section. The U.S. National Arboretum also has a collection. Z6b.

Chyrsanthemum

Revered in Japan, the white **Chrysanthemum x grandiflorum** (morifolium), known as *shiragiku* represents the Imperial family. The chrysanthemum is the crest of the Emperor of Japan. It is known as *kiku* and many *kiku* festivals are held in autumn (fall). The Japanese particularly favour the spider group. They were first grown in the Saga Imperial Villa in the 9th century and are known as *saga-giku*. At the festivals plants are displayed in many innovative ways. In the UK, they are best grown in a cold greenhouse. When 15-20cm (6-8") tall they should be pinched out to encourage branching. After flowering they can be cut back to 23cm (9") and over-wintered almost dry. 40cm (16") or more. Z5.

Hydrangea

Flamboyant sums up these Japanese natives. They do best in full sun to partial shade. Too much shade hinders the production of blooms and they dislike cold winds and too much nitrogen. These are the only plants I know where you can change the colour of the flower by adjusting your soil for blue or pink blooms. It all depends on the soil pH and the aluminium in the soil. Basically the more aluminium in a low pH soil (acidic) the bluer the flowers and vice versa for pink. Test your soil, if it is alkaline and you want blue flowers, amend your soil accordingly. White flowers stay white. Mophead hydrangeas have very showy flowerheads, lacecaps are more delicate. Z5.

Imperata

The green form is not often planted, but the red form, known as blood grass, has become sought after for its vibrant colour. **I. cylindrica** 'Rubra' is a handsome, deciduous grass but beware its tendency to be promiscuous. 'Red Baron' is no different. Erect leaves emerge lime-green with a touch of red at the tips. As the season progresses, the colour works its way down the leaves. It likes full sun to bring out the best colour and is especially attractive with the sun shining through the leaves. It really likes to be moist, more so when in full sun. It also works well as a container plant. Divide in April to June. 30cm (1ft). It is used more in modern gardens than in a traditional Japanese one. Z5.

Next page top left : Paeonia 'Black Pirate'; centre left-Dry garden at the Japanese Bonsai Nursery, Cornwall; bottom left: Iris ensata; all photos on right taken at the Japanese Tea Garden, San Francisco.

Iris ensata

Japanese iris is often used to enhance waterside plantings and can be grown in any lime-free, moisture retentive soil in a sunny site. Crowns must not be submerged in winter. These heavy feeders do not like freezing conditions. Divide every two to three years after flowering and plant rhizomes up to 5cm (2") deep. Named cultivars typically have large flowers. Ensata Gardens in America produce superb quality cultivars. These flowers have been hybridized in Japan for hundreds of years and they are especially beautiful ranging from whites to pink and purple and all shades of blue

Juniperus

J. procumbens 'Nana' is a dwarf juniper suitable for a number of uses in the garden. It can be trained to shape and clipped. The super tight foliage is ground hugging and makes a handsome green swathe. When used in this way, it is best not clipped. It grows moderately to 30cm (1ft) with a 1.8m (6ft) spread. It needs to be grown in full to part sun. Water regularly until established, then less so. It will appreciate a feed with a general purpose fertilizer before new growth starts in spring. Prostrate forms are highly suited to the Japanese garden. Z4b.

Ophiopogon

This is a rhizomatous grass, known as mondo grass in the USA. The dwarf species are used as groundcover. It is not actually a grass, but a member of the lily family, related to *Convallaria* (lily of the valley) and *Liriope* (lilyturf). It makes a dense carpet of green with **O. japonicus** and **O. jaburan** the main species. Flowers appear in summer and are followed by persistent berries. Water well in the first year until established. It tolerates most soils that are well-drained and is good in pots. Give protection below Z6.

Paeonia

Herbaceous peonies originated in China and were introduced into Japan in the 8th century. They are a symbol of prosperity. The predominant colour is pink or white available in single, semi or fully double flowers of great but fleeting beauty. Foliage is handsome too, so the contribution is not so brief. Semi-double P. 'Charismatic' is just that with its vivid pink blossoms and matching pink-tipped stamens. P. 'Old Faithful' is a rich, rose-like form of double red petals held on strong stems. P. 'Mistral' has wonderful flat-faced pink flowers. P. 'White Wings' is an enchanting single having a boss of golden stamens. Peonies prefer a sunny or lightly shaded site. Plants in full sun, especially doubles produce more flowers, in shade plants tend to produce fewer blooms but these often last longer. Soils must be adequately drained; they do not mind heavy soils and prefer slightly alkaline soils. Tree peonies such as P. 'Black Pirate' are dramatic. The semi-double, deep mahogany red flowers open like trumpets against the finely dissected foliage. P. delavayi makes a handsome spreading shrub to 1.5m (6ft) tall. Its deeply dissected leaves are tinted red and flowers range from blood red to chocolate. It can be grown from seed. Z2.

Phyllostachys

Both **Phyllostachys aurea** (golden) and **Phyllostachys nigra** (black bamboo) is used in large groves. Bamboo can also be used in fencing or edging and in boundaries. It symbolizes happiness and longevity. Bamboo is often trimmed to form shapes representing hillsides. Z7.

Pinus

Sharp-needled pines are the most frequently used in sculptural ways pruned into shape, often in cloud form. Pines symbolize longevity and happiness. **Pinus thunbergii** (black pine) represents the male and is used in coastal scenes and **P. densiflora** (red) symbolizes the female and is used for mountain scenes, imitating their use in nature. **P. densiflora** prefers sun in slightly acidic soil, **P. thunbergii** is very tolerant of most conditions.

Rhododendron (azalea)

Offer a splash of vibrant colour. Pink is the most often flower colour used. They symbolize fragile and ephemeral beauty. They give the effect of miniature mountains and wooded landscapes.

Left: Hydrangea serrata

Outside Japan, interesting Japanese-style gardens can be found at:

Kew Gardens

The finest traditional Japanese building in Europe is found in the grounds of Kew gardens. The intricately carved wooden Chokushi-Mon, or gateway of the Imperial Messenger. It was originally made for the 1910 Japan-British exhibition and is a replica, on a small scale of the Karamon of Nishi Hongan-ji in Kyoto. After the exhibition, it was moved to Kew. The gateway was restored in 1995 with its present, traditional copper tiles. It is set on a mound in a dry stone garden.

Pine Lodge

Designed by Ray and Shirley Clemo this is a garden created by passionate gardeners. The Japanese garden is based on a design seen on a visit to Japan. The viewing lodge overlooks the lake and one can see all the way down the sloping lawn to the artificial lake at the bottom of the garden. The plants are well-chosen, beautifully placed and the simple rendition evokes the feeling of serenity with which we associate Japanese gardens.

Japanese and Bonasi Garden, Nr Newquay

In a totally different style, this garden is a series of different areas; associated with Japanese gardens. The planting is surprisingly dense; the garden was created from 1991-7. Various buildings, a hill garden and a Zen garden, a bamboo grove, a moss garden, stone lanterns, a *shishi-odishi* (deer scarer), *tsukabai* (water basin), *bonsai*, waterfalls, pond, bridges, islands and viewing points with rich planting. 250 tons of rock was carried by hand into the garden. The garden also has a nursery.

Kyoto Japanese Garden, Holland Park

The garden was built for the 1991 London Festival of Japan, created as a joint project between the Royal Borough of Kensington and Chelsea and Kyoto Chamber of Trade in Japan. Designed by a Japanese designer and built by a Japanese team, it is a fine example of a 'strolling' garden. However, pruning was carried out in the western style. Penny Underwood studied the techniques under the Japanese designer, Tanaka-san and carried out correct maintenance and pruning in 2003.

The garden features a waterfall, pond with koi, a winding path and some nicely placed rocks, plants and lanterns.

Tatton Park

In 1910-1913, Alan de Tatton Egerton brought over Japanese gardeners to create an authentic Japanese garden. A tea house is connected to an island with a Shinto shrine. There were lanterns, a pagoda, a temple and representations of 'Mount Fuji'. The ground was covered in moss and the original garden, surrounded by a bamboo fence, was reached by crossing a bridge. It was restored to its original form in 2000-2001 with the aid of photographs and with research conducted by the Osaka University of Art, Japan. Today, the garden is viewed from a low fence or from the gateway.

Japanese Friendship Garden of San Diego

This garden is nicely executed; it was first built as part of the World Expo in 1915 in part of Balboa Park but stayed for 30 years after the exhibition. In 1950, San Diego formed a relationship with Yokohama and the new garden was constructed to celebrate their friendship. The name of this garden is *Sen-Ken-En* meaning 'three-scene garden' being water, pastoral and mountain. It was named in honour of the garden of the same name in Yokohama. Guided by the original principles of traditional Japanese design, the garden incorporates the local regional landscape and climate in San Diego. Walk through the gate on the broad, winding path. As you approach the exhibition house designed in traditional *sukiya* style, you are greeted by a maple and lantern. There is a viewing room for contemplation of the dry garden. Outside the exhibition house, the winding path leads on to the *tsukabai* and another lantern. The arching trees, rocks and plants provide a serene landscape.

Japanese Garden, Butchart Gardens

Begun in 1905, the tranquil gardens are one of the oldest parts of the Butchart estate. The garden was created with the help of a Japanese designer. It retains some of the original plantings including the maples, dogwoods and Tibetan blue poppies. The Torii Gate is vibrant red, a colour echoed in the bridge. The garden is absolutely stunning in autumn with colour provided by maples and chrysanthemums as well as two purple beeches. Beautiful cloud trees grace the garden.

Previous page: The Japanese Tea Garden, San Francisco

Japanese Garden, Portland

Long shall I remember the walk to this garden, I must surely have reached heaven. No-one could believe I was walking from the Zoo to the garden, via Hoyt Arboretum. Nestled in the scenic hills, west of Portland, my mind, body and all my senses were at peace once I had arrived. Designed by Professor Takumo Tono and created between 1963 and 1967, many have claimed it as the most authentic Japanese garden in the USA. The garden includes a formal Japanese tea house, meandering streams and a view of Mount Hood. The 5.5 acre garden is split into five areas – a strolling pond garden, a tea garden, a natural garden, a flat garden and a sand and stone garden. The mature Acers provide glorious colour.

Yao Japanese Garden, Bellevue Botanic Garden

Named for its sister city in Japan, the garden here at Bellevue, was created by Robert Murase and Associates. It combines some Pacific Northwest plants with those normally found in Japan, a meeting of East and West. One of the garden docents, friend and writer, Linda Urbaniak was kind enough to show me around the garden on a freezing February day. The garden is accessed via a traditional Japanese gate. Columbia River basalt and stone lanterns are skilfully placed. Rhododendrons, azaleas, viburnums and maple provide lush planting. Japanese primroses line the banks of the stream. In summer the peonies are breathtaking. The garden is surrounded by a rustic fence.

Butchart Gardens, Victoria, BC

The Japanese Tea Garden, Golden Gate Park

To walk through this garden is to walk in the realm of angels. This garden touches the soul. Harmony speaks from every surface – plant, path or pavilion. The gardens are carefully manicured in the Japanese style, the bamboos are often trimmed to shape, cloud pines abound and shrubs form typical rounded shapes. Azaleas and iris add colour. The lake reflects plants and pavilions.

This type of Japanese garden is known as a 'wet walking' garden but the visitor encounters a small Zen garden too. It was first created as the Japanese Village at the 1894 California Midwinter International Exposition, or the World's Fair in what is now the Music Concourse. It is the oldest Japanese Garden in the United States. Makoto Hagiwara, a Japanese landscape designer had the idea to convert the temporary exhibition garden into a permanent feature. He constructed the gardens, its pavilions and tea house. The one acre exhibit increased to five acres and moved from its original site.

The Hagiwara family lived in and maintained the gardens from 1895 to 1942 importing many statues, plants, birds, a Shinto shrine, a wooden Buddha and a porcelain lantern amongst other objects. The garden we see today is different but is still a representation of the original.

The Zen or dry garden was designed by Nagao Sakurai symbolizing a miniature mountain scene with a stone waterfall and small island surrounded by a gravel river. The red Buddhist pagoda has been moved to replace Hagiwara's Shinto shrine. The 1915 Temple Gate near the Pagoda was also removed and rebuilt. The South Gate, dating from the 1915 Panama-Pacific exhibition was also partially rebuilt. The Drum Bridge is from the Exposition of 1894. Two Meija large bronze lanterns from 1912 sit either side of the Torii Gate. This is my favourite of all the Japanese Gardens I have visited outside of Japan. So far I have clocked up three visits, I hope there will be many more to this quiet corner of San Francisco.

There is also a tiny courtyard garden at **Birmingham Botanic Gardens** built by the Japanese Garden Society (U.K.) in 2005. A modern interpretation of a Japanese garden can be seen at **Barnsdale Gardens** with a central bridge and gravel surfacing. Many U.S. cities have Japanese gardens.

Garden styles

We come like pilgrims to shrines, to worship and adore. We gaze and seek inspiration, learn and take away precious memories of a garden often more spectacular and far grander than any we could ever hope to own. We learn, absorb, interpret and add something new

Gardening is an evolution. Good gardens do not happen over night. They develop with their owner as one learns the process, improving step by step. Gardens do change, even historic gardens have changed, sometimes drastically over the years.

Gardens are made, not just of plants and features but of a time and place influenced by many factors including emotion and atmosphere. For example growing all the pretty plants you like most does not make a cottage garden just as a couple of rocks, a lantern and a maple does not make a Japanese garden. It is always a good idea not only to look at individual plants growing in a given setting, but also to see complete gardens and engulf their raison d'etre. Period garden styles can provide inspiration. The list is by no means exhaustive. I have chosen examples that typify each period. It is not intended that they are copied slavishly for to do so would be to ignore the spirit of the place which cannot be carried from one garden to another.

The enduring style in England on large estates is the English landscape Movement. Country gardens still mainly emulate the cottage garden style. The town garden is in the grasp of contemporary design. Towards the end of the twentieth century a number of styles emerged reflecting a more personal character.

Many English landscape gardens had fallen into disrepair leading to restoration of many gardens from the 1980's onwards. One of the most famous restored gardens is **Heligan**, discovered after 75 years of neglect and restored to much acclaim. Here the gardens are divided into the subtropical jungle with plants brought back by Victorian plant hunters and the Northern gardens consisting of the productive gardens (a fantastic kitchen garden) and the pleasure grounds including New Zealand and Italian areas. So too, overseas, many gardens have been restored. The restoration of **Paleis Het Loo** in the Netherlands led to that of the Privy Garden at **Hampton Court Palace.** The two were linked by history since both were created for William and Mary.

It is difficult to find a solution for today's gardens in the gardens of the past. However, by understanding the elements and components of each period, we can understand how well these great gardens were suited to their time, place and intended use. Each garden served a purpose, it had a function.

From medieval gardens to contemporary gardens in England with additional features on several gardens from around the world, here are gardens to inspire. Some retain their original design and features whilst others have been faithfully restored or renovated.

Exact plans are of little use as a garden must respond to its individual setting; reflect its purpose, its context. Inspiration is a springboard for the designer or gardener to imprint his or her skill and interpretation according to individual needs. Preconceived ideas are not intuitive. Allow the site to influence a free mind and spirit that is open to ideas and possibilities. I see no problem in following slavishly period gardens to match a period home. However, it is always admirable to give the garden more individuality than that would allow. When we come to the present day, the contemporary garden may borrow and learn, but must, above all, interpret and re-invent. Oddly enough a contemporary garden can suit a period house; just as many period interiors are now decorated in contemporary fashion. The key is the sympathetic treatment. The modern garden serves the home owner as an extra living space. Smaller houses send us outdoors for recreation and to escape the feeling of four walls.

Influences from earlier gardens are present in some of the styles highlighted. The Egyptians, who were known to have imported flowers, created gardens with a central theme of fertility amply represented by the presence of water. The idea of the Paradise garden came from Persian and Moghul gardens. Rose gardens were known in ancient Greece. The Chinese gardens influenced Japan as well as the West. The great French, Italian and English landscape gardens were created to impress. Each style has its beginnings in a given place, adapted to climate and country. Gardens have evolved. The overriding reason for creating a garden today is pleasure, a desire to expand our living area and to be stress-free.

In British gardens, most flowers are not natives but come from all over the world. The Ice Age swept away many British natives and plant hunters brought plants from all over the world to beautify British gardens. British garden styles were influenced by overseas styles through the centuries and vice versa. Nowadays, the new perennial style has been translated to British gardens, but subtle changes need to be made in the planting, as we do not have the same climate as Germany and the Netherlands where the style evolved. Think carefully if you are borrowing a style that essentially belongs to another country. Consider if it suits the landscape and if the same plants can be grown.

The earliest gardens we know of in England are from Roman times, walled courtyards from large villas and palaces. From AD43 the Romans created gardens for enjoyment and pleasure. They grew both edible and ornamental plants. Rectangular or semi-circular pools and fountains were part of the garden. Pergolas were constructed for shade. Statues of gods, urns, busts and sundials were popular. In AD75, the palace of Flavia was begun, the finest surviving example, is now known as **Fishbourne Roman Palace** in Sussex, which has been reconstructed. The symmetrical planting of low, box hedges is divided by gravel paths. Hedges are punctuated by small niches which probably held statues. The formal garden near the house leads to a landscaped area and on to the waterside below. A small, kitchen garden grows fruit and vegetables popular in the period. In AD 278 vineyards were part of British horticulture, and 5-10 years later, even as far north as Lincolnshire.

The Medieval Garden at Prebendal Manor

Some Museums and gardens show designs and styles from more than one period.

The Geffrye Museum
The Geffrye Museum exhibits a number of small but good interiors. The exterior shows gardens from periods throughout history but when I visited one August the gardens were not that well kept. Entrance is however free. The Museum has an Herb Garden showing 170 different herbs and associated plants. The 12 beds are arranged according to use such as cosmetic, medicinal or culinary. The garden is based on a traditional plan with a fountain at the centre of the axis. Three arbours provide secluded seating beneath climbing plants and roses.

The Museum includes a seventeenth century Late Elizabethan Garden. Based on medieval gardens, they were functional with herbs grown in raised beds. The gardens of town houses were mostly of modest size.

The mid to late Georgian garden consists of roses grown in low, circular box hedging.

There is also a mid to late Victorian display (1860-90) showing tall *Cannas* in a bed of fancy-leaved *Pelargoniums*. The *Canna* is indicative of the fashion for exotic, tropical and colourful plants.

The Edwardian Garden (1900-1914) shows an informal style with 'old-fashioned' plants. A stout pergola supports roses and there is a pond and iris.

Weald and Downland Open Air Museum
Fifty historic buildings ranging from the 13th to 19th century are housed here together with period gardens, woodland walks and a picturesque lake. The first building was dismantled on its original site and rebuilt here in 1968. Toll cottage has a traditonal garden from the 18th and 19th centuries when tolls were used. Bayleaf Farmstead is a reconstruction of a typical working farm with its garden and orchard as found in the Middle Ages.

Mapperton House
Gardens from three periods include the Italian garden dating from the 1920's complete with terraces, grotto, fountains, statuary and topiary. 17th century fishing ponds have survived. An orangery was added in the 1950's. View the fourteen acre site from the lawn.

Medieval Gardens

The medieval garden is a place of contemplation and serenity, both qualities in much need in the 21st century

No gardens from this period have survived in tact in Europe. Documentation is scarce on the plants grown, however books and paintings provide information. A record of Canterbury Cathedral in 1160 shows an herbarium in an infirmary. In c. 1190, De Naturis Rerum by Alexander Neckham was published in which he listed 200 plants. Many gardens were attached to monasteries and religion played a big part. The medieval flower garden was often known as *hortus conclusus* – an enclosed garden. The secluded gardens were meant for contemplation and walking. Medicinal and edible plants were useful and fruit trees were grown in orchards.

Decorative gardens were only for Kings and the extremely rich. Monasteries were self-sufficient and had gardens for useful plants and fish ponds known as stew-ponds. Peasants lived off the land. Medieval gardens might have three distinct areas. They were simple, regular and formal in style. Large or small gardens were enclosed by hand-made brick or stone walls, thorn or wattle or a popular quick-set of bramble and whitethorn. They would include a space to grow medicinal plants and those for strewing on the floor or to make hand waters. Plants often had multiple uses, being used for food, scent, medicinally or for dyes. Plants had to be useful they were not merely decorative. An herber or herb garden, flowers and turf with flowers grown in the grass was common. The castle or manor garden featured a pleasure garden with sheltered seats and flowery meads for ladies to walk in, dance, play chess or listen to music. Extensive grounds might include a park with hunting woods and wild beasts; William the Conqueror used the parkland at Windsor Castle. In southern Europe the garden might also include a vineyard. The years from 1066-1400 were some of the warmest England has known, enabling tender plants to be grown in the north of England and Scotland. The contemplation garden was influenced by the Garden of Eden and had religious significance. Red and white were popular colours, the former representing the Blood of Martyrs, the latter the purity of the Virgin Mary. Flowers with five petals represented the wounds of Christ, fruit trees for the tree of knowledge, grapes for everlasting life.

Typical elements

Hortus conclusus the enclosed garden contained few flowers, amongst them *Viola* (violets), *Aquilegia* (Columbine), *Lilium* (lilies), iris and roses. Colour was provided by fruit trees and herbs.

The lawn area was first dug over then flooded with boiling water to kill seeds in the soil. Turf was laid and mowed with scythes twice a year. It was not the grass we see today. Feeding was not the done thing and slow-growing grass often included chamomile.

Raised or sunken beds were raised or lowered and edged with boards or woven willow to improve drainage. Used mainly in vegetable and medicinal gardens, they were simply spaced at a minimum 1.2-1.5m (4-5ft) wide and the length of the enclosure, subdivided to a manageable size, say 1.2m (4ft) to allow for weeding. The paths were a minimum of 30cm (1ft) wide. Beds were almost always rectangular and set into a regular pattern like a windowpane. A centrally-placed feature came along not long after 1600, a time when triangles were also introduced. Sunken beds were primarily used in Islamic gardens, such as those at the Alhambra. This was necessary to stop the garden from drying out.

Paths consisted of cheap grass or dirt but had many disadvantages. The most common paths in medieval times were laid in gravel. Sand and stone paths were also used and sometimes there were ornamental tiles. Walkways were often covered with vines. Arbours could also be found in the medieval garden.

Turf seats, often found in the herb garden were popular and are perhaps the most recognized feature of medieval gardens. They were built along the same principles of raised beds. The walls were higher and were constructed of wood, bricks, wattle or sod. The 'exedra' is a seat with a high-backed support. Wood, turf, stone and marble were also used to create seats often covered with an arbour. Marble tables were also used for entertaining, eating or playing games.

Water was an essential feature, usually surrounded by lawns. Wells and well heads were popular. Springs often opened into a pool or trough from which water could be drawn for the practical use of washing. Tiered fountains were in use before the 1500's. At this time a 'fountain' might just be a basin fed by a pipe. Apart from fountains, statuary does not seem to have played a part in the medieval garden. Water was also used for irrigation and there were ponds for keeping fish.

The moat, a means of defence used from Roman times, often surrounded a garden, though none are intact. At Windsor Castle one can see the remains of a moat.

Large gardens especially might have a labyrinth, cut from turf in Roman times, like a grass maze. In the Medieval garden they featured herbs and small shrubs. **The Royal Botanic Gardens, Edinburgh** has a Celtic Labyrinth as a tribute to the Queen Mother. It was inspired by a Celtic Cross close to Glamis Castle. The plantings of *Myrica gale* (bog myrtle) are in the shape of the letter E for Elizabeth. Trellises supported a number of plants and were often used for boundaries or for the back of a seat. Arches and pergolas were also in fashion.

Topiary animals appeared late in medieval times and examples were seen at **Hampton Court** in 1599.

Ceramic urns, 'Italian' style pots and wide-mouthed jugs were popular. Woven baskets were used for transportation. Potted plants were used to extend the growing season, much as they are nowadays.

Typical plants

Grapes, rosemary, jasmine and roses were grown over trellis. A rosary was a shrubbery devoted to roses.

Orange, bay and pomegranate were often raised in tubs. Gilliflowers – carnations and pinks were supported in pots. It is said that *Dianthus caryophyllus* came with the Norman invasion, clinging to imported stones.

The herb garden would feature sage, hyssop, thyme, lavender, basil, costmary, balm, rue, southernwood, wormwood, poppy, clary, mint, pennyroyal, celery, betony, agrimony, tansy, catmint, rose, borage and chamomile.

Apple, cherry, plum and pear trees were common even in peasant's gardens. The word orchard was synonymous with the word garden. The orchard was also a place for recreation. Apples, often pearmains were the most commonly grown fruit. Warden pears were used for pies. The vegetable garden included peas, beans, onion, leek, gourds, melons, radish, cabbage, kale, leafbeet, parsnips, turnips, garlic, chives, fennel, parsley and watermelon.

Box, germander, rosemary, privet, roses and yew were used for hedging. Mixed hedges were common.

Seats and lawn features employed scented chamomile. Pleached allées, fruit trees and trees possessing a pleasant aroma or look were included. Trees such as beech were coppiced to provide a plentiful supply of branches for fencing. Both chestnut and almond were grown for their edible nuts.

Medieval Style Gardens

Bede's World Herb Garden

This garden is based on plants grown in Anglo-Saxon and medieval times. Designed by Rosemary Cramp and Richard Hill in 1978, it draws upon a typical physic garden with trellis work, a central arch, gateway and beds with medicinal, culinary and aromatic herbs. Inspiration was taken from a 9th century plan.

Deans Court Garden

A herb and kitchen garden growing very old varieties of vegetables, fruits and flowers without artificial fertilizers or chemicals. The monastery fishpond is of interest. The thirteen acre garden is enclosed by a serpentine wall.

Norton Priory

A medieval herb garden has been created in the grounds. An 18th century walled kitchen garden holds the national collection of *Cydonia oblonga* (quince). The sixteen acres of woodland contain Georgian summerhouses and the modern herbaceous borders are colourful.

Prebendal Manor House

The medieval gardens designed by Mike Brown have been recreated from several authentic plant lists. They represent both the practical (self-sufficient) and decorative features used in gardens from the 13-15th centuries. The gardens include a trellised herber and a typical decorative garden enjoyed by the wealthy. The Manor House is the earliest surviving dwelling in Northamptonshire. The grounds include two medieval fishing ponds, a wild garden and a 16th century dovecote. The 18th century tithe barn houses a museum.

Queen Eleanor's Garden

This castle garden is just outside the Great Hall of Winchester Castle, where King Arthur's round table is kept. It is an accurate recreation of a 13th century medieval herber including turf seats, a bay hedge, a Purbeck stone fountain, chamomile lawn, hazel tunnel arbour and many herbs and flowers of the period. Holly, ivy and bay are grown representing the medieval ideal of faithfulness. Strawberries, columbine and roses were symbolic of Christian spirituality. The garden was opened in 1986 by the Queen Mother. It is said to be the most authentic garden of its kind. The garden measures 9 x 27m (30 x 90ft), its small size is typical of the period.

Tudor England (1485-1603)

The pleasure garden was a serene space for walking and playing bowls

The House of Tudor (1485-1558) brought a new look to gardens. Henry VII's ornate gardens at Richmond probably influenced Henry VIII's **Hampton Court**. Nothing of either garden remains. In 1597, John Gerard published one of the most famous garden books – Herball. In 1621 the first botanic garden was begun in Oxford. In 1629, John Parkinson published the book Paradisi in Sole Paradisus Terrestris. Gardens are rare as few survived the new wave of design, farming or estate management.

Gardens were usually enclosed and had formal layouts based on a grid with knot gardens and heraldic emblems as well as topiary. Tudor gardens were designed to be seen from above, from the first floor of the house. The garden started to become an extension of the house as seen at **Montacute**. In the 16th century, flowers were grown for pleasure for the first time; gardens were still for the rich, including arbours or covered walks of pleached trees so that the ladies did not spoil their pale skin. The garden might also include a maze, a wilderness and an orchard. The first parterre was created in France by Claude Mollet in 1580. Until the end of the 17th century, the word 'knot' is more often used in England. There are few, if any, original parterres in existence in England.

Jasmine, Antirrhinum and African marigolds, Narcissus and hyacinthus appeared at this time as well as many new vegetables such as broad beans and trained fruit trees. Explorers such as Sir Francis Drake and Sir Walter Raleigh brought back plants from their expeditions. In 1492, Christopher Columbus sailed to the New World; bringing back many new plants to Europe.

Typical elements

Just as the Mount offered a view of the garden, the *claire voie* offered a view of what was beyond the garden through an iron grille. The Mount first appeared to give a view of the intricate knot, developed from the watchtower of medieval gardens. Mounts were raised structures and often created as spirals or pyramids 100m (30ft) high with a spiral path leading to the top often with buildings at the summit. They introduced height into the garden.

The knot is an intricate woven pattern of plants in geometric form best viewed from above. Popular in the 16th century, using *Buxus* (box from 1595 on), *Santolina* (cotton lavender) or Thyme low hedging. The first plant used to create knots was *Armeria maritima* (thrift). Grass, coloured sand or gravel was used to infill. Later, flowerbeds began to make an appearance within intricate low hedges. Topiary, practised since Roman times, began to feature once more in geometric form or animal shapes, showing Italian influence.

Mazes were a popular feature at this time. They began as turf labyrinths and developed into pathways with tall hedges. Mazes are usually made from yew, but can be made from many materials including glass.

Fountains were a sign of prestige and wealth with white marble taking centre stage. Grottoes and water features appeared. Elaborate water features came into being during the Jacobean period.

Raised walks afforded a view of the garden. In Elizabethan times these were often referred to as terraces.

Painted wooden heraldic devices on poles were used in the reign of Henry VIII, **Hampton Court Palace** featured many such images of animals as did **Holdenby House**.

Tudor gardens did not usually feature the popular turf seats of previous times. Seats were still often covered with arbours hewn from native woods.

As in medieval gardens, the shrubbery (rosary) where roses were grown was still popular. In 1560 at least 24 varieties of roses were available.

The Kitchen Garden or cook's garden would have a boundary of hawthorn unless the owner was very wealthy and walled the garden. The orchard was quite varied, a place to grow apples, pears, plums, walnuts and filberts as well as apricots, almonds, peaches, figs. Some even grew capers, oranges, lemons and olives.

The Elizabethan Garden at Plas Mawr, Conwy

Tudor Gardens

Buckland Abbey

The former home of Sir Francis Drake is graced with a new Elizabethan garden. Here the National Trust created something new that they felt was fitting to the property. The garden consists of a circular pool, granite steps, topiary and box hedging with plants grown in Elizabethan times. There is a grassy meadow and a small orchard with old varieties of fruit. Founded by Cistercian monks, the Abbey was already old when Drake took possession in the 16th century. The herb garden was created by Vita Sackville-West in the 1950's.

Cawdor Castle

The Castle was the 14th century home of Thanes of Cawdor. The earliest garden dates from the 16th century and has a maze. The walled garden dates from 1620. Vegetables and soft fruits were grown. In 1981 it was fashioned into a holly maze, based on a mosaic floor from the ruined Roman Villa of Conimbriga in Portugal. It depicts the minotaur's labyrinth at Knossus in Crete. Within the walled garden, there is also a paradise garden, knot, thistle garden and an orchard planted with old Scottish fruit trees.

The flower garden was begun in 1710 and completed fifteen years later. There was a bog and mound and fruit trees. In 1850 oval lavender borders were filled with roses. In the 19th century the house was only in use in the shooting season, so a seasonal display of late herbaceous plants was installed. These borders still exist and the season has been extended. There is a holly garden bordered by laburnum tunnels.

The steep, wild garden between the Castle and the stream was planted in the 1960's with Rhododendron, Azaleas, willows, bamboos, bulbs and includes a giant redwood. Through the Big Wood, 750 acres of fine trees, lies **Auchindoune Gardens** with its original inspirations and plants from Tibet brought back by Frank Kingdon-Ward. The kitchen garden was laid out by Arabella Lennox-Boyd. It has used organic principles for over a quarter of a century. Cut flowers, soft fruit, orchard trees and vegetables are grown in traditional beds edged in box.

Above: The late Elizabethan garden at The Geffrye Museum, London
Centre: The Red Lodge, Bristol
Bottom: Labyrinth, Garfield Conservatory, Illinois, USA

Helmingham Hall Gardens

An early rare Tudor House from 1480, a moated manor featuring a beautiful parterre redesigned in 1978. In 1982 the knot garden was created using an infill of plants introduced into Britain before 1750. The garden was designed by Lady Xa Tollemache. The old 400 acre parkland dating from the early 17th century, grazed by deer, features an old mound topped by an 18th century obelisk. A wooden palisade was replaced by brick walls in 1745. The garden is in keeping with its Tudor spirit. Worth seeing is the double herbaceous 100ft long border and a formal garden with billowing hybrid musks.

Holdenby House

Contains the outlines of a beautiful Elizabethan garden replanted in 1980 by Rosemary Verey using plants available in 1580 with clipped yews and a sundial. The fragrant border was planted by Rupert Golby and there is a silver garden. A bowling garden, parterre and terraces were constructed in 1580 to impress Queen Elizabeth I on her journey through England.

Little Moreton Hall

Is an example of a lovely timber-framed Tudor house with a knot garden restored to its former glory with flowerbeds edged in box with yew designed by Graham Stuart Thomas. There is also a freshwater moat and an orchard. The one acre garden has a mount.

Lytes Cary Manor

The medieval manor house and fourteenth century chapel were once owned by the medieval herbalist, Henry Lyte. It is surrounded by an enchanting garden in Elizabethan style. As you enter the garden large topiaries greet you, representing the twelve apostles. An almost hidden door takes you through to a more informal style border. Hidden paths enclosed by high hedges add a sense of surprise and an air of mystery. The border along the South Front is stocked with plants grown in the 16th century by Henry Lyte. At the foot of the garden is an orchard. In 1907 the manor was purchased by Sir Walter Jenner who restored house and garden which are now in the possession of the National Trust.

Lyveden New Bield

The garden is one of the oldest layouts in England of an Elizabethan pleasure garden. It features an elaborate water garden terminating in the Garden Lodge. The formal symmetry typical of the period is retained with an example of a mount garden. It is a rare survival of the important water gardens of the sixteenth century with an ambitious system of canals. The largest orchard in the care of the National Trust has just been restored to its original plan of 1600 with central walks, ancient apple varieties, plums, pears, cherries and walnuts.

Montacute

The corner pavilions and long terrace are typical of the Elizabethan garden that must have once graced the Elizabethan House built in the 16th century for the lawyer and MP, Sir Edward Phelips. The Long Gallery houses Elizabethan and Jacobean portraits. By 1630 the garden contained courts, an orchard and park. There was possibly a mount, removed for the present day fountain. The original layout is retained, yet the planting is 19th century. The golden Ham stone walls remain around the East Court which was made into a garden in 1787 when the principal entrance was moved from the West Front. The north garden was designed in the 1840's and replanted in an excellent manner by Phyllis Reiss in the 1950's. The Orangery was built in 1848. The Park covers 300 acres and includes an oak and lime avenue. The house and grounds were given to the National Trust in 1931.

Owlpen Manor

In 1926, Sir Geoffrey Jellicoe described the garden at Owlpen as possibly the earliest domestic garden to survive virtually intact. The grass terraces and hedges date originally from the 16th century, altered in the 1720's and then restored in the Old English style by Jewson in 1926. He planted the box parterres and topiary yews. Yew rooms, overhanging terraces and steep paths are linked by gravel paths. The simple plan is enclosed by stone walls with coping. The core of the garden is Tudor and has been remodelled since 1980 styled on the turn of the 18th century formal tradition.

Previous page: Lytes Cary Manor, Somerset
Next page: Montacute

Packwood House

The 16th century house features a yew garden said to represent the Sermon on the Mount with some of the yews over 18m (59ft) high. The yews representing the twelve apostles are thought to date from the early 18th century with yews below perhaps from a later date. The garden begun in the mid-18th century is now largely a mid-Victorian recreation. There are 'bee boles' dating from 1756 and a raised area for viewing. Notable topiary, courtyards, mellow brick gazebos and the park are reasons for visiting. The Fountain Court features a plunge bath from 1680. At the turn of the century the herbaceous borders hovered between the order of the Victorian period and the looser more relaxed Arts and Crafts style. The seven acre garden is owned by the National Trust.

Plas Mawr

To mark the 400th anniversary of the death of Robert Wynn in 1998, Cadw planned a beautiful restoration of the courtyard garden of this, the finest surviving example of an Elizabethan townhouse. Plas Mawr was built between 1576 and 1585. The building is an architectural gem noted for the quality of its plasterwork.

The Red Lodge

A fine example of an Elizabethan-style walled knot garden of box hedges. It is a replica of the pattern from the lodge's bedroom ceiling. The garden is a simple knot with a two-tier box in the centre and having a surrounding herbaceous border. All the plants grown here could be found in England in 1630. The surrounding fence is typical in style and similar to that used at Plas Mawr, Conwy.

The Tudor House Museum and Garden

The House received Lottery funding in 2006 to undergo restoration. The reconstruction of a Tudor garden in the grounds was designed by Dr. Sylia Landsberg and includes a knot, fountain, secret garden and herbs. There are heraldic beasts, rose arbour, vine tunnel, bee hives and period plants. The garden is just 30m square (100ft).

The maze outside the Getty Museum

Renaissance to Restoration (1603-1702)

The splendour of the Baroque garden, particularly the French style, is a magical world in which one is dazzled and amazed, filled with wonder and enchantment

The oldest 'slip' gardens date from Jacobean times. They gained popularity much later in the mid-18th century, utilising a narrow strip of land usually outside the kitchen garden and most often used as a nursery. The compost area was also often found here.

From 1649-1660 many ornate English gardens owned by the aristocracy were destroyed by Puritan rule. In 1660, Charles II was restored to power with the end of the Civil War and gardening began to flourish once more. With Charles came an elaborate and flamboyant style influenced by the great French gardens (see the section on France).

William and Mary came to the English throne in 1689, bringing with them the Dutch influence, seen at **Hampton Court Palace** and sweeping away the Tudor garden. Baroque gardens were created in Holland, France and Italy and the style later filtered through to England from 1660-1725 with characteristically geometric gardens based on mathematical precision. Parterres replaced knots. John Evelyn (1620-1706) wrote the Kalendarium Hortense, the first calendar for the gardener. The Chelsea Physic Garden was created in 1673 to teach apothecaries to identify plants. Plants became more important, increasing in number and availability. Exotics and tender plants arrived from all over the world with glasshouses and conservatories to enable the gardener to look after them. Bananas came to Britain and tea was imported from China. Salads became popular and included many ingredients including the young leaves of primrose, tansy and marigold as well as flower buds, roots and herbs. Gardens increased in size and might include the wilderness - formal pleasure grounds.

The labyrinth, Kenilworth Castle

Typical elements

A parterre is an arrangement of symmetrically patterned beds, like a carving. Some had a distinctive, embroidered appearance of fine cut turf in arabesques, flowers, birds and so on with the small alleys or intervals filled with several coloured sands but with few flowers. Pioneered by Andre Mollet, they first appeared in England in 1639.

Elaborate water features were fashionable as exemplified by **Chatsworth House** with its Grand Cascade and the copper fountain trees. Many basins have disappeared. I think of the basin as a bowl and this was its more general use. The word also referred to a geometric pond found in formal gardens. The octagonal basin at **Wimpole Hall and Gardens,** Cambridgeshire is a rare survivor. The French were famous for ornamental canals. Charles II not wishing to be totally outdone emulated the fashion. He had a canal built in St. James' Park by the Frenchman, Andre Mollet in 1660. It is no longer in existence, having been changed into an informal lake in the 18th century. The Long Water at **Hampton Court Palace** was created shortly after and still forms part of the palace gardens.

By 1680 statues were being used as a focal point for formal gardens and their popularity was to increase from this time on. Herms also became popular at this time. A tall pillar topped by a classical bust, usually depicting Hermes, messenger of the gods. They had been a feature in ancient Greece. Urns were favoured ornaments at this time too.

The side garden at Haddon Hall, Derbyshire

Typical gardens

Aberglasney
Dating from the seventeenth century is a unique and very rare example of a parapet walkway in the restored cloister garden and a yew tunnel. The parterre features tulips and orange trees. The yew tunnel north-west of the house is thought to date from the 1700's, though Patrick Taylor dates it much later. The formal, rectangular pool is thought to date from Jacobean times.

Boscobel House Garden
The garden has a fully restored knot to the original seventeenth century plan. Here the future King Charles II hid in a tree from Cromwell's army in 1651, now known as the Royal Oak. The flowers in the garden, seen from the upper floor of the house, represent a forbidden Catholic symbol, unseen at ground level. The formal garden has a raised viewing platform.

Bramham Park
Formal, French-style gardens include a parterre dating from 1698 to 1713. Most gardens of this period were swept away, so this is a rare survivor. The layout is thought to have been designed by Robert Benson, who rebuilt the house as a grand Queen Anne, Palladian-style mansion. A dominant axis runs south-east from the façade. A temple by James Paine dates from the mid 1750's and an Ionic temple and great obelisk, cascades and ponds feature amongst the tall beech hedges. A second axis runs almost parallel to the south-west. Benson's daughter Harriet added follies, temples and the Black Fen woodland to the 68 acre gardens.

Castle Bromwich Hall Gardens
These English Baroque gardens are being restored as near as possible to their glory of 1680-1740. The present day holly maze was a 19th century addition, based on a plan by London and Wise is a distorted mirror image of the maze at **Hampton Court**. The ten acre walled garden features over 600 period plants. A yew parterre in the North Garden was replanted in 2001 and created by pollarding old yews growing in the grounds. The west Claire-voie has been restored. The holly walk leads to an elegant summerhouse with views to an early Orangery known as the Green House. Historic vegetables and herbs are grown in an early 18th century layout.

Above: Ham House, Richmond, Surrey
Below: The yews at Hampton Court Palace, Surrey

Above: Ham House, Surrey
Below: Hampton Court Palace

Grimsthorpe Castle

The castle was built in the 13th century and transformed in the 16th by the Willoughby de Eresby family in whose hands it remains to this day. The garden laid out in the 1680's closely resembles what we see today. In the formal garden to the south lies a new topiary garden containing small ornamental pools. A rose and box parterre and fine topiary enchant. A walled kitchen garden redesigned in 1961 has apple and pear espaliers alongside quince and pear trees. Grimsthorpe is surrounded by 3,000 acres of landscape with ancient woodlands. The twenty-seven acre garden retains the atmosphere of the past.

Haddon Hall

The house dates mainly from around 1600. It is one of the best surviving examples of the framework of a 17th century garden in the Italian style. The stone steps appear to disappear, lost amongst the greenery – a sure way to create a sense of mystery. The present day gardens were created by the 9th Duchess in the early 20th century and contain superb rose gardens. Sixty types of *Delphiniums* grow in the herbaceous borders.

Ham House

The Stuart garden features an interesting lavender parterre surrounded by a hornbeam tunnel. A maze-like wilderness with gravel paths, statuary, seating, plats and a raised terrace with recreations of the original summerhouses are all enclosed by hornbeam. The recent restoration dates from the plan of 1671-2 displayed in the library closet. The Orangery dates back to the 1670's. A walled kitchen garden has been restored to its 17th century plan. An original plant list of 1653 shows that vines, pears, peaches, cherries and apricots were grown here. The inventory of 1682 shows that oranges, lemons and myrtles were grown in pots. The garden is owned by the National Trust.

Hampton Court Palace Gardens

Hampton Court was bought by Cardinal Wolsey in 1514. Henry VIII, whom the Cardinal had hoped to impress, liked it so much, he acquired it in 1525. In the 1530's three new gardens were created running down to the river – the Mount, Pond and Privy gardens. The Palace and gardens were made famous by Henry VIII; in his time the Privy orchard contained many sundials created by Nicholas Kratzer. The garden also contained many wooden carvings of heraldic beasts mounted on poles.

The Banqueting House, dating from this period is now open once again. The Mount, planted with apple trees, had a glazed arbour atop, crowned with a leaden cupola. The Privy garden lay beneath the windows of the King's apartments – the garden being a status symbol.

In 1662, Charles II made a great Patte d'oie east of the palace, thought to have been designed by Andre Mollet. The central avenue encloses the Long Water.

William III's Dutch influence transformed the gardens. The East gardens, originally Henry VIII's parkland, are now a spectacular semi-circular parterre with 12 marble fountains and the Great Fountain as seen in the painting by Knyff in 1702 which still hangs in the palace. The grilles, an exquisite claie-voie were created at the same time by Jean Tijou, originally made for the Great Fountain Garden; they now afford a view of the Thames at the far end of the Privy Garden. The maze, all that remains of the original wilderness was commissioned in 1690 by William. Its trapezoid shape covers a third of an acre with over a half mile of paths. The original hedge was hornbeam, but it has been repaired so many times that it is almost all yew nowadays. The knot garden is an example of a 16th century garden planted in the 1900's. The great vine was planted by Capability Brown in 1768 but he did not install a landscape garden here. The northern gardens were Henry VIII's wilderness, but now feature clipped yews and bedding planted in the time of William III. His Privy Garden was restored faithfully with plants growing in 1701, statues were copied from the originals and Tijou's grilles restored. Queen Mary's bower, the Wych Elm arbour running along one side of the Privy Garden had been affected by disease and was reinstated using hornbeam. Roses, fritillaries and other flowering plants from the period are grown in typical style, well-spaced apart in slightly raised beds. The pond garden is a sunken formal garden.

Levens Hall in 1880

Above: The Sunken Garden
Previous page: The Privy Garden, The Knot
all at Hampton Court Palace, Surrey

Hatfield House

In 1611, John Tradescant the Elder, a plant hunter, established the gardens at Hatfield House for Robert Cecil. The Tradescants were both Royal gardeners. John the Elder travelled to Europe, N, Africa and Russia, whilst John the Younger travelled to America. He introduced phlox, michaelmas daisies, lupins and goldenrod. The Elizabethan park and Jacobean gardens include an herber, knot and wilderness. De Caus laid out a water garden with a diamond-shaped lake having an island and banqueting house. The park contains ancient oak trees. The garden has largely been redesigned in the formal style by the Dowager Lady Salisbury including plants grown by Tradescant. The East Gardens, a parterre in 1890's style is enclosed by avenues of lollipop evergreen oaks on 2m (8ft) trunks that surround the formal beds. In front of the Old Palace is the knot garden. Based on a traditional design, four central beds surround a small pool, the corners of the beds distinguished by box pyramids. Three of the beds are knots, the fourth a gravel maze. The Elizabethan fruit garden contains pomegranates in summer and there is an organic kitchen garden. The maze has been reconstructed.

Kenilworth Castle

The garden here is sheer delight. The flat labyrinth structure is textured and clearly defined. The remains of Henry V's Pleasance can still be seen.

Levens Hall

The present house is largely from the 16th century, but parts date back to the 13th century. Work began on the gardens in 1694 for James Grahame with the aid of the Frenchman, Guillaume Beaumont. In 1695, he created the first ha-ha in England. Beaumont's 1730 plan of the garden still exists and has remained largely unchanged, restored at the beginning of the 19th century. The long axial walk of beech hedges has a roundel at its centre. The gardens include the world-famous topiary garden with pretty flowers contained in box-edged beds. Chess pieces, spirals, animal forms and geometric shapes are hardly contained by the formal design. Arbours and high yew hedges are brought to life with *Tropaeolum speciosum*. Parterres are bedded out with 15,000 plants annually. A new fountain garden has been made and there is a nuttery. The oak avenue through the park is in the landscape style. The gardens retain their eccentric extravagance being one of the prime examples of topiary.

Moseley Old Hall

A one acre garden recreated in 17th century town garden style consisting of a knot, parterre and walled garden as well as a nut walk. All plants and trees are typical of the period. They include plants used for dyes, washing and medicinal purposes as well as fruits such as apples, pears, quinces, medlars, cherries and mulberries. The garden is owned by the National Trust.

Museum of Garden History

The Dowager Marchioness of Salisbury designed the garden as a reproduction of a 17th century knot with authentic planting in 1981. The hedging is dwarf box, *Buxus sempervirens 'Suffruticosa'*. The traditional, geometric design incorporates a small square, a circle and four half circles. Four sections of the hedge are planted in contrast and with the box hedging, form the letter T for John Tradescant, repeated symmetrically within the design. *Santolina* (cotton lavender) and *Helichrysum italicum* (curry plant) have also been used here to create the T. A mixture of shrubs, roses particularly *Rosa x alba*, which tolerates the poor conditions and thin soil, herbaceous perennials, annuals and bulbs are used.

In summer it appears quite informal, whereas in winter, in its bare bones it is more formal. The central topiary is a holly spiral, using *Ilex x altaclerensis* 'Golden King'. Beneath the east window are two columns of *Myrtus communis* (myrtle) and near the fountain *Viburnum tinus* shaped into lollipops.

Pitmedden

Pitmedden is one of the oldest gardens in Scotland. The house was destroyed by fire in 1818 and the garden fell into decay. Imagine five miles of box hedging enclosing intricate parterres as originally laid out in 1675 by Sir Alexander Seton and recreated by The National Trust for Scotland in the 1950's. The recreation was undertaken with guidance form the late Dr. James Richardson and George Barron. The Great Garden is a walled garden containing three formal parterres taken from designs possibly used in the Palace garden at Holyrood House. Original stone walls enclose a sunken area with a pair of pavilions and a double staircase. A fourth parterre is a heraldic design taken from Sir Seton's coat of arms.

The six parterres are filled with 40,000 plants offering vibrant colour in summer, obviously not a historical representation but visually effective. Over 80 varieties of apple trees adorn the high granite walls. There are also herb and wildlife gardens, a woodland walk and the Museum of Farming Life. The garden features sculpture by local artists.

Powis Castle

The estate dates back to at least the 12th century. The gardens are an example of the Italian and French styles with grand 17th century terraces probably designed by William Winde in the 1660's having original lead statues from the 18th century, an orangery and aviary. Four long formal terraces were inspired by the Palace of St. Germain-en-Laye with statues and old yews built into the rocky slopes beneath the castle. In 1705 a water parterre was laid out on the flat ground at the foot of the terraces, unfortunately changed into the Great Lawn in 1771 by William Emes. An informal woodland wilderness dating from the 18th century has a colourful display of rhododendrons. The kitchen garden was turned into a flower garden in the 20th century. The Castle and walls dominate the garden magnificently, yet if you visit in summer the walls are softened by Rosa banksia and Acca sellowiana. The 24 acre garden owned by the National Trust occupies the steep slope to the south-east.

The knot at the Museum of Garden History, London

The Queen's Garden, RBG Kew

The 17th century style garden carried out with a true regard for authenticity was the idea of Sir George Taylor in 1959. Work began in 1963 in an area behind Kew Palace, often flooded by the Thames. It contains arcades and steps associated with the Dutch House. Amongst its sculptures are five 18th century terms commissioned by HRH Frederick, Prince of Wales in 1734-5. An ornate gazebo graces the mound, a boscage of hornbeam entices. A parterre is enclosed by box hedging with a central water feature and a copy of Verrochio's 'Boy with a Dolphin'. Next to the parterre is a sunken nosegay garden with scented plants such as sage, bergamot and artemisia. All plants in the Queen's garden were grown in England during the 17th century for their medicinal properties and culinary use, including *Buxus*, *Santolina*, *Rosmarinus*, *Taxus*, *Cynara*, *Tulipa* and *Lavandula*.

Westbury Court Gardens

The four acre garden created between 1697 and 1705 is an example of the Dutch style. In 1967 the National Trust began a programme of restoration using the original planting plans. Hedges fringe the large canals with topiary pyramids and formally planted parterres. A T-shaped canal features a statue of Neptune. A small walled garden planted with old roses and plants grown before 1700 is surrounded by box hedging. Beds, known as carp beds are raised to form a ridge planted with specimen flowers such as tulips. A simple quincunx of old fruit trees includes quinces and medlars. The holm oak at the end of the T-shaped canal is thought to date from the 1600's. The vegetable garden grows plants known to have been in cultivation before 1720.

Above: The ornate gazebo on the mound and previous page: Queen's Garden, Kew
Below: The Regency Garden at RHS Harlow Carr Gardens, Harrogate, North Yorkshire
Next page: Chatsworth House

Georgian and Regency (1714-1837)

The new town gardens were stylish in their simplicity and graceful accomplishments

Georgian town style was simple consisting of beds with shrubs and roses. Georgian gardens were often accessed via the servant's quarters. Vegetables and fruit were not widely grown in town gardens but the pineapple made its appearance on large estates. **Heligan** has a working pineapple pit. From 1760-1800 town gardens were increasingly seen as an extension of the house, a place for recreation and entertainment. The garden tended to cater more to the tastes of its owner; the prevailing taste was for simplicity and tidiness. A central lawn with flower beds and gravel paths or stone paving for the wealthy was typical. Gardens were in the formal style at first but the landscape and picturesque styles became influential. This period is one of rapid development and change.

In 1735 Carl Linnaeus published Systema Naturae. In 1768 Sir Joseph Banks sailed across the Pacific with Captain Cook to bring back new plants. By 1789 Kew gardens had over 5,000 plants in cultivation and plants became of interest in themselves. *Rhododendrons, Kalmias* and *Hydrangeas* were popular. In 1804, the Horticultural Society was formed, it later became the RHS. In 1822, John Loudon published the famous Encyclopaedia of Gardening. Four year's later he founded the Gardener's Magazine. The lawnmower was invented in the 1830's.

Georgian Garden
The Georgian Garden in Bath is an example of an original layout from 1760-1770. The garden was restored in 1985-6 under the guidance of Lorna McRobie, created with plants from the period, although the specific plants used were unknown. The townhouse garden is an 18th century innovation. By the end of the century the upper classes had beds and borders. The original garden at 4 The Circus was covered with a mixture of clay and gravel. A central axis with three flowerbeds having a rounded bed at the far end with trellis screens. The simple layout is enhanced by variegated foliage and double flowers. An authentic Georgian roller is used to keep the gravel looking tidy.

The English Landscape Movement (1750's – 1780's)

In these vast landscapes, appearing at one with nature, the quiet can be astounding as if nothing else exists

From the 1700's almost every gentleman of means took a European tour. They came home hoping to create on their own country estates something of what they had seen in Greece and Italy. Gothic, Rococo, Chinoiserie (the pagoda at Kew 1762) and Palladian styles emerged with Elysian or Arcadian fields. The natural garden, sympathetic to nature arose as a direct reaction to the forced landscapes of the 17th century. The park-like landscape idealized nature. These peaceful and idyllic settings were manipulated by Kent, Brown and Repton. Many of the gardens have survived with great lakes, majestic trees and sweeping, undulating lawns. Kent was one of the forerunners of the natural movement, which was developed into the landscape style by his pupil and son-in-law, Lancelot 'Capability' Brown, who epitomized the movement. He swept away many formal gardens, which would have been better preserved. Nevertheless, Brown's genius typifies the English landscape. His vision was romantic and it is true that in England no other style has evolved that evokes such feeling of splendour and peace. His landscapes are this England, this green and pleasant land. They are timeless.

Brown set up his own landscape business in London in 1751. In 1772, George III employed Brown to remodel parts of Kew Gardens. His predecessor, Kent, had worked on the original plans for Kew in 1730. Repton largely carried on Brown's work, but re-introduced flower beds and gravel walks. His first commission was in 1788.

Lucid lines, long avenues, gently rolling contours and vistas were key elements of the landscape style executed with proportion and balance, employing simplicity and a clarity of vision seldom repeated to this day. Trees such as Scots pine, beech, oak and sweet chestnut were planted in natural clusters. Flowers were relegated to walled kitchen gardens. A relationship existed between the house (often a Palladian mansion) and the Elysian landscape, which merged imperceptibly into the surrounding countryside. Sweeping lawns gave movement, instigating the invitation to explore.

The Pagoda at Kew, built in 1762 when Chinoiserie was at its height

Toward the end of the period from 1780-1830, the Picturesque movement took hold, a reaction against Brown's 'natural' landscapes. This was followed by the Gardenesque style in 1832, made popular by John Loudon. The chief components were non-native and exotic plants in individual beds. In 1840 the most popular plants were chrysanthemums, dahlias and roses. York stone was used for paths from the eighteenth century onwards.

It was a period of great plant hunting trips with Joseph Banks a leading figure. He became the first Director of **Kew**. It is believed that he introduced over 7,000 plants to horticulture.

Typical elements

Charles Bridgeman (1690-1738) was the first to make widespread use of the ha-ha in England. The hidden ditch created a subtle barrier between garden and the countryside beyond and prevented cattle from entering the country estate. The ditch usually falls away perpendicularly on the garden side, with a slope rising into the countryside.

Temples were frequently used such as the Temple of Ancient Virtue at **Stowe**. Aesthetically pleasing they became an essential part of the landscape garden – the classical ideal, picturesque temples were found in the French artist, Claude's paintings. Inspired by visits to Europe, classic statuary was the main ornament used.
Echoes of the Italian water garden, grottoes were festooned with shells and stalactites. These cavern-like structures I find an odd eccentricity, much odder than the folly. They were costly yet fashionable.

In the landscape garden, seating became more important and was positioned to take advantage of the view. Trellis-work was used for screening especially around seats. Iron seats were created. Although found in the previous century, gazebos gained popularity affording a view of the garden and being widely interpreted.

Inspired by Arcadian ideals and the landscape painters, the serpentine lake became the forte of Capability Brown. The setting was idyllic; the man-made lake became part of the natural landscape. The extent of the lake is disguised.
Originating with the Romans, the cold bath featured in many 18th century gardens, though few, like the one at **Stowe**, remain. They were medically beneficial!
The heyday of bridges as a garden ornament came with the creation of the serpentine lake. Palladio's designs were the supreme example of bridge construction. Only four remain in the world, three of them in England.

Although in existence in the 17th century, glasshouses became more popular in the 18th century as the number of exotic plant imports increased. Their numbers increased further in the following century as glass tax was abolished. Similarly, the orangery was popular in this period for raising oranges with protection. They were often quite elaborate buildings. The south-facing side of the building featured glass.

Landscape gardens

Adlington Hall
The gardens, landscaped by Brown include a ha-ha. Lime Avenue was planted in 1688 and leads to a woodland wilderness with winding paths revealing temples, bridges and follies in the Rococo manner. A path through the *Laburnum* arch leads to a formal rose garden then onto the maze of yew. A new parterre has been created.

Blenheim Palace
Designed by John Vanbrugh, the palace was built to celebrate the military prowess of the Duke of Marlborough from 1705 - 1716 and completed by Nicholas Hawksmoor in 1725. An evergreen garden known as the Military Garden was laid out by Henry Wise at the same time. An Anglo-Saxon hunting lodge, Woodstock Manor was found on the estate but demolished in 1723. Henry II had created a 12th century garden with a well as a centrepiece known as **Everswell** that still exists today.
The 2000 acre parkland is considered one of the finest examples of Brown's work with his most famous lake. In 1764 he naturalized the existing landscape. Vanbrugh, the architect, envisaged the marsh transformed into a lake by damming the River Glyme traversed by the Grand Bridge based on designs by Palladio. The bridge was not completed as Vanbrugh planned with large arcades and towers, but it is still very grand, 120m (400ft) long, containing thirty-three rooms.

Studley Royal, Yorkshire

Later on, Capability Brown flooded the valley, thereby fitting the bridge suitably into the landscape. The beech hedges lead to woodland pleasure grounds.

The gardens nearest the house are a very fine example of formal style, designed in the early 20th century by Achille Duchene. The Italian garden lies immediately to the west of the palace with four *parterres de broderie* around a central, neo-classical mermaid fountain. The Water Terraces, west of the palace, were built between 1925 and 1930. The upper terrace has scalloped pools and fountains framed with parterres. A fountain decorates the lower terrace. There is also a Grand Cascade, Arboretum and Rose Garden. The Secret Garden, made by the 10th Duke in the Japanese style, was opened in 2004. The world's second largest symbolic hedge maze, The Marlborough Maze, covers just over half an acre. Two wooden bridges act as vantage points. The palace was the birthplace of Sir Winston Churchill.

Castle Howard

Sir John Vanbrugh's masterpiece exhibits the transition from classicism to romanticism. Work started on the house in 1699 but was still incomplete when Vanbrugh died in 1726. In 1700-1750 Ray Wood became a woodland garden and the Temple Terrace was constructed. The sweeping lawn leads the eye down to the magnificent lake. There is also an irregular eighteenth century wilderness. The winding walks and placement of statues have led garden historians to believe that this was a precursor of the landscape style. The south parterre was created by Vanbrugh. He was responsible for many of the temples and statues in the garden including the famous Temple of the Four Winds from 1724-28. Hawksmoor carried on the work creating the mausoleum that Walpole declared 'would tempt one to be buried alive'. Although famous as an 18th century garden, much of the garden is also influenced by Victorian tradition. The remains of a 19th century parterre has at its centre my favourite feature, the Atlas fountain. It is magnificent, one wants to gaze and gaze. It expresses such power. The fountain carved by the sculptor John Thomas was installed at the same time as Nesfield's parterre in the early 1850's. Nesfield designed the large formal garden that lays behind the house, from here the landscape garden takes over merging with the wood and countryside beyond. The walled garden was dedicated to growing vegetables and fruit. It is now used as a rose garden and a plant centre.

Chiswick House Gardens

Designed by Charles Bridgeman and William Kent for the art patron, Lord Burlington between 1727 and 1729, the gardens feature a ha-ha and wonderful vistas with herms, temples, statues, an exedra and classical ornaments punctuating the parkland planted with trees. Kent, responsible for the classical allusions, designed a rustic cascade and serpentine canal between the years 1720-30. There was an orange tree garden, with the oranges grown in tubs in Burlington's time. The maze built between the house and canal in 1730 was the first of its kind in England. The house was designed by Burlington himself and became an influential Palladian design. Since Kent became popular, his design has remained largely intact although only one of the decorative buildings, the Rustic House remains. Some of Burlington's temples were destroyed in 1858 by the Dukes of Devonshire. The formal Italian garden and Conservatory were added by the Dukes of Devonshire in 1812-13, created by Lewis Kennedy and are in good order. The 65 acre garden and house were granted a Lottery Fund for restoration.

Claremont Landscape Garden

The house was redesigned by Vanbrugh in the early 1700's. The garden was created by some of the most famous names at the time, Vanbrugh, Bridgeman, Kent and Brown. Bridgeman built a great turf amphitheatre overlooking a formal circular pool. Kent introduced a serpentine ha-ha and made the formal pool into a natural lake with an island at its centre and a classical pavilion. On the southern bank of the lake, he created a cascade, transformed into a grotto in the 1760's. Capability Brown obliterated the amphitheatre and rebuilt the house. The first gardens were created around 1705 and the National Trust bought the 49 acre grounds in 1949 with restoration commencing in 1975. The gardens now feature the lake with Kent's pavilion set on an island, the grotto, Bridgeman's 18th century grass amphitheatre and the belvedere on the hill built by Vanbrugh.

Duncombe Park

The 18th century garden is a masterpiece of the Palladian style. The 35 acre (14 hectares) garden features the great lawn, terraces, Doric and Ionic temples, a yew tree walk, woodland walks and a scented secret garden. The conservatory was designed in 1851 by Banks and Barry. The 18th century parkland believed to date back to medieval times, is now part nature reserve.

The Atlas Fountain, Castle Howard

Euston Hall

One of the finest examples of Kent's work – the layout of the park and serpentine lake were completed by Brown. Kent's temple, an unusual octagonal folly and archway entrance survive. Mature belts of trees, lime and beech avenues lend the look of nature.

Farnborough Hall

By and large, this landscape garden from the 1740's remains unchanged. In the mid-18th century, the gardens were much improved by Sanderson Miller. An S-shaped terrace walk with a series of pools, an Ionic temple, the Oval Pavilion with a blue and white interior leading to an obelisk on top of a hill take one around the garden, though there is overgrowth of vegetation, spoiling some of the views. The land in front of the Hall slopes down towards the lake. The gardens were completed by 1751 and are owned by the National Trust.

Gilbert White's House

This thirty acre garden has been largely restored to its 18th century style. There is a small landscape garden, wooden ha-ha, interesting quincunx with five cypress trees on a mound, 'Six Quarters' and a wildflower garden.

Goldney Hall

These 18th century formal gardens over ten acres are best known for their five follies. They feature a bastion, ornamental canal, Gothic tower, rotunda and shell-lined grotto. The planting is currently bedding in colour-themed borders. The ornamental canal is attractive with a statue in the water and formal beds at one end. The gardens, the creation of Thomas Goldney are on a hilltop overlooking the city and are owned by the University of Bristol.

Kensington Gardens

Originally part of Hyde Park, the gardens were formed in the 18th century. Queen Caroline took 300 acres in 1728 and employed Charles Bridgeman to create a new garden for Kensington Palace. He made a round pond in front of the Palace with avenues radiating from it. The Westbourne stream was dammed to create the Long Water, a natural-looking lake. The most ingenious landscape feature, the ha-ha, a ditch and not a fence was used to separate the gardens from Hyde Park. After Queen Victoria moved the Court back to Buckingham Palace, the gardens lost favour and the ha-ha was mostly filled in. The Italian gardens were created in 1860.

Mount Edgcumbe

The Edgcumbe family acquired the state in the 16th century and enclosed a deer park in 1539. Originally a 17th century wilderness and a formal landscape garden, these gardens laid out in the 18th century by the Edgcumbe family were the earliest landscaped park in Cornwall and now feature ideas from French (Regency), Italian (1790's) and English formal styles. The zigzag walks were laid out in the 18th century above the cliffs with ornamental buildings. The Earl's Drive was created in the 18th century and features rare trees including a 400-year old lime and a Lucombe oak as well as a Victorian shell seat. The orangery housed orange trees, taken out in summer into the formal Italian garden with its mermaid fountain and classical statues. The French garden is overlooked by a conservatory formally laid out with flower beds and box hedges. The English garden has irregular lawns with a pretty garden house dating from 1729. The American and New Zealand gardens complete with geyser are more recent. Colourful flowers and heathers grace the restored Victorian East Lawn terrace. The gardens also hold the National Collection of Camellias and there is a fern dell. The house and Earl's garden are at the top of a hill, on the coast with views over Plymouth Sound.

Painshill Park

One of the 18th century great landscape parks has been restored to its former glory. The castellated Gothic Tower was completed high on a wooded knoll in 1750 when Windsor Castle could be seen from the top. Charles Hamilton created what are known as the Hamilton Landscapes between 1738 and 1771. Hamilton was deeply influenced by the Italian painters. The symbolic objects are revealed along a broad river with valley sides planted with azaleas and rhododendrons, amongst the first in England. There is a Turkish tent commanding views of the 14 acre serpentine lake, a folly taking the part of a ruined abbey by the water's edge and other interesting features including an amphitheatre. An island on the lake with a restored grotto decorated with stalactites and crystals through which you can row a boat is connected by a chinoiserie bridge. The garden including the vineyard has been faithfully restored.

Next page: Plas Newydd, Wales

Painswick Rococo Garden

This is a flamboyant gem with amazing features that was a forgotten garden until 1982. In the mid 1700's there had been a garden with walks through woods, a kitchen garden, water and buildings. It is one of the most fascinating gardens in England. The wooded valley is overlooked by ornamental buildings, the Gothic Red House and the Eagle House. The white Gothic exedra is my favourite and overlooks the diamond-shaped kitchen garden. A brand new maze built by Angela Newing celebrates 250 years of the gardens. Six acres of Cotswold garden combine formality in its near symmetry and alignment of paths with an informal treatment. The garden is famous for its snowdrops in spring.

Petworth House

The estate dates from at least the 12th century when it was owned by the Percy family, who later became the Dukes of Northumberland. In the late 18th century, it passed by marriage to the Wyndham family (Earls of Egremont). The present house was built from 1688 and with it the pleasure grounds were replaced by George London with a layout of formal groves and walks. A bowling green, banqueting house and black marble fountain accompanied flower pots on piers. In 1751 to 1763, the 682 acre landscape park was designed by Brown, who created new pleasure grounds on the original Elizabethan site, a 30 acre woodland garden. One of his first projects as an independent designer, considered one of his finest. West of the house, he formed a serpentine lake with islands, Doric temple and Ionic rotunda. A flower garden blossoms with one million daffodils in spring. The 30 acre garden and 700 acre deer park, inhabited by the largest herd of fallow deer in England has been owned by the National Trust since 1947. The landscape was made famous by the paintings of Turner.

Plas Newydd

The house was built by James Wyatt for the 1st Earl of Uxbridge around 1795 on the base of a previous property. The gardens, laid out by Humphrey Repton in 1798 have lawns and trees featuring a spring garden, woodland walks, an Australasian arboretum and formal Italianate terraces created in the 1930's with an enclosed pavilion. The thirty-one acre estate was given to the National Trust in 1976 and enjoys spectacular views over the Menai Straits to Snowdonia. See photo previous page.

Prior Park Landscape Garden

The Palladian mansion was built between 1735 and 1748 to the designs of John Wood the Elder for Ralph Allen. Created with advice from his friends, Alexander Pope and Brown. The gardens have now been partly restored by the National Trust including a Palladian bridge (one of only four in the world), three lakes including a Serpentine lake, Gothic Temple, Grass Cabinet and Mrs. Allen's Grotto. The informal woodland has a winding path which leads to the bridge. The 28 acre garden, very modest in size for an 18th century landscape garden is set in a dramatic landscape running down a steep valley to the south of Bath. The views of the Palladian bridge are spectacular and deer roam the park. see photo next page.

Raby Castle

The Medieval castle is surrounded by formal 18th century walled gardens designed by Thomas Wright. The 5 acre garden sits within a 200 acre deer park. The walls were made with local bricks with flues that could be heated to grow subtropical fruits such as apricots and figs. Features that survive are the two yew hedges that are 200 years old and an ornamental pond dominating the central garden. The garden has been reworked in the 20th century to include herbaceous borders.

Rousham House

The garden laid out by Bridgeman in the 1720's sits in the curve of the River Cherwell. Kent was called in 1738 to complete the garden that set the tone for the period; informality had taken over from the formal garden. He left Bridgeman's work intact and amplified upon it. Bridgeman's amphitheatre can still be detected though slightly obscured. Kent designed an Augustan scene with Roman statues peppering the landscape, intended to be viewed in a certain order from a winding path. Each statue and vista is carefully arranged. A serpentine rill flows through the garden, a grotto with a small cascade and a classical temple overlooking the River Cherwell. An open air cold bath designed by Kent in 1738 was fed by the rill. A Tudor and Stuart style exists nearer the house, an attractive walled garden with box hedging. An historic dovecote is still in use. Kent's standing as the father of the landscape style ensures this garden a place in history as one of the first to be executed. The 30 acre garden has changed little and remains with original features still intact in the hands of the Dormer family.

Stourhead

The Palladian villa was designed by Colen Campbell for Henry Hoare, a banker, in the 1720's. The garden is an outstanding example of the landscape style designed by Henry Hoare II and laid out between 1741 and 1780 after his visit to Italy. Its beautiful setting in a steep-sided valley was used to advantage to create the picturesque lake by damming the river Stour. The garden was designed to be approached by a shady walk from the house. The path comes suddenly to the edge of the combe where the drama of the lake is visible below. Classical features include the Temple of Flora and the Pantheon which are set around the central lake. On the west bank is a grotto built in 1755 with part of its ceiling decorated with seashells. Inside there are marble statues, a river god and nymph framing a view across the lake to the Temple of Flora. On one hill, overlooking the beautiful landscape below is an obelisk and King Alfred's Tower. This brick folly is 50m (180ft) tall and was designed by the architect of many of the ornamental buildings, Henry Flitcroft in 1772. On another hill, The Temple of Apollo offers a vista of cascades and temples. Some of the original features were removed in 1785 by Richard Colt Hoare who also built a second lake. Most of the original garden remains but the effect has been drastically altered by the plantings of Rhododendrons, Laurel and other shrubs since its creation. The arboretum was begun in 1791, but the planting in the garden is largely 19th and 20th century. Stourhead was Lady Penelope's residence in the Thunderbirds. I always wanted to be Lady Penelope, to drive that pink car and where better to drive home to than Stourhead. Yes M'Lady. Since 1946 the 100 acre estate has been owned by the National Trust. It remains the finest example of gardening of its period.

Stowe

The Temple family have owned the estate since the 16th century. Created by William Kent, the garden evolved from Baroque style to Landscape Park. In the 1690's, Stowe had an Italian-style Baroque parterre which has not survived. From 1710-20 Bridgeman and Vanbrugh designed an English park for Sir Richard Temple. Bridgeman built what is probably the longest ha-ha anywhere. In the 1730's Kent was engaged and created more temples. The Elysian Fields were begun in 1731, a paradise for heroes of the Gods with temples, fountains and statues with vistas and controlled viewpoints. In 1741, Brown was appointed head gardener.

Bridgeman's octagonal pond and eleven acre lake were given a natural shape. Stowe is a series of gardens. The western garden with its theme of illicit and unrequited love has the Temple of Venus amongst others. The Eastern with monuments and temples designed by James Gibb, The South Vista - the principal axis of the garden since 1676 was once the siting of the formal Baroque garden, swept away by Brown in the 1740's. The Grecian Valley thought to have been created by Brown in the landscape style, fuses architecture and landscape. Statues gaze upon, as do our eyes when looking down from the temples, this peaceful, green and pleasant land, with water to reflect the leaves of trees, the skies. Peace, peace. The gardens are owned by the National Trust.

Studley Royal Water Garden

This Georgian water garden created in the 18th century represents one of the finest examples of the picturesque style contrasting with the earlier formal work. The garden was the idea of John Aislabie in the beautiful wooded valley of the river Skell. After his death in 1942 the work was continued by his son who purchased the remains of Fountains Abbey. He preferred the landscape style over the formality of his father. It is considered England's most important water garden of the 18th century. The earliest part of the formal garden is a water parterre with a canal running alongside the Moon Pond, a circular pool flanked by crescent ponds. The surrounding lawn is dotted with statues and overlooked by the Temple of Piety which was added later in 1742. Up above in the woods, is a tower built in 1728 and gothicized 10 years later. On the other side of the valley, Colen Campbell designed a Banqueting House. The visitor takes the serpentine path past follies, statues and temples that grace the landscape. Anne Boleyn's Seat, shrouded in the woods, gives a view of the Abbey, England's largest monastic ruin. The 360 acre deer park is the oldest feature of the gardens, thought to be from medieval times and is home to 500 Red, Sika and Fallow deer. Leaving by the East Gate, the towers of Ripon Cathedral are framed by the gateway. Since 1983, the estate has been owned by the National Trust. It is best to ignore the route they ask you to take. The intention was to start with the Moon Pond and end with Anne Boleyn's seat affording a surprise view of the Abbey.

Previous page: Prior Park, Bristol; next page: Top: Blenheim Palace; Centre: Stourhead; Bottom: Stowe

Victorian gardens

Arley Hall

This 2000 acre estate is owned by the Warburton family who have created the twelve acre gardens over the past 250 years having owned the site since the 12th century. The park was landscaped between 1760-80 by William Emes. A ha-ha separates the area from the pleasure grounds. The eight acres of formal gardens lay south-west of the house and were laid out in the 18th century. The walls and surviving alcove at the far end were built in around 1790. The arboretum, named The Grove lies north-east. From 1832 the house was re-built in the neo-Jacobean style. The double herbaceous borders created in 1846 are the most famous feature of the garden, the first border of its type laid out on a grass walk descending from the alcove and backed by yew hedges with topiary and buttresses delineating the space. The small fish garden was created in the 1920's and is representative of the fashion for sunken gardens. The Victorian Vinery is 28m (100ft) long and houses fig trees as old as the building and a selection of tender plants such as olives. The gardens also feature a pleached lime avenue and a Quercus ilex walk where the oaks are shaped into great cylinders. Much of the garden and planting is 20th century.

Ascog Hall and Fernery

The rare, sunken Victorian fernery was restored in 1997. In Victorian times, it had housed many exotic tree ferns and featured in the Gardener's Chronicle in 1879, complete with an inventory of plants growing at that time. A new roof, identical to the original was erected in 1995 with the aid of a grant from Historic Scotland. The fernery, newly planted, re-opened two years later. Over 80 subtropical ferns from around the world can be seen as well as *Todea barbara,* the only survivor from the original fernery thought to be over 1,000 years old.

The Victorian potting shed at RHS Harlow Carr

Biddulph Grange

Long I wanted to visit this garden, I found its Victorian eccentricity utterly charming, a most unusual garden that fascinates. Jellicoe refers to it as cosmopolitan classicism. It was designed by James Bateman and his wife in the mid 19th century to display his collection of plants. In 1840, they enlisted the help of their friend Edward Cooke who designed many of the architectural features and rockwork. They devised a series of connecting gardens each with a theme. The visitor is on tour, as various gardens inspired by different countries are revealed like wonders of the world. Close to the house, the sloping ground is terraced in Italianate style. The formal Italian garden leads to a lake surrounded by Rhododendrons. A dark tunnel leads to a fabulous Chinese temple with a brightly painted bridge. The Dragon parterre is watched over by a golden buffalo. The Egyptian garden has a temple guarded by sphinxes and yew topiary. There is also a Scottish glen, a stumpery, a tower for viewing the Dahlia walk with its buttressed yew 'walls'. The amazing framework of the garden conceals each extraordinary compartment. What an exciting adventure this garden is, full of delights and surprises. The original house was destroyed by fire in the 1870's. The fifteen acre gardens have been restored by the National Trust. If you want to see something different, Biddulph provides it.

Brodsworth Hall

The house replaced an 18th century house, in neo-classical style for Charles Thellusson in the 1860's. Fine turf terraces were built at the same time and flights of steps installed. The white marble urns and statues of whippets along with other sculptures were made by Casentini, an Italian sculptor. To the east are old cedars predating this period, and to the west a flower garden with a tiered fountain flanked by monkey puzzles and beds cut into the lawn. To the west also, on the site of a former quarry, is the Grove. Here is one of those oddities of the Victorian era – a pet cemetery. A rare collection of 350 ferns have been planted in the dell. The elegant 18th century pavilion, the Target House stands at the end of the archery lawn. The rose garden is full of 19th century varieties. The gardens include a formal croquet lawn, summerhouse and rock and woodland garden. A series of grand gardens in miniature with period bedding plants have been restored by English Heritage, returning the 15 acres to their former 1860's glory along with the house.

The Egyptian Garden at Biddulph

Cragside

One of the largest rock gardens, which tumble down the valley towards Debdon burn. At the bottom is one of the tallest Douglas firs in the country at nearly 60m (150ft) tall. The Italianate terrace garden where exotic fruits were nurtured in glasshouses displays carpet bedding and ferneries. Thousands of trees were planted to hide the bare hillside, which feature many 19th century *Rhododendrons*. The house was the home of Lord Armstrong, an industrial millionaire. The garden was the idea of his wife who grew many species from overseas and is now owned by the National Trust.

Drummond Castle

The castle was built in the late 15th century for the first Lord Drummond. In the early 17th century the castle was re-worked and the gardens laid out in the Renaissance style as a terraced garden. The fine 19th century gardens have been restored with the magnificent parterre based on St. Andrew's cross with the original polyhedral tower sundial from 1630 at its centre. The old yews and many period trees remain. There is a copper beech planted by Queen Victoria to commemorate her visit in 1842.

Erddig

The late 17th century house was refashioned in the early 18th century. The thirteen acre estate was given to the National Trust in 1973, which restored the decaying property and land. It is an example of 18th century life with recreated formal gardens consisting of a large walled garden and Victorian parterre. The walled garden shown in an engraving by Badeslade in 1740, houses a large collection of historic apples, pears, plums and apricots. Some, like the pear, *Bon Chretien d'Hiver*, date from the 15th century. Extensive parkland, the canal and a yew walk survive. Immediately behind the house is an Edwardian garden of parterres with bedding and a fountain set between two gabled outbuildings. A Victorian flower garden leads between urns into the woods. There is a national collection of ivies. Emes designed the unusual cup and saucer waterfall in 1774. The device creates an internal, cylindrical waterfall with the stream a few yards away beneath a bridge-like arch.

Previous page: The Chinese Pavilion and the Dragon at Biddulph Grange, Staffordshire
Next page: Glendurgan, Cornwall

Glendurgan

This is a prime example of the Victorian garden with treasures from far off lands. Built in a ravine the garden has *Dicksonias*, *Trachycarpus* and *Gunneras*. Extensive colour is provided by *Rhododendrons* then *Hydrangeas* later in the year. A wonderful laurel maze overlooks a *Taxodium* by the pond. **Trebah**, almost next door is equally beautiful and also created by the Fox family.

Gwydir Castle

The Tudor mansion with an Elizabethan arch and terrace are undergoing restoration. The gardens contain cedars said to have been planted to celebrate the wedding of Charles I. The 19th century parterre was designed by Barry, although gardens had existed here since the 1590's. Peacocks roam the gardens.

Harlow Carr

The gardens were founded in 1950 as the display gardens of the Northern Horticultural Society and have been in the hands of the RHS since 2001. The area of ancient woodland features many old trees. The Victorian Garden at Harlow Carr created in 2004 has a Chinese folly and a gravel parterre influenced by Biddulph Grange. There is also a shrubbery and a geometric bedding scheme beneath a balustrade. *Araucaria araucana* grows in the garden; it made its first appearance in gardens at this time.

Larmer Tree Gardens

An extraordinary example of Victorian exuberance laid out by General Augustus Pitt-Rivers as a public amenity. Specimen trees, ornate buildings and arbours mingle with peacocks and other exotic birds. The gardens have been restored since the 1990's and some new features added to the eleven acre site.

Osborne House

The Royal Palaces and gardens were in a shocking state when Victoria came to the throne. Albert and Victoria bought Osborne House on the Isle of Wight in 1844. Prince Albert designed the Italian terraces where Victoria would take the air. A central fountain was embellished with Victoria's favourite flowers such as *Magnolia grandiflora*, jasmine, roses and honeysuckle. On the other side, an avenue of trees extends the line of the house into the parkland. In the grounds was a children's garden with a chalet, an innovation in those days. The gardens have been restored.

Sheffield Botanic Garden

First opened in 1846, the lawns have been restored to a design by Robert Marnock in the Gardenesque style incorporating the National Collection of Weigela and Diervilla. Far more famous are the fully restored curvilinear glasshouses. The linking walkways between the three glasshouses were demolished in 1901 and they too have been rebuilt using stainless steel frames. The plants in the 90m (over 300ft) long glasshouses are watered by hand with rainwater collected in tanks from the roofs. The gardens also include an authentic Victorian bedding scheme and the rose garden restored to its original Victorian planting, herbaceous borders, a rock and water feature with plants native to the Pennines, an original bear pit and a fossilised tree. Mediterranean plants are in the most sheltered area, an Asia Garden and a Prairie Garden with North American perennials flowering in large drifts.

Shugborough Hall

A complete working estate where one leaves the 21st century and steps back in time. The walled garden dating from 1805 has just been restored. In its day, it was renowned for its innovative gardening techniques to produce fruit and vegetable. It was designed by the famous architect Samuel Wyatt for Thomas Anson. Eight monuments and follies are found in the Grade I listed riverside gardens dating from the 19th century. The ten acre National Trust gardens consist of an herbaceous border, riverside walk, formal terraces with topiary and an arboretum containing fifty oaks, a rose garden restored by Graham Stuart Thomas and a butterfly garden.

Right: The 1890's parterre at Gwydir Castle, Wales
Next page: Top: all Victorian garden, RHS Harlow Carr Displays at Kew and RHS Wisley in the Victorian style

Waddesdon Manor

Spetchley Park Gardens

This formal Victorian 30-acre garden is a home to many rare and unusual plants. The owner's aunt was Miss Ellen Willmott and many plants date from this time. Good herbaceous borders and interesting features include the root house and the Lucombe Oak on the cork lawn. The gardens continue to evolve and new designs and plants have been added.

Waddesdon Manor

The house was built by Hippolyte Destailleur for Rothschild and completed in 1889, resembling a French Renaissance château. The grounds were landscaped by Elie Laine at the same time. This garden is chiefly known for its unequalled massed bedding requiring some 50,000 plants, the Victorian masterpiece. At the centre of the terrace, which was restored in the 1990's, is a pool and fountain. Since 1957 house and garden have been owned by the National Trust.

Arts and Crafts Movement 1880-1920

Flair and taste, style and colour, enliven the garden

Structure and planting behave as one as architects and artists come to the fore. Evocative of the craftsman style one of its main figures was William Morris with his home, **The Red House**, Bexleyheath, Kent where the garden clothed the house. The National Trust acquired the house in 2003. Few records exist of its original appearance, but the subdivisons still clearly exist.

Local, handcrafted products were essential. The style often harked back to medieval times. The garden was an essential part of the home, consisting of a series of rooms, getting closer to nature further away from the house.

Edwin Lutyens, the architect and Gertrude Jekyll, the gardener, created 125 gardens that epitomize the style. She had many favoured plants which have become standbys in many modern flower gardens.

Garden rooms became popular filled with twists and turns, avenues and vistas to discover surprises. The garden is not seen in one glance; some parts being hidden from view.   One can create different experiences in different rooms, but the whole must gel together. Give the garden a backbone, a broad axis, crossed by secondary paths. In this way the space available seems so much larger. *Taxus*, yew will suffice for most of the hedging, but you might also employ allées of trees, *Tilia* (lindens) where space permits, preferably pleached, *Pyrus* (pear) or *Crataegus* (hawthorn) in smaller spaces. Hedges provide the means of dividing the space, ornament the means of linking the different rooms.

Crafted seat at Hestercombe

Arts and Crafts elements

Topiary
Curved steps
Hardscaping softened with plants
Ornate thatched garden structures
Claire-voie
Handcrafted, rustic furniture
Garden rooms
Alpines, rock gardens
Clipped box and yew
Colour co-ordinated herbaceous borders
Sunken waterlily pools
Rills ending in pools
Pergolas with scented climbers
Planting between cracks in paths
Link to the landscape beyond

Cottage Style

Quintessentially English, the cottage garden has reigned supreme and goes as far back as Saxon times. The original cottage gardens were utilitarian with vegetables, herbs, chickens and maybe a pig. The rural cottage garden remained a plot to grow food to stave off hunger whereas in towns, factory workers began to grow flowers such as pinks, auriculas and carnations.

The cottage garden style was developed by William Robinson to encompass the range of new plants coming to Great Britain from the New World and the Far East. It was then developed further by Gertrude Jekyll to embrace the herbaceous border. It is still popular today and is open to wide interpretation. The image of the sweet, chocolate box garden, complete with thatched cottage is one that many gardeners aspire to.

The profusion of colourful flowers and wildlife living in harmony is irresistible. I have for some years now been an exponent of bringing the cottage garden up-to-date by injecting the 'pretty' colours with vibrant darker colours. It is remarkable how many cottage garden plants are now available in these dark colours. It gives the cottage garden an intriguing slant and brings it into the 21st century. Ornamental grasses have already made their way into contemporary cottage style. The lawn is gladly still anathema to cottage gardens.

The classic cottage garden can be re-created with large, wide borders overflowing with herbaceous perennials, annuals, old English roses, shrubs, fruits and vegetables. Fruits such as raspberry canes and apple trees are popular. The planting is layered with shrubs, such as *Hydrangea* or *Cotinus* (smokebush) and herbaceous perennials. Sweet peas beckon from tripod supports, honeysuckle clothes walls, lavender spills onto paths. *Clematis* and roses languish over the door, framing the entrance to the house. It is an inward-looking style created with walls, trellis or fencing. The cosy style can sometimes seem overwhelming, yet the garden is abundant and giving. The hardscaping is timeless with old brick paths and rustic styling. A picket fence is often the best type of enclosure, frequently found painted in white. Ensure there are plenty of places to sit and admire the garden.

Cover arbours with scented plants such as climbing honeysuckle. One thing often lacking in modern gardens is scent. This is where a good cottage garden triumphs. So many of the classic cottage type plants are full of scent that pervades the garden and makes the visitor swoon with delight. If you use the garden in the evening, *Matthiola incana* (night-scented stocks), *Reseda odorata* (Mignonette) and *Nicotiana* (ornamental tobacco) provide delicious perfumes to enliven flagging spirits. The informal garden lends itself to romantic gardens full of roses, honeysuckle and jasmine. Delphiniums tower, pansies edge borders, stone walls ooze Wisteria and are relieved by heads of *Alcea* (hollyhocks).

A rustic gate would lead to the path and there might also be an orchard. Hardwood or wirework furniture is appropriate in this setting. Gardens overflow with plants and can be time-consuming to maintain but one is rewarded by the profusion of colour and scent. There is always something new in flower and the garden maintains interest in this way.

Savour those scents, wallow in that colour, bask in the glory of prolific plants, watch the bees buzz

Previous page: The White Garden, Barrington Court
Right: The pergola, Hestercombe
Next page: Chiffchaffs glorious garden

Cottage gardens

Alfriston Clergy House
A fine, scented cottage garden, restored with traditional flowers laid out in the 1920's. The 14th century cottage is surrounded by a one acre garden full of colour. To the side is an orchard and lawned area. The back garden has a terrace with an herbaceous border overlooking the River Cuckmere. There is also a vegetable garden. It was the first house to be acquired by the National Trust in 1896 for the princely sum of £10.

Barnsdale, Oakham
This is a favourite garden and one I have returned to many times. It is a series of gardens, created for the BBC Gardeners' World television programme, hosted by the owner of the garden at the time, Geoff Hamilton. Much of the planting is cottage style, the garden shows flair and skill in combining well-loved English plants such as roses, campanula and stachys.

The individual gardens are not huge and suit today's lifestyle. Three cottage gardens have plenty of room for growing vegetables, fruit and flowers. In one a picket fence encloses the garden and there is a home-made shed. At either end arches are smothered in roses. There is a glasshouse for summer bedding plants and for propagation. The garden was originally built for the Daily Express at the first ever BBC Gardeners' World Show live. The Artisan's Cottage Gardens was intended for those on a small budget and included do-it-yourself ideas and plants selected for their ease of cultivation and propagation. The Gentleman's Cottage Garden was built to demonstrate how to tackle a garden that is wider than it is long. The design is quite formal. The gardens as a whole have a romantic air.

Chiffchaffs

This is such an interesting garden with wonderful views. Designed and maintained by Mr. Potts since 1978 this is sheer delight and shows just what a cottage garden can be with an eye on relaxed design as well as beautiful plants. The garden is densely planted; an herbaceous terraced garden rises from the lawn with curved stone steps. There is a woodland walk with spring flowers and autumn colour. The three and a half acres overflow with good plants, good taste and good structure.

Dorneywood Garden

This is a cottage style garden with fine herbaceous borders and a rose garden created in the 1930's style. The Queen Anne style house was built in 1920. The gardens are open by written appointment only. Eminent British politicians have gathered beneath the wisteria-clad loggia since the house was donated for use by a senior member of government in 1947.

East Lambrook Manor

Margery Fish created a garden at Lambrook Manor which is quintessential cottage style. However, this garden needs a lot more tender loving care than it has received in recent years. The bones of the original garden are still there. I visited in 2000 when the restoration began and again in 2006 and found it rather disparaging. The long border, white garden and terrace have already been restored. The garden has a nursery and a good tea shop and gallery with changing exhibitions. It is here I discovered the brilliant watercolours of artist Moish Sokal.

Gant's Mill

The Mill dates back at least 900 years. It has recently been restored and opened to the public. The garden is an exquisite English garden with a plantswoman's touch. Very small, it is instructive of how to use space filled with colour and excitement. I fell in love with this garden. Blue delphiniums and poppies are replaced by dahlias and rudbeckias in late summer. More than 60 irises bloom from May to June and there are a good number of hemerocallis (daylilies) and clematis too. Water is abundant in the exuberant gardens. The ornamentation changes each year with sculptures by local artists. The vegetable and kitchen garden is practical. There is a 400 yard riverside walk culminating in the top weir. The mill is also open.

Lower Severalls Garden

The Pring family have farmed and gardened here since 1929. The owner's daughter took over in 1985; the garden has matured with fine herbaceous borders, island beds, a woodland walk and a bog garden known as the 'Wadi'. In 2003 a green-roofed octagonal pavilion was erected. The gardens are set in front of the handsome 18th century Ham stone farmhouse.

This page: Lower Severalls, next page: Gant's Mill

Herbaceous Borders

A must in the 1920's and 30's, the herbaceous style had been recommended by John Claudius Loudon as early as 1840, but it took Jekyll's writing and skill to bring the style to the fore. Even if you do not have the time or the wish to garden in this way, herbaceous borders are typically English and are brilliant to gaze upon.

They are most successful planted with some shrubs and bulbs, often referred to as the mixed border. Choose herbaceous plants not only for their flowers but also for their form, habit and foliage for they must look equally good when not in flower. This is why I detest asters with their awful foliage and I would say uninteresting flowers too, In fact many of the daisy family possess unprepossessing foliage. Too many daisies are planted in herbaceous borders when they need variety in species.

A strong backbone is necessary. The spine is a 1.8m (6ft) minimum wall or hedge because of the height of many herbaceous perennials. The border also needs great width to balance the height. Buttresses give the border rhythm or plant shrubs at intervals - **Arley Hall** uses *Berberis*. The herbaceous borders at **RHS Wisley**, some of the best I have seen are weighted with *Sambucus* (elder). *Yucca* and *Phormium tenax* are distinctive in leaf and provide solidity and provide interest during winter. *Echinops* and *Cynara* offer further sculptural qualities. *Acanthus, Eryngium, Hosta, Bergenia* are all interesting leaf plants to include and some of the *Iris* hold their own too.

Be ready for plants that finish early, leaving behind bare stems. Grow later perennials to take their place or use a vine such as *Vitis* or *Clematis*. Plants that look as good in seed as in flower are valuable in this situation. *Achillea filipendula* is one such and the flat flowerheads add contrast. Peonies and flag iris are interesting in seed too. The best herbaceous borders are those with a restrained colour theme. It is still difficult to better Gertrude Jekyll's colour plans. In shade, white with a touch of green works well. Blue, as Jekyll noted is best with a touch of pale yellow and works well with silver foliage. Deep purple foliage works well with red and orange flowers. An all-yellow border can work admirably but watch the quantity of daisies and their similarity. Multi-colours need careful consideration and should never be in solid blocks but woven tapestry-like. Separate colours can be harmonized by using silver foliage or green as the go-between. It is easy to employ *Lavendula, Stachys Artemisia* and rosemary to good effect.

Arts and Crafts gardens

Barrington Court Garden

The Court House is thought to have been built by William Clifton who purchased Barrington in 1552 from the Daubney family. It is a typical Elizabethan E-shaped design in mellow Ham stone. This is a particularly delightful garden influenced by Jekyll in the early 1920's. The white garden is supreme and proves the point that white gardens can work without a yew background yet it is just one of the rooms in this garden with separate colour themes. The rose and iris garden is at its best in June. The lily garden is full of colour. There is a large walled kitchen garden built as a square divided into four with a central axis. Fruits are trained on walls. Great attention is paid to the floor of the garden. The National Trust has owned the property since 1907 and leased it to the Lyle family in 1920, which created the estate as we see it today. It has been managed by the National Trust since 1991. The adjoining Court House is leased to Stuart Interiors, who show period furniture.

Bodnant

The Edwardian garden is in a beautiful setting in Wales on wooded slopes above the river Conwy, with stunning views over to Snowdonia. Henry Pochin bought the estate in 1874. He planted many conifers by the river Hiraethlyn some of which survive in the Dell. He also created the *Laburnum* tunnel with its metal curved framework. His daughter married Charles McLaren who became Lord Aberconway. Their son, an avid plant collector, added to the garden with many *Rhododendrons, Camellias* and *Magnolias* fired by the interest in Chinese plants. He built grand terraces, the formal rose garden overlooking the croquet terrace and the ornamental gardens that descend the slope. The Lily Terrace has a large lily pool. The pergola is shrouded in roses and leads to the Canal Terrace where there is an 18th century pavilion, the Pin Mill. One can gaze at it from the William Kent garden bench surrounded by yew hedges clipped in an unusual arrangement. The deep herbaceous border is backed by a wall. The 80 acre garden has been owned by the National Trust since 1949 and retains its unique qualities as a garden of moods.

Next page: Bodnant, Wales. The herbaceous border and Pin Mill and canal with the shady seating area guarded by two sphinxes

Cothay Manor

Designed in the 1920's by Reggie Cooper, the garden was influential. Cooper counted Lawrence Johnston at **Hidcote** and Vita Sackville-West at **Sissinghurst** amongst his friends. The garden has been restored by the Robbs since 1993. It looks superb, each part as sumptuous as the last, hidden by the yew hedges. My only regret is that although it sits beautifully with the house, the fine manor perhaps deserves a period garden – there is now a Mount planted with wildflowers and bulbs. Yet this is a special garden of its type and a tribute to Mrs. Robbs' hard work.

Eaton Hall

At the turn of the century, Lutyens designed an Italian parterre in the spirit of the Victorian garden, the old style was still in favour with many garden owners. The garden can still be seen today virtually as it was designed. The simple parterre is surrounded by box topiary and includes statues and a grand fountain. At Eaton there is also a small but very effective white border, a kitchen garden, rose garden featuring a white area and delightful pillars with a view of a church spire. The garden has been opened to the public since 1845 but is presently only open three times a year.

Great Dixter

Who could dislike Dixter? This is such a fantastic plantsman's garden set against the Lutyens dream of a house dating from the 15th century in parts but added to by Lutyens in 1910. How lucky was Christopher Lloyd to garden here. His father, Nathaniel, created the topiary. Lloyd's mother, Daisy, made an Arts and Crafts style garden with the advice of Lutyens in keeping with the house. The five acre garden is exuberant as an English garden should be. Christopher was perhaps the greatest English gardener yet. With a backbone of yew topiary and hedges and good bones, he added much to the garden. He was flamboyant, a great colourist with no fears. He mingled purple, orange and pink like a child playing with colour achieving great, bold plantings. He launched several humble plants into stardom, among them *Ranunculus 'Brazen Hussy, Dahlia 'Bishop of Llandaff'* and *Verbena bonariensis*. He created the Long Border, a mixed border, extended the meadow, ripped out the rose garden and replaced it with an exotic, subtropical planting much in vogue in the 20th century.

Next page: the enclosures at Cothay Manor

Great Fosters

Framed on three sides by a Saxon moat, the gardens were originally designed by W. H. Romaine Walker and Gilbert Jenkins in the Arts and Crafts style. The knot garden is full of flowers and herbs contained by clipped hedges and topiary. Central to the design is the sundial belonging to the direct descendants of Sir Francis Drake, believed to date from 1585. The tiered steps of an amphitheatre have been carved into the hillside. In the 50 acre estate is a lake, a grand lawn leading to lime trees and a wisteria-draped Japanese bridge that leads to a sunken rose garden and lily pool.

Hestercombe House Gardens

From 1750 the estate belonged to Coplestone Warre Bampfylde who created a 35 acre landscape garden between 1750 and 1786. The restoration of the gardens began in 1995. The gardens include a Gothic Alcove, Trophy Seat, Temple Arbour and Witch House on a steep hillside. The fine wooded valley already contained an obelisk and ornamental tower created by his father. By 1771 a waterfall and root house had been added. A lake was created at the foot of the valley fed by a stream from the cascade. A mausoleum was added yet none of the buildings are as distinguished as Stourhead.

The Jekyll and Lutyens gardens were laid out from 1903-8 for the Hon. E. W. B. Portman and oversahdow the older garden. The site on the far side of the Victorian house that replaced the Queen Anne house offers incredible views of the Vale of Taunton. The main area is the Great Plat, the rill, the Pergola walk. The Great Plat featured one of Jekyll's beloved plants, *Bergenias*. Small enclosed courts with circular pools terminate the (30m) 100ft long rills that were planted with iris. The pergola is a marvellous feature, affording views across the countryside. It is some 70m (230ft) long with alternating round and square pillars in sturdy local stone pillars with crossbeams in rustic oak wood of ample proportions to balance the stone. *Clematis*, Russian vine and roses clothe the pergola in all the finery of Sunday best. There is a circular Rotunda, linking the axes to connect the Plat to the Dutch Garden, a paved parterre. The Orangery was designed by Lutyens. The architecture oozes plants in this textural paradise. The stone steps come alive with *Cerastium tomentosum* (snow-in-summer) and *Euphorbia* which plays on the tones of the stone. In 1973, Somerset County Council restored the gardens. It is a masterpiece.

Hidcote Manor

The 17th century house was bought by an American in 1907, Gertrude Winthrop. Her son, Major Lawrence Johnston, created Hidcote Manor Gardens from 1907-1948. It is, broadly speaking, an Arts and Crafts garden. He was an avid plant collector who visited Africa and China in 1927. The White Garden formerly the Phlox Garden included roses, campanulas and crambe. The topiary birds were deliberately unsymmetrical. The garden has strong lines, structural yew hedges and a fine layout of garden rooms, unrelated to the house. One of the principal and endearing vistas is from the cedar lawn through to the stilt garden. The Pillar Garden contains slender, evergreen pillars softened by flowering plants. The Stream Garden bisects the formal plan introducing another element – a naturalistic streamside is created for one to walk beneath trees with colour injected by spring bulbs and in autumn, the changing colours of leaves. A stone bridge and rustic handrail add texture. Since 1948 the ten acre garden has been in the hands of the National Trust and the layout remains with what is thought to be new planting. It has been a strongly influential garden.

Munstead Wood

Jekyll laid out her own gardens as colour-themed borders. Plants were massed and inter-linked. Cool tones enhanced brilliant ones. One of the borders was 4.3m (14ft) deep and 60m (200ft) long. Although the length could be shortened, the depth is good to aim for, without it one does not achieve the necessary layering. The house was built to Lutyens design and completed in 1897. In one corner, Jekyll made a formal garden, a kitchen garden and a nursery. To the east and south was wild woodland with broad walks. The Green Wood Walk offers a view of the house. The house and ten acres remain of the original fifteen. The present owner has restored the garden. In 1912 there were large specimens of *Euphorbia characias ssp wulfenii,* one of Jekyll's favourite plants used to provide dramatic punctuation. In the spring garden, Lutyens placed a wooden gate, homely and fitting. Here morello cherries were grown amongst a mist of arabis, tulips and crown imperials. One of the four beds in the Grey Garden was planted with *Artemisia, Alcca* (hollyhocks), *Echinops* (globe thistle), *Lilium* and a blue *Clematis.* Whilst a blaze of lupins and flag iris brightened June; the September borders with pale yellow snapdragons, rose pink sedums and blue heliotropes and a plethora of asters were a highlight of the gardens.

The hardy flower border was a stroke of genius with red pelargoniums, Dahlia 'Fire King' and *Salvias* backed by hollyhocks in a red and orange colour scheme.

Rodmarton Manor

This beautiful garden retains many of its original features. It was one of the last houses to be built and furnished in the Arts and Crafts style with local stone and timber executed by local craftsmen between 1909 and 1929. The garden was designed by Ernest Barnsley under the direction of the owner, Margaret Biddulph and her head gardener William Scrubey. It most closely adheres to the ideals and principles of William Morris. A series of outdoor rooms were separated by holly, box, beech and yew hedges. The holly hedges, the limes by the circle, the beech hedges and pleached beeches are original as is much of the topiary and yew hedges but some are out of scale now with the original, obscuring the views. The double borders are flanked by grass and a paved path leads to the pavilion. The herbaceous borders, including many unusual plants lead to a summerhouse.

Sissinghurst Castle

Sissinghurst was not bought by Vita Sackville-West and her husband Harold Nicholson until the 1930's as the scattered remains of an Elizabethan house. The imposing tower that remained was used by Vita as her study. They were avid and experienced gardeners, who began the garden before the house was habitable. The bones of yew, box and pleached limes were employed along with romantic roses and herbaceous plants. The exquisite structure of the garden - the pathways, vistas, turns and surprises of a tempting view of what lies in wait - was created by Harold Nicholson, often from the top of the tower, shouting down instructions. The planting created by Vita's capable hands owes so much to the Arts and Crafts Movement, to Hidcote and to the earlier white gardens of India yet it had originality and flair. The white garden is surrounded by green hedges. The white *Rosa mulliganii* grows in profusion with silver grasses, *Stipa barbata.* The little mentioned purple border is another single colour border with *Clematis* and *Cotinus* along with the sunset garden of oranges and lemons. The National Trust took over in 1968 and the original ten acre garden is intact. Nicholson described it as 'a perfect proportion between the classic and romantic, between the element of expectation and the element of surprise.'

Above: Hidcote Manor, Gloucestershire
Top left: Hestercombe
Below left: Edwardian Planting at RHS Harlow Carr

Tintinhull House

The elegant 17th century manor house with 18th century additions was bought by Phyllis Reiss in 1933. Dr. Price, the previous owner had made a garden and the Eagle Court was in existence. Phyllis skilfully worked on it to make a garden of rooms in under an acre. This is one of the finest executions of how to use space in small gardens. Colour (Phyllis admired dark shrubs such as *Berberis thunbergii Atropurpurea Group*), texture, form and shape are all used to great advantage. She used the existing features such as old yews, trees and walls and built on them. Herbaceous plants were used in sophisticated schemes. Her plan was innovative. The vistas are tremendous. Large topiary domes line the path to the front door with spatial acumen. This is a tranquil oais of calm pools, busy borders and an air of seclusion, The divisions are perfect. The garden is well-balanced and appears much larger than it is. There is a fine azalea garden, kitchen garden and fountain and the gardens retain historic planting. In 1953, Reiss gave the garden to the National Trust and it has had a number of tenants, including Penelope Hobhouse. Reiss is rarely given the credit she is due. It remains an important garden, a testament to her ability.

20th Century Gardens

Small gardens arrive on the scene

Wartime meant that everything came to a halt, large estates lost their gardeners who went to war never to return. Labour and money were scarce for the upkeep of gardens. Practicalities led to less opulent gardens. With the advent of WWII much land, even the Royal Parks were turned over to producing food. The Dig for Victory campaign was started in September 1940. People were asked to grow leeks, sprouts and potatoes. The campaign was amazingly successful and the nation was a lot healthier for it. In 1941 a million acres of potatoes were grown. One in five homes had an allotment. Many dug up their existing lawns and borders to grow food.

Gardening had been for the rich, for those with land. In the main, head gardeners no longer ruled, women had come to the fore of garden design. Architects and artists created interesting gardens in the twentieth century. The boom in house-building meant new ideas were needed for smaller gardens. The ordinary householder with a small plot was a new emphasis. In this era concrete came to the fore as a garden material.

Many styles are found in the 20th century. After the war years, slowly a time of prosperity came hence new thinking and new ideas came to the fore. Media gardening began in 1934. Design gradually moved on from the Arts and Crafts through modernism and the outdoor room to contemporary style.

An Cala
Designed by Mawson and planted by the actress Faith Celli in the 1930's, the gardens show much of his typical style and retain their feel. Meandering streams, winding paths and formal terracing with wide lawns are key features. Much of the original planting still survives. A 4m (15ft) high wall protects the garden from Atlantic gales and the Gulf Stream means that *Abutilons* and other tender plants grow here. The lush, sheltered five acre garden has views across to the Inner Hebrides.

The Festival of Britain inspired these gardens at RHS Harlow Carr, right and previous page

Festival of Britain (1951)
In 1951 Battersea Park was transformed into the Festival Gardens for The Festival of Britain and it was the first sign of an emerging modern look. A grand piazza was created with fountains along with a tree walk that had raised wooden platforms suspended between branches so that you could walk amongst the treetops. The gardens have recently been restored.

Concrete modern houses with smaller gardens demanded a new style. Concrete, cheap and available, became a popular material for the garden. This new style was less fussy and plants were used to soften the concrete. Single colour blocks of flowers epitomize the style. There is a typical garden in the festival style re-created in 2004 at *RHS Harlow Carr*.

Russell Page, the English landscape designer was involved in the design of the gardens for the Festival of Britain. The main garden features – the Vista and Flower gardens have been restored. The first subtropical garden open to the public was here at the festival, yet the gardens were a fusion of ideas and styles, the rosary looking back to the 19th century. In 1962, Page wrote The Education of a Gardener, an influential book on garden design.

The Italian revival continued, considered a weak rendition of the earlier Italian glory, the revival simply imitated the earlier style with no injection of new blood. Topiary was still in vogue.

The Peto Garden

Peto travelled widely and placed his collection of Italian and Spanish artefacts in a strongly formal structure with planting influenced by Jekyll and Robinson, both of whom praised his work. Ilford Manor is medieval in origin, the classical facade is 18th century, added at the same time that the woodlands were planted. The terraces lend themselves to the Italian garden style. Cypresses, broad allées, walks and statues form the main stage of the 2.5 acre garden with flowers taking a subsidiary role. The garden has been restored to the original vision and planting of Peto. He also created the Italianate water garden at **Buscot Park**.

Portmeirion

The creation of Sir Clough Williams-Ellis, who designed and built the Italianate gardens between 1925 and 1972 is in a beautiful coastal position. Although Portmeirion is nothing compared to the former grandeur of the Italian Renaissance, it is nevertheless an intriguing garden. The garden contains architecture and buildings of baroque character like a stage set. The plants are bold, *Trachycarpus* (Chusan palms) and *Taxus baccata* 'Fastigiata' slender Irish yews, *Eucalyptus* and many tender plants thrive here adding a luxurious air to the fragmented buildings. The woodland purchased in 1941 adds a wonderful green backdrop. It is perhaps equally well-known for the pottery of the same name and for The Prisoner. I am not a number, I am a free woman.

Renishaw Hall

The Sitwell family had lived nearby since the 14th century. Sir George Sitwell inherited the estate in 1887 and began to lay out the garden. The garden is an Italian Renaissance revival garden. I love the vista from the top terrace, it is glorious. The terraces are linked by stone steps from the axis of the house. Yew topiary and hedges, fine statuary and urns mingle perfectly. In the centre of the final lower terrace is a pond with a single water jet, which shoots magnificently in the air. Cross vistas lead into woodland and there is a waterlily pond. There are several nooks and crannies around the garden. It is a garden divided into twelve rooms.

The Peto Garden at Ilford Manor

Sir George was not interested in flowers. However his successors have created mixed borders resplendent with shrub roses, whilst keeping the Italianate framework.

Trentham Leisure

The Italianate gardens have been restored with the famous copy of the Perseus statue by Cellini standing at the foot of the Lower Flower Garden featuring 60,000 plants and bordered by a mile-long lake. The new planting scheme has been designed by Tom Stuart-Smith and the East and West Pleasure Gardens designed by Piet Oudolf. The amphitheatre has also been restored as well as the landscape gardens originally created by Brown. Whilst the restoration respects the past, new blood has been injected into the gardens.

Modernist

The **Homewood** in Esher is a 20th century modernist house and garden designed by Patrick Gwynne.

Geoffrey Jellicoe was an English landscape architect and garden designer. He designed what is considered to be the last Italian garden in England at **Ditchley Park** with its beautiful parterre and stilt hedge. His heart was in the Modernist movement. His **'Sky Garden'** created in 1956 on the roof of Harvey's store now House of Fraser, Guildford demonstrated his revolutionary ideas, employing concrete islands and planters that went to the very edge of the roof. Water is rarely absent from Jellicoe's work and here it creates the effect of spaciousness by reflecting passing clouds. To have such expanses of water on a rooftop is miraculous. The gardens were restored in 2000. Designs by Jellicoe also include **Shute House,** Dorset with its magical water gardens including the musical rill and **Sutton Place**, Surrey. He also designed the canal at The **RHS Gardens, Wisley**. He is responsible for the garden rooms at Sandringham. In 1975, he wrote The Landscape of Man.

Sylvia Crowe (1901-1997)

Sylvia Crowe was a landscape architect. Her landscapes and gardens expressed the fluidity of concrete and employed many ideas still used today such as Ali Baba pots, small accessible herb gardens near the kitchen door, shallow pebble ponds and round concrete planters. She designed the **roof garden** for the Scottish Widows Head Office overlooking Holyrood Park in Edinburgh.

Christopher Tunnard

He created relatively bleak landscapes of modern gardens that perfectly matched the lines of the buildings, designing **Bentley Wood** in the 1930's. A large expanse of concrete was not 'English' in many eyes, yet the hardy and easy to grow plants he employed are those now found in many town gardens - *bamboo, Viburnum davidii, Pachysandra terminalis, hostas, Phormium* and *grasses*. The terrace is a sparse in many respects. The surrounding woodland was thinned. Space, balance and unity were of far more importance than plants. The Henry Moore sculpture is no longer there and the planting has now changed. He is the author of 'Gardens in the Modern Landscape'.

This page and next page: The gardens at Renishaw Hall, near Sheffield

Arne Jacobsen (1902-71)

St. Catherine's College, Oxford was designed by Arne Jacobsen (1902-71), one of Denmark's most influential designers in 1964. The gardens form an integral part of the building design. The skeleton of the design has remained relatively unchanged. A three-metre grid is unified by rooms separated by yew hedges with choice trees and shrubs.

Outdoor Room (1960-80)

Labour-saving inventions came to the fore. The popularity of outdoor entertaining grew in the 1970's. Pre-cast concrete became available in garden centres and the construction of patios increased.

The creation of the outdoor room owes a lot in this country to John Brookes, who was in turn influenced by designers in Scandinavia and the USA. Simple, low-maintenance ideas that were easy to create by the home handyman and DIY enthusiast typify the style. Many of the ideas and their continued evolvement can be seen in Brookes' own garden, **Denmans**. Most of the earlier gardens have been swept away as they look so much of their time. Gravel, stepping stones and concrete reigned supreme. Low-growing groundcover plants smother weeds. Architectural plants, big and bold were used to effect. The pergola, popular in the Arts and Crafts style made a come-back in a simple form to be used with vines to create a shady retreat in the modern garden. It was the Mediterranean in Britain, a style that has continued to increase in popularity. Planting was pretty much the same in all gardens, the demise of the specialist nursery in the 1950's and the advent of the garden centre. *Juniperus squamata* 'Blue Carpet', *Fatsia japonica, Hosta, Rheum palmatum* and *Cordyline australis* were grown in many gardens and are still popular today.

Bottom right: The 1970's garden at RHS Harlow Carr
Top right: The canal at RHS Wisley designed by Sir Geoffrey Jellicoe

Previous page: Steven Wooster designed the Minimalist Garden for Capel Manor
Above left: A typical town garden with raised beds and trellis, RHS Wisley model gardens
All gardens below are at Witan Street, RHS Wisley, Woking, Surrey, each represents a different approach to a 9x6m rectangular plot
Above right: Revolutions by Juliet Sargent
Below left: Intersections by Catherine Heatherington
Below right: Our Garden by Andy Sturgeon

Contemporary gardens

Much of contemporary design is devoid of that feeling of actually being in a garden space at all. The outdoor room still requires a clothing of plants as decoration

Contemporary gardens have little in the way of universal elements; they are defined by their differences in style. Diversity and inspiration are the key words. Influences come from modern art, formal gardens and a desire to garden ecologically. Gardening has become one of the most favoured pastimes from tending your own patch, to plant 'hunting' to visiting gardens.

In many modern gardens the role of plants is side-stepped by perspex, wood and concrete in any colour to match your mood. Gardens have entered the unexpected with art fuelling the phase. The garden might be designed by the homeowner, architect, artist or a garden designer.

It is essential to know what you want. Certain themes are current and each one expresses a totally different idea of gardening from minimalism to naturalism. In each movement you can see the threads of the past. The TV programme, Ground Force has often been highlighted as the cause of today's interest in gardening. The makeover shows appeal to busy people who need a quick fix. It is essential to sit down with a designer and to have a clear idea of what you want otherwise the result might not be what you imagined.

The current popularity of gardening is as much to do with financial and social change, personalities and garden trends. More people have disposable income and leisure time. More women work nowadays and their primary interest is gardening. We are lucky to have resources that once would have been the domain of the exclusive designer. We have become more design conscious. The garden has become stylish; truly an extra room. Gardening magazines, books, gardens and garden shows all inspire. The small garden has finally come of age.

Yet there is one concern I have to say out loud, the outdoor room should not look like a living room, it should not be seating, cushions, TV, diner, kitchen. This is devoid of the term garden. What one should strive to achieve is a livable, usable space outdoors, not a reflection of what we already possess indoors.

Above: The Chelsea Flower Show features contemporary garden design; Next page: Top left and right: Diarmuid Gavin; Centre: Sogo Garden by Lizzie Taylor and Dawn Isaac, part of Designing-Gardens; Bottom: Eve at The Eden Project

Contemporary style for the trendy and style conscious is popular in small gardens in towns and cities where space is short. It suits modern houses with a small, allotted space. It tends to be low maintenance in line with today's busy lifestyles but often at the cost of plants. In most contemporary styles, pairing of objects is important. Containers are used in twos or threes, in differing sizes. Single species are often used in repeat planting. Andy Sturgeon has gained fame for his clean, sophisticated look. Many modern gardens include art and statuary. Johnny Woodford and Cleve West's designs have pushed them to the forefront of contemporary garden design. Woodford's sculptures are inventive creations with powerful energy. Cleve West's designs combine bold landscaping with texture and colour. The gardens are often symbolic, emblematic or explore specific themes. I believe most of Diarmuid Gavin's gardens fit their purpose with a fresh style that encompasses good plantmanship. Arabella Lennox-Boyd combines traditional features with a quiet flamboyance in planting. Dan Pearson led the naturalistic movement fitting plants into their surroundings ecologically. Tom Stuart-Smith represents a traditional viewpoint with modern plants. Christopher Bradley-Hole continues the modernist look with more abundant planting than expected. They have all showcased at the Chelsea Flower Show, diplaying the best of the current design.

Natural Gardening

In contrast to the concrete and plant-less designs of some contemporary gardens, many modern gardens embrace ecologically sound principles. In many ways they have their beginnings with William Robinson. These natural gardens in their various forms are all in tune one way or another with nature. As gardeners we believe we are creating natural surroundings when we create a garden, but gardening is a false representation. We try to tame yet we are often too dominant, too demanding.

Wildlife Garden

Gardens should surely be at one with nature. Shape, form and style follow the landscape. The wildlife garden is not untamed just as it is not abandoned. There is a certain untidiness that does not take over the look. It explores ways to encourage wildlife into the garden. Wildlife gardens present a whole new experience, light years away from the concrete and chairs of many a modern garden. Elements include an herb garden, a pond, plants that provide berries, a bird table and corners for hedgehogs to hide. A pond is ideal, but a bird bath or even a pebble pool will attract wildlife. Natural garden pest predators will be attracted to the garden. The Wildflower Meadow features native flowering plants in drifts. Native grasses can be used alone and paths mown right through them giving structure and shape.

Few wildlife gardens have borders but if you opt for one, make it natural. Ideal plants are *Digitalis* (foxgloves), *Anthemis* or *Aquilegia* (columbines). It is best to plant natural species not hybrids, a mixture of natives and non-natives. Go for nectar-filled flowers, berries and native trees. Grow a wide variety of plants that flower at different times of the year to ensure pollen is available over as long a period as possible. Cut back herbaceous plants in spring instead of autumn – they provide a welcome home for wildlife through winter. Seedheads make an attractive late-season display and are useful food for birds. Oats and barley will feed birds through winter. Hoverflies and lacewings are attracted to flat-faced flowers such as *Limanthes douglasii*, the poached egg plant. The compost heap is home to insects and invertebrates and is the best way of disposing of much kitchen waste. Climbing plants on walls provide yet another home. Add bird and bat boxes, beehive, hedgehog houses and a pond to encourage wildlife.

Above: Nectar-rich Sedum spectabile and cultivars attract bees

If you feed birds, they come to rely on you and food must be provided all year round. Rotting logs encourage beetles. Ladybirds eat hundreds of aphids each day. Beech provides a natural, solid hedge for privacy. *Cotoneaster, holly* and *hawthorn* provide berries to attract birds. Hedges encourage wildlife but trim before March or after August so as not to disturb nesting birds. Regularly mulching bare soil encourages more earthworms. The wildlife garden must be managed organically.

Choose natural furniture made from willow or hazel. Think carefully about choosing objects and items that do no harm to the environment. Employ wood from sustainable forests, potting compost that does not destroy peat lands. **The Wildlife Trusts Lush Garden** at Chelsea 2005 featured a pond, a garden building with green roof, nest boxes, decaying wood pile, a mature orchard and wildlife meadow. **The Moat and Castle Eco Garden** was very contemporary with a central feature of a natural swimming pond where plants filter the water. The soil dug out to create the pond was used as a natural landform for the meadow and wildflowers to encourage wildlife. **The RSPB/SITA ET Garden** used native plants and recycled products to create a contemporary wildlife garden. It featured a semi-raised pool and bog garden full of nectar-rich flowers. A decorative frieze was created from household rubbish.

Plants for natural gardens
Wildflowers - natives
Groundcover
Lawns for insects
Nesting boxes
Bird baths
Pond
Native trees

Include a balance of nectar and berries.

Nectar	Berries
Arabis	Berberis
Aubrieta	Cotoneaster
Buddleja	Crataegus
Erysimum	Fuchsia
Helianthus	Hedera
Lavandula	Ilex
Lonicera	Leycesteria
Muscari	Pyracantha
Ribes	Sambucus
Sedum	Sorbus

Seedheads
Achillea
Angelica
Centaurea
Clematis
Cynara
Dipsacus
Echinops
Filipendula
Helianthus
Lunaria
Solidago

The Meadow Garden

Meadow gardens provide a conservation area for natural flora of the region in turn providing food and shelter for wildlife. Hedgerows have all but vanished from the English countryside, but this is one way of making recompense for the damage done. Some local authorities have planted wildflowers by motorways following the examples set in Holland and Germany. A fine conservation area is found in **Thijsse Park** which is part of Amsterdamse Bos, Amstelveen, Holland. It was remarkable for its innovative use of wildflowers and the ecological movement.

Meadows tend to be very colourful and bright, falling into two categories – flowers or grasses or a mixture of the two. Prairie meadows are populated with wildflowers and warm-season grasses. If you do not have acres to spare, consider the following to help establish a site.

Wildflowers look best in a semi-natural setting. You can find seed mixes suitable for all types of site from dry, shady through to wet. To establish this kind of meadow takes intensive ground preparation, denuding the soil of seed and vegetation. Warm-season grasses are slow to establish and require one or two seasons before broad-leaved plants can be introduced. Meadows are not maintenance free to begin with and require special management until well-established. The main work is to clear the site and then to keep weed seeds down. Most wildflower mixes are very adaptable. On clay soils it is better to work in sand first. Sandy soils are best with the addition of humus to make them moisture-retentive. You have a choice of planting seed, plugs or full-size plants according to budget.

Sow seed evenly and simply press into the soil without covering. This establishes contact and enables seed to germinate. Sow when rain is anticipated, seed must be watered in by hand. Seedlings will need to be kept moist but not wet until they are 20cm (8") tall. If you have designed the area, you will need to dig every year and re-seed to maintain it as you want it to be. Otherwise nature will take over, seeds will sow themselves at will and weeds will invade. Once established, mowing takes place just once a year. Sometimes different parts of the meadow are mowed each year, say a third at a time. Mowing in autumn on a high setting means that all your flowers have seeded themselves to fill gaps.

This annual mowing also cuts down any weeds that have drifted into the area. Fill in any bare patches in spring with new seed. You can even mow a path through the meadow to get a closer view. In the USA a natural meadow requires no irrigation whatsoever, wherever you live. A thick mat of plants will eventually discourage weeds. Fertilization is ill-advised as plants simply do not need it. There is an exemplary meadow at **Great Dixter**, Rye. Meadows have recently been incorporated into garden design and used in modern ways. The chief exponents are Dan Pearson and I love the way Arabella Lennox-Boyd uses wildflowers with mown paths.

Grass Gardens

Based on gorgeous grasses, this stylish look has gained a lot of followers. It is linked to meadow gardens. Silky plumes that look so soft and touchable sway in the breeze, bringing colour, movement, often strong architectural qualities and texture to the garden. Grasses bring silvers, blues, bronzes, greens and even blood-red to the garden in leaf or in flower. Soft or spiky, grasses add much needed texture. No wonder they are so popular. This natural planting style has a contemporary look.

Give some thought to the heights of different grasses as well as the growth rate. Some are quite frankly space-eating monsters. Grasses tend to fall into sun lovers and moisture lovers so plant them in groups according to your soil. Plant in large clumps with taller varieties planted mid border or even towards the front if they have see-through qualities such as **Stipa giantea** (giant golden oat grass) a fine architectural grass with golden seedheads in summer. Blues are provided for by the invasive **Leymus arenarius** – a very difficult plant to keep under control but beautifully steely blue, **Helictotrichon** and the better known **Festuca glauca** and its cultivars with their spiky blue needle-like leaves. The exotic Japanese Blood Grass, **Imperata cylindrica 'Rubra'** is best admired when backlit, but this too can run, so much so that in some parts of the world it is designated as invasive. **Stipa tenulfolla**, the pheasant grass is silky soft as is **Pennisetum**, which I find really hard not to stroke. If you like something really unusual, try the rush, **Juncus 'Curly Wurly'** with its stems that look like they have been wound like a coil. None come bolder than **Arundo donax** which is most attractive in its variegated forms. Some grasses grow much faster than others and it takes skill to get the grass garden to look just right.

Although the seedheads of many grasses are attractive and extend the season, watch species like **Briza media** and **B. maxima**, you will never get rid of them if you allow them to seed in the garden.

Left top: The meadow at Great Dixter
Bottom: The meadow at RHS Harlow Carr in autumn

Organic Gardening

There can be few who no longer know what organic gardening is. I have always gardened organically with one exception, I sometimes use blue pellets to kill slugs. Principles of organic gardening, much publicized by Geoff Hamilton, include making the soil as healthy as possible, choosing companion planting – plants that work together beneficially and encouraging natural predators into the garden for a true ecosystem. Organic gardeners are environmentally conscious; usually make their own compost and recycling. They also collect rainwater and use local plants where possible. We should all garden organically. With the news in the U.K. that we shall soon be charged for the water we use and have water by the meter instead of a fixed bill, and with many areas of the world facing serious drought, now is the time, if you have not already done so, to think carefully about the plants in the garden. If we all xeriscaped, we would lower our water bills, thereby making water available for other uses. Less time is needed for maintenance, watering takes time and effort, especially if done by hand.

All the above themes garden with nature, to do so
Use drought-tolerant plants
Collect rainwater in a water butt
Make leaf mould

Great plants for the drought garden include
Allium
Artemisia
Convolvulus
Cynara
Echinops
Eryngium
Euphorbia
Lavandula
Oregano
Rosmarinus
Salvia
Sedum
Stachys
Teucrium
Thymus
Verbascum
Succulents

Sustainable Gardening

Sustainable gardens require low inputs of energy, water and fertilizer. A garden hose can use between 600 and 1000 litres of water an hour. We need to look at rainwater harvesting. Bradstone came up with a great idea for water conservation. An underground reservoir lined with a waterproof membrane is made in the garden and houses a hidden pump. Covered with specially designed boxes, the reservoir can be paved over or laid to lawn. When it rains, rainwater seeps through and can be used to water the garden with the aid of a hose pipe. Reservoirs could even be built inside garden walls.

EcoHouse is an organic garden designed on permaculture principles in Leicester. Their mission states that their aim is 'a world where actively caring for the environment is second nature'. Visitors can find tips on growing vegetables, herbs and flowers in a way that is not harmful to the environment. On site there is a wildlife area, butterfly garden and beehives. Advice is given on installation of ponds and on attracting wildlife to the garden. They give plenty advice to those with small gardens too.

We are finally moving towards a different kind of garden and home; one which cares for the environment.

Ecohouse at the DC festival

Worldwide gardens

The Red Sand Garden (above) and the Ephemeral Lake (below) are part of the innovative gardens at RBG Cranbourne, Australia

AUSTRALIA

A news poll in Australia revealed that nine out of ten people aged 25 and over (approx 12.3 million) find a sustainable, environmentally-friendly garden to be the most desirable type of garden. (source NGIA). The same report discovered that 74% found native plants more appealing. 71% of Australians want an outdoor room. So Australians face up to the challenge of the 21st century garden. There are many gardens embracing Australian native plant style.

The British-born landscape designer, **Edna Walling** transformed gardening in Australia. An instant success in the 1920's when she started writing for Australian Home Beautiful. At first she was much influenced by Jekyll, but later developed the use of Australian native plants. The drive leading up to **Cruden Farm,** Victoria, one of her early designs, is planted with lemon-scented *Eucalyptus citriodora*. The coloured bark, almost white makes a distinctive contribution. She is renowned for her use of stone, native plants with dense greenery and few flowers and for linking house and garden. She worked with existing landscapes and features to find inspiration for her designs. She used architectural principles to give the garden structure, softened by plants. She kept maintenance to a minimum believing that gardens should not be hard work. Her informal cottage style is best seen at **Bickleigh Vale Village**, Moorrolbark, Victoria. She created garden rooms such as those at **Mawarra**, Dandenongs, Victoria. The gardens feature her signature elements – an ornamental pool, stone steps and terraces with dense planting and remain as she designed them. **Markdale Garden**, Binda, NSW was redesigned by Walling in 1949 and again is intact. The five acre site shows the harmonious elements of Walling's vision.

The Australian Native Garden, Australian Embassy, Japan
This is not actually in Australia but in Japan. Designed by Jason Sher it showcases Australian plants including State floral emblems. The design contrasts with the existing Japanese garden. The dry river bed has a wooden bridge. A railway sleeper pathway leads to a timber deck.

The Australian Garden
The garden was designed by landscapers Taylor Cullity Lethlean in association with Australian plant expert, Paul Thompson. Explore Australian plants and their environment. The first eleven hectares of this garden opened in 2006 and will be followed by the opening of more features by 2010. This innovative garden truly inspires rendering the falseness of many hybrids laughable. The exhibition gardens show ways to use native plants in the home garden. The Red Sand garden is an amazing landscape – a realisation of just how beautiful native landscaping can be. A vibrant red sandscape features large circles of saltbush, *Aptriplex* with seasonal wildflowers echoing the natural colours of the Central Australian landscape. The Ephemeral Lake sculpture created by Mark Stoner and Edwina Kearney is equally amazing with its liquid-shaped ceramic plates on sand. The Diversity Garden shows plants from different climatic zones within Australia. The Water Saving Garden demonstrates how to group together plants according to their water needs and how to choose drought tolerant plants. The Future Garden features alternate ways to garden with mulches and plants. The Kid's Backyard uses natural plant materials recycled into a play area avoiding the use of plastic and metal. The Arid Garden and Dry River Bed demonstrate the role of water in the Australian landscape where many areas are subject to alternate drought and flood. It examines the power of water to shape the land. Here is a Desert Discovery Camp for children to learn and play. *Kingia australis* is used in this area. The Eucalypt Walk has five areas, each featuring a well-known eucalyptus, the ironbark, box, peppermint, bloodwood and stringybark. The Rockpool Waterway lies beneath the Escarpment Wall, a sculptural wall over 100m high designed by Greg Clark and inspired by natural features found in central Australia such as Uluru and King's Canyon.

Each part of the garden tells a story about the Australian landscape and its plants. Desert like areas and other parts of Australia are best planted with natives. The planting at **RBG Cranbourne** is anything but boring. They have really pushed the boundaries here and used that landscape and its plants to the full proving that natives can be innovative. At the **Royal Botanic Gardens** there is also a Bushland area, an Australian Rainforest Walk, California Garden, Grey Garden and Water Conservation Garden appropriate to gardening in Australia.

FRANCE

The true meaning of the word grandeur and a sense of theatre is understood in French gardens

In France, we encounter the home of the Baroque, the *bosquet* as well as a number of gardens inspired by English style.

Le Nôtre revolutionized French garden design. He organized space like a mathematician, but it's the nicest form that maths can take. The vision he followed was simple: garden and house were part of the bigger landscape, axial lines, woodlands, unity, scale, rhythm, illusion, movement. In effect all the things we look for in a garden today. Le Nôtre carried out his vision without faltering, excluding all that was unnecessary and created some of the most fantastic and enduring landscapes.

In France, the Renaissance began with the return of Charles VIII from Italy in 1496, with him he brought many Italian craftsmen. In the 16th century, medieval gave way to classicism. The great gardens of the period consisted of skilfully proportioned sites that disappeared into the bosque, the woodland, as if by magic. For the first time architecture was subordinate to the landscape.

Below and previous page: Vaux-leVicomte

Vaux-le-Vicomte

There are gardens in which one wants to linger, almost never to leave, Vaux-le-Vicomte is one. The garden was highly innovative and famous in its day, the brainchild of Fouquet and Le Nôtre. Carved out of a wild area of 100 acres (40 hectares) the garden imposes order and a sense of perspective to outmatch the beautiful château built between 1656 and 1661. Perfect harmony exists between the architecture, the garden and the surroundings, yet the house itself is secondary to the landscape. 3km (one and a half miles) is divided into a sequence of terraces with *parterres* on a strong axial design that sweep up into the woodland. There is an elaborate grotto, flat expanses of water, lawns and fountains.

This was the age of elegance, and this garden is truly elegant. The skilful manipulation of the site means that one appears to see the whole garden in one glance. However, from the château the sunken canal is hidden from view at first; an element of surprise has been employed. It is a work of art, to lay paradise at one's feet. From the château looking south, one's eye is taken along the axial to the lake and canal and finally up the hill into the woods. The gilded crown in the centre of the sunken garden is a lovely touch. Keep turning back to see the château as you walk along the axial path, or veer to either side. The garden and château fell into disrepair after Fouquet's demise. In 1875 it was purchased by Alfred Sommier, he and his descendants have brought Vaux back to its former glory restoring the gardens and replacing the statuary. It is not a slavishly historic rendering of the garden, some liberties have been taken including the yew pyramids which were not part of the original garden.

The scale is immense but not overpowering. Some of the elements are traditional, the moat surrounding the château, the canal and retaining buttresses. Le Nôtre was virtually unknown at the time; his father had created the gardens of the Tuileries in Paris. Fouquet, patron of the arts, entrusted the design to Le Nôtre who did not fail him. It stands as the greatest garden of the Baroque Age, Vaux is worth more than one visit, it is glorious and Andre Le Nôtre's finest work. It is still awe-inspiring. One feels the immense importance of being Fouquet, and the jealousy and envy felt by his contemporaries for the man who owned such magnificence. Many of the original sculptures and plants were taken by Louis XIV for Versailles.

Versailles

Louis XIV commissioned André Le Nôtre to design the gardens at Versailles between 1661 and 1670. It is often considered the finest French garden, being the culmination of Le Nôtre's work, his final masterpiece perhaps, yet I prefer the scale of Vaux. Of course, Versailles is grander in many ways, but Vaux is more intimate. However, intimacy was not the reason for Versailles, the most outrageous expression of absolute monarchy in existence. Versailles Palace too was enlarged by Le Vau, architect at Vaux. The work at Versailles was finished by d'Orbay after Le Vau's death in 1680. The plan is influenced by the Piazza del Popolo in Rome, the grand allée. The gardens are magnificent, worked on an axial, one descends passing fountain after fountain. The *parterre* is a more intimate compartment, the part I like the best. *The Parterre du midi, Parterre d'eau* and *Parterre du Nord* are found below the west wall of the château.

It is difficult to imagine the genius of Le Nôtre's mind, the innovator and creator of this marvel. Le Nôtre's job was to show the Sun King as supreme ruler, he managed it perfectly with monumental scale and little sense of enclosure to satisfy the King's immense ego. The gardens disappear into infinity. Just one fountain would have been grand, but their numerous quantities seem to be overkill. Apollo gazes down the never-ending length of the Grand Canal, created in two stages 1668-9 and 1671-2 to the distance beyond, to the heavens. Nevertheless, I admire its extravagance; unique and marvellous in an overpowering, awesome way. The canal itself is 1670m (5,413ft) long. Its east-west axis points towards the setting sun, Louis XIV was known as The Sun King and the imagery is important throughout the garden. The orangery dates from 1684-6 and is a vaulted chamber containing over 1,000 oranges. In May 1664 the garden was sufficiently complete for the King to begin festivities.

Previous page and below: Versailles

Above and right top and bottom: Versailles
Below: Villandry

Villandry

Villandry was built shortly after 1532 by Jean le Breton and the gardens were famous in the 16th century. In the 18th century they were destroyed and replaced by an English-style park. What we see today was created in the early part of the last century. In 1906, the garden was in disarray, a new formal layout was carried out by its new master, a Spanish doctor named Carvallo. He also restored the château to its Renaissance appearance. A canal flows from the ancient Baroque pool separating the ornamental garden from the vegetable garden. The potager modelled on the 16th century is its most famous feature. Divided into nine squares each with intricate beds edged with dwarf box, in which are grown two seasonal crops not of flowers, but of vegetables, many ornamental. Annuals and biennials are found at the perimeter of each square. At each corner roses grow on trellised arbours providing shade for the viewer. Beneath the salon windows, the ornamental gardens are dedicated to the theme of love, hearts enclosing flames represented by box hedges and red flowers. The garden of music featuring lyres and harps of topiary, water jets, box hedging and beds of flowers. In its spirit it communicates well with the house although many of the plants were unknown in the sixteenth century. The earliest layout Carvallo could find for the gardens was dated 1762. All that remained of the original was a Baroque pool and canal.

Le Labyrinthe

The original potager has been restored. The garden is known as *le jardin du cinq sens* – the garden of the five senses. Ancient roses, palisaded fruit trees, medicinal and aromatic plants and fountains adorn the garden. It is in keeping with the ancient city of Yvoire.

Fontainbleau

A pretty garden with a wooded area, a lake and folly and a formal garden surrounds a very pretty château with the statue of Diana and her hunting dogs in the grounds.

Luxembourg Gardens

The elaborate bedding is in essence Victorian style and it is exquisitely executed. There is a surprise in one water feature – a floating face.

The Tuileries

In a magnificent setting by the Louvre on the banks of the Seine are the Tuileries. I had always wanted to visit since I read about them in French Literature as a student. Wirtz has created a parterre here. The borders further along, near the Louvre are interesting, the bedding given a new slant with the use of black plants.

Below and next page, top left: Fontainebleau
Top and centre right and bottom left: Luxembourg
Gardens, Bottom right: Parc André Citröen

Monet's Giverny

The garden of the artist, Claude Monet is one of the most famous and most visited gardens. If you pull into the car park, you will be struck by the beauty of the natural planting for this is the nicest place anyone could park a car. Across the road is the house and garden where Monet came to live in 1883 and create the gardens in two parts. The house is built on a hillside bordering a small river, in front of it is a pattern of long, narrow flower beds and gravel paths. The lines are softened by exuberant, floriferous planting and colour. The sunset border is here in vibrant oranges and yellows. Enchantment is alive in the arches that drip roses and sweet peas in a most romantic way. In 1893, Monet bought the land that faced the house, beyond the road and railway tracks. A tunnel under the railway leads to the water garden made famous by his water lily paintings. The recently renovated Japanese style bridge is draped with white wisteria, along with the bamboo and willow, it is a natural setting. The gardens have been restored but some of the plants have changed. With a spell all of its own; it really makes you want to garden, to pick up your brushes and paint.

The colourful plantings of Monet's Giverny
Top right: Zinnia orange; Centre right: Rudbeckia
Below: Yellow viola with Aegopodium podagaria
'Variegatum'

HOLLAND

Holland is still known as the land of tulips, yet her horticultural status in the 21st century is predominant. Here you will find many tributes to the tulip, botanic gardens, notable arboretums, English and Dutch baroque style gardens as well as very definite interpretations of contemporary style. J. P. Thijsse influenced the ecological parks, the *heemparks*.

Hortus Botanicus, Amsterdam
In Amsterdam, the Botanic Garden stands in a lovely setting backed by water. As early as 1638, there was a physic garden attached to the University of Amsterdam. The Botanic Garden was laid out as an herb and pleasure garden in 1682. The modern, three-climate glasshouse opened in 1993 with a walkway through the temperate house offering a view of the pond. There has been new landscaping too.

Hortus Botanicus, Leiden
Clusius regaled as bringing the first tulips into Holland, was the founder of the Botanic Garden at Leiden in 1594. The reconstruction of his garden with brick-edged rectangular beds forms part of the present site. A Japanese garden was created in 1990 to commemorate Von Siebold who sent many plants to the garden when working as a doctor in Japan. 65 *Passiflora* species and *Aristolochia* are to be found in the glasshouse.

Hortus Bulborum
This is a favourite of mine, a garden of heirloom bulbs, mainly of tulips, but also having a good collection of daffodils and some hyacinths. It has none of the pizzazz and showmanship of Keukenhof, but all the thrills of old varieties, many of which are still grown today. Colourful bulbs are paraded in straight lines.

Keukenhof, Lisse
The sheer numbers of bulbs on display bowls you over. Keukenhof has brought the floral exhibition to a grand if sometimes garish art. It was created in 1949 as a showcase. The park itself had been laid out by J. D. Zocher the Younger in 1854 with handsome woodland glades. Today, over six million bulbs are shown on the seventy-nine acres. It is often described as the place to see *tulips* and although *tulips* reign here, hyacinths, daffodils, muscari, crocus and other bulbs such as Crown Imperials (*Fritillaria imperialis*) are displayed in enormous masses, drifting in elegantly shaped beds amid water features and trees. Some of the plant combinations are good. In addition, you will find large glasshouses and a few show gardens. The gardens are only open for a short period each year at the height of the flowering season.

Left: Strongylodon at Hortus Botanicus, Leiden
Below and next page: Keukenhof

Paleis Het Loo, Apeldoorn

Het Loo was a summer retreat for the Royal family and both the palace and gardens have been restored to their original 17th century splendour. The Dutch Baroque garden, the most richly planted and exuberant of their time, lies behind the house. It was really hot when I visited in May, the only shade is provided by the semi-circular pergola at the far end of the garden. The perfect symmetry, axial layout and gravel walks with water features designed by van Cleef, parterres and statues were all under the blazing sun. The original design was executed by Le Nôtre's nephew, Claude Desgotz. The plan was not carried out in full and the garden does not dominate the landscape. The main garden has a raised walkway. In the eighteenth century, the garden was swept away in favour of an early landscape-style garden featuring classical and *chinoiserie* type buildings. The gardens went through further modifications including the creation of two large lakes in 1818-24. In 1962, the garden and house were donated to the State. In 1970 the restoration began being completed in time for its tri-centennial in 1984. The restoration was based on a plan by Christiaan Pieter van Staden c.1714. However it is not an exact replica of the original, some of the trees from the landscape park being kept. One gets the feel of the original with its handsome water features. I love the quiet canal flanked by lines of trees. The box hedges are punctuated with pencil-thin junipers and filled with authentic plants from the 17th century. Rosa mundi, crown imperials, tulips, dictamnus, rue, monkshood, flag iris, peonies and bear's breeches are all grown here. It is a charming garden without being overwhelming.

Mien Ruys Tuinen

The famous Dutch garden designer has been very influential. Gardens were created at her parents' nursery that became world-famous, Moerheim. She created gardens from 1925 and they stand as testimony to the ideas she developed in her lifetime. The gardens range from the earliest Wild and Experimental to grasses and the 90th birthday celebration garden which featured 90 different annuals in mixed borders. Her ideas have been adopted into popular design and the gardens offer much inspiration today. The nursery still exists too.

Piet Oudolf

Regarded as one of the finest plantsmen of contemporary garden design, Oudolf has made his mark. His nursery grows some of the most desirable hardy herbaceous perennials, attached to a garden providing ideas for all those seeking low-maintenance plants. Oudolf has designed gardens in many Euorpean countries and in America. He says of his work

"The vision I have developed on gardening and especially in my work with perennials is based not only out of respect for nature but also the power, energy, emotions, beauty and aesthetics it gives."

The Oudolf sumptuous new perennials border at RHS Wisley in autumn

ITALY

European gardens had their effect on what was fashionable in England. Chief amongst these styles was the Italian Renaissance, although the style never adapted so well to the English climate and landscape. These exquisite gardens were usually built on hillsides using evergreens such as cypress, ilex and box. Topiary, stone, stairways and arbours were features that fitted harmoniously and naturally into the composition.

Garden and home were planned together as a unit. The climate encouraged outdoor living and the gardens reflected this. Line was borrowed from the house and harmony reigned. We learn the lessons of formality, symmetry and geometry combined as an art form to surpass nature itself. The gardens although grand are not as pretentious as the French gardens. Nature is tamed rather than subjugated.

Villa Lante

Although it did not assume this name for 100 years, it was designed by Vignola (1507-73). The water features were nothing short of genius. Tomasso Ghinucci from Siena was the hydraulics expert who made it happen in the 1560's. The gardens just seem to drip water, built on a series of terraces with water gods, grottoes and fountains. There is a water parterre with a central fountain vying for attention amongst the green parterres. The water cascade runs into the famous Fountain of the River Gods, the gods reclining in splendour. The Cardinal's Table has a central trough of water. Water jokes, spray the unsuspecting. Vast plane trees and stone carvings complete the landscape. The perfectly symmetrical design is on four levels with a main axis. The Villa, designed as a summer refuge is two pavilions, one built in 1578 and one in 1612, from here the gardens appear to be suspended.

Villa d'Este

The villa was created from 1550-1572. It truly is the most spectacular water garden. Ancient Roman elements are included, sculptures even being taken from the nearby Villa Adriana (Hadrian's Villa). Its creator, Pirro Ligorio also alluded to the debt in his creation of a classical temple. Overall, the gardens dominate the landscape, cascading down a hillside below Tivoli with a central axis interspersed with offshoots and linked by stairways and ramps. The Organ Fountain (1661) and the Terrace of One Hundred Fountains are its most famous features. Hydraulics was used to add theatre and drama to water features. The water cooled the hot temperatures found in this area. It was designed for Lucrezia Borgia's son, Cardinal Ippolito d'Este and it intended to impress. The garden has been restored, still impressive today, imagine what it was like when first revealed to visitors.

Villa Capra

The villa also known as Villa Rotunda was built by Palladio in 1550. It marked the end of an era in landscape design and at the same time influenced the revolution of the 18th century in English landscape design. It sits on a low hill near Vicenza.

Villa Gamberaia

The transition period between the Renaissance and Baroque was called Mannerism and is best characterized by the Villa Gamberaia which overlooks the Arno Valley, Florence. The water garden consists of four flat expanses with a central fountain, topiary and hedging. The Villa was built in 1610 and the gardens were initially made with a large bowling green as the main feature, but enlarged and transformed over the centuries. Princess Ghyka came in the early 20th century and employed Italian landscape designers to restore the gardens.

Villa Garzoni

The Baroque period followed with central radiating avenues culminating in a central feature as found in urban planning. These features were translated into the garden. In Rome, the Piazza del Popolo was created in the late 1580's. The Baroque climax in gardens came in 1652 with the creation of Villa Garzoni near Lucca. The semi-circular parterre is at the foot of terraces that culminate in a wood area (bosco) of holm oak, cypress, bay and box with a magnificent cascade with pools flinging water into the air. Green dominates the scene.

Villa Capra

Above: Villa Garzoni, Right: Villa Lante
Below and below right: Villa d'Este from the
100 fountains.

MOROCCO

The Majorelle Garden

If Morocco and Marakkech do not conjure up a certain feeling within you, you are already dead. The very essence of the place is exotic, full of scents and notions. This garden is truly at one with its setting, all the elements belong. Jacques Majorelle (1886-1962) was a painter who came to Morocco in 1917. Palms, cactus, ferns and tropical flowers abound in the garden created in the 1920's. The blue buildings combine with gold pots and ornate gold window screens to create atmosphere. This is a garden not created by head and hand alone, but by the soul and spirit. Following the death of Majorelle, the house and gardens were bought by Yves St. Laurent. Majorelle's studio now houses the Museum of Islamic Art.

RUSSIA

Peterhof

Founded at the beginning of the eighteenth century by the Emperor, Peter the Great, this palace embodies the essence of Russia at the time. Created near the new capital, just 29 km from St. Petersburg, it was intended to become the most splendid summer palace. After 1917, the palace came under State ownership and turned into a museum, the Peterhof State Museum-Reserve.

The magnificent gardens provide the right setting for the palace. In the surrounding parks are 176 fountains, four cascades and incredible gilded statues, sculptures, majestic palaces and works of art to impress even the most unimpressionable. The grounds include six palaces, grottoes, an Upper Garden and Lower Park as well as the Alexandria Park. The Great Cascade is one of its finest features and Peterhof has earned the name of 'Capital of fountains'. The Sea canal is the north-south axis of the site. It was sketched in the original design by Peter the Great himself and construction began in 1715. The canal divides the 102 hectare Lower Park in two parts, east and west, each containing further water displays. The Great Cascade is a beautiful Baroque fountain. The fountains were created and improved over many years, with periods of reconstruction and restoration. Finally the cascade was given a new lease of life in 1995. 138 jets spurted water into the air.

Terraced slopes stretch for 100m either side of the Great Cascade, they are interspersed with single jet fountains. Amongst the miraculous fountains found in the grounds, is the Pyramid Fountain with its 505 jets, in seven tiers, on four sides forming the geometric pyramid shape. The Sun Fountain is a favourite, set in a large rectangular reservoir called the Menagerie Pool. Gilded dolphins spout water and a single tube rises from the centre with a golden disc having holes from which water spurts. Three trick fountains were created in 1784.

The Upper Gardens cover 15 hectares (40 acres) and were designed to provide a formal approach to the Great Palace. There are *parterres* and pairs of square, radial and circular patterns. Each *parterre* is enhanced by trees and shrubs along the perimeter and by the fountains, marble statues, covered walks and arbours. They were restored in 1972.

The Lower Park follows the natural run of the land forming a flat strip of coast bound by a terrace on the southern side and by the Gulf of Finland to the north. The Marine Canal is almost 600m long. Straight avenues link all the features consisting of fountains, palaces, pavilions and cascades. Its unity has been preserved.

To the east is Alexandria Park where construction began in 1826. The Romanovs created the Imperial summer residence here in the second half of the 19th century. The park with its vistas, glades and hills embellished with sculpture, buildings and trelliswork clothed with climbers is romantic. Nicholas Avenue forms the central axis transversing the park from west to east.

SPAIN

The distinctive patio gardens were a leftover from the Moors and the Moorish gardens still form the best of Spanish gardens. Parks form part of most major cities with tree lined avenues. Gaudí's Güell park still has an air of freshness and newness about it.

The Alhambra, Granada, Spain

The Alhambra was built by the Moors and is much influenced by Islamic and Persian gardens. Water was brought from the nearby Río Darro and between 1273 and 1309 there were public baths inside the fortress. The glorious architecture is a perfect complement to the simple courtyards where water reflects the heavens. The outdoor courtyards all feature water – in flat expanses or fountains, many used for ablutions. Part of the buildings date from after the expulsion of the Moors in 1492. The Patio de Los Leones (The Court of Lions) was originally planted with orange trees. The simple water rill channels towards the magnificent fountain, the basin held aloft on the backs of lions. The Jardines de Daraxa were constructed between 1526-38 and contain cypress, acacias, orange trees and box with a large, central marble fountain made in 1626 and decorated with a poem. The Jardines del Partal covering the area between the Ruada exit and the Torre de Las Damas (Ladies Tower) are planted with lush green trees such as cypress near a flat canal of water.

The main garden is the Generalife, the pleasure palace. It features a cypress hedge walkway through an arch cut into yew. The canal known as the Patio de la Acequia (Irrigation Patio) is 48.7 metres long and 12.8 m wide. It is interspersed with jets at regular intervals that shoot water out over the channel. At present there are myrtles, roses, cypress and orange trees but the planting, like the house has changed over the years. The lower gardens are accessed through an arch. The Patio de los Cipreses (Cypress Patio) consists of a myrtle hedge surrounding a central pond. A 19th century stone staircase leads to the upper gardens, the hanging gardens. They include vegetables, myrtle, box and cypresses over 100 years old. The courtyard gardens are an exquisite example of a style (Persian) adapted to a new climate and surroundings. The Generalife gardens are built on the lie of the land, falling away and as such are a forerunner of the hillside terraced gardens of the Italian Renaissance. The patio gardens are an early example of gardens as an extension of the house. The Alhambra, the red palace, is at one with its position.

I first visited the Alhambra as a student, I wrote about it in my thesis on Islamic Architecture in Spain as part of my degree. I revisited in my early 30's. It is a garden I would like to revisit often, it holds a special magic for me, an aura of calm even when bursting to the seams with tourists. One can feel rushed by the crowds, but this is a garden in which to take your time, relax and contemplate encouraged by flat expanses of water. The scale is human, each courtyard open to the sky. In its heyday it was the final stronghold of the Moors in Spain. This is one of the greatest gardens in the world, yet it is not just the garden that thrills, it is the building, the setting, it's a complete package. If my Arabian Prince ever comes, I hope he whisks me off to this most romantic of palaces.

Alcázar, Sevilla

A Moorish palace, not as ornate as the Alhambra yet the architecture is still magnificent. It has been changed several times and most of the palace dates from 1384 in the style of the Moors, constructed for Pedro the Cruel. The Patio de las Doncellas contains a rectangular tank with sunken gardens on either side.

Casa de los Pilatos

A large 16th century mansion with a mix of Moorish, Gothic and Renaissance architecture with a beautiful courtyard having azulejos with Greek and Roman statuary and a central fountain. The house is full of antiques and paintings and is in private hands.

Parque María Luisa, Sevilla

This park contains 1920's Art Deco and mock Mudejar architecture. Palms, orange trees and Mediterranean pines are lush amongst ponds and beds of bright flowers. The Plaza de España is the central feature with its mosaics and water feature. Constructed as part of Sevilla's world exposition, nearby is the Royal Tobacco Factory, immortalized in Bizet's Carmen. It houses the University where I studied for part of my degree.

Next page: Top left: Generalife gardens, Alhambra, Right, top, centre and bottom: The Alcázar, Córdoba Bottom left: Alcázar, Sevilla

The Moorish Mosque, Córdoba

The Mosque now houses a Cathedral built in 1523 by Charles V, but it is the Moorish architecture that stays in one's mind. The horseshoe arches here are rightly famous and they link visually to the lines of orange trees in the Patio de las Naranjas in the enclosed courtyard. The Great Mosque was begun in 785 and added to and expanded over the next two hundred years. It is the third largest structure in the Islamic world. The oldest entrance, dated 786 is the Minister's Gate (Bab al-Wuzaara) on the west façade which remains to this day, almost unchanged. This truly is a wonder of its time and remains so to this day.

Antoni Gaudí

The public park, Parc Güell, Barcelona (photos this page) acquired by the city of Barcelona after WWII was designed by the Spanish architect, Antoni Gaudí; Güell being the patron. Work began on the mountainous site north-west of the city centre in 1900. The decoration is what one remembers, the mosaics, the organic forms.

USA

America was much influenced by what went on in English gardens. Only recently has there been an increasing interest in native plants with the enduring Californian style and local plants in all States. America is greening up with green roofs and urban design.

Beatrix Farrand became the only woman founder of the American Society of Landscape Architects (ASLA). Her most famous work is **Dumbarton Oaks** in Washington DC, transforming the gardens from cow fields between 1920 and 1940. It is now in the ownership of Harvard University, but it was created for Mildred and Robert Woods Bliss. The Italianate style planting is influenced by Jekyll and yet Farrand uses her skill to instil the garden with a sense of place. Ten acres of landscape include small formal gardens with rich planting, a Roman-style amphitheatre, ironwork largely designed by Farrand. The *Prunus* Walk, Cherry Hill and the cowpath, now planted with *Scilla* and other spring flowers are romantic. The strong yellow of *Forsythia* Hill is joyous in spring. The Ellipse is simple yet so effective, formed by a double row of *Carpinus* (hornbeam) on stilts. The federal style mansion was built in 1800 with the Orangery added in 1810. Farrand's clients came to live here in 1920.

She also designed the **Eolia Italian Gardens** at the mansion of The Harkness Memorial State Park, Connecticut. Farrand is well known for saving Jekyll's drawings from destruction. She donated them along with her own collected works to the University of California.

Fallingwater fits its surroundings like a hand in a glove

Frank Lloyd Wright (1869-1959)

Pure genius, he knew how to live at one with nature whilst producing an extraordinary landscape.

Robie House, Chicago 1910, is considered one of the most important buildings in the history of American architecture - a quintessential prairie house. Wright himself fought to save it from demolition twice. The exterior restoration of this modern masterpiece was completed in 2003 and the inner is being restored. The garden will be restored to reflect the relationship Wright created between the building and nature. Three large elm trees existed on the 1910 site and there were built-in flower boxes. The cantilevered roofs overhang the straight lines of the walls. The roof means that the sun hardly hits the glass-walled southern exposure of the living quarters which are above ground level. The building was designated a Chicago Landmark in 1971. Today it serves as a Museum for the Frank Lloyd Wright Preservation Trust.

Fallingwater, Pennsylvania 1935 is my favourite design of this genius. In 1991 it was voted the best all-time work of American architecture in a poll of members of the American Institute of Architecture. This is organic architecture at its best promoting harmony between man and nature through integrated design. It expresses the idea of unity perfectly. Do the trees grow around the house, or is the house set amongst the trees? They appear as one, impossible to divide. The waterfall, known as Bear Run, flows as if by magic from the stone of the building, an integral part of it. The house has almost as much outdoor as indoor space; the terraces are cantilevered to mimic the jutting rocks. Its original furnishings are still intact. The house built for the Kaufman family was donated to Western Pennsylvania Conservancy in 1963.

When Hilla Rebay, the art advisor to Solomon R. Guggenheim, was looking for an architect to design a new building to house his paintings, he wrote to architect, Frank Lloyd Wright in 1943

"I need a fighter, a lover of space, an agitator, a tester, a wise man... I want a temple of spirit, a monument!"

Wright was dead before the building was completed in New York, but it stands as testimony to his genius. The spiral, an inverted ziggurat with an open rotunda allows visitors to view several layers of galleries. The design has been much copied, as old as it is; it still looks fresh and new. Standing on 5th Avenue with Central Park nearby, it is a relief from the dominance of New York architecture, the icing on a sculpted, geometric organic cake.

Thomas Church led the California school of garden design and developed the concept of the outdoor room, a complete departure from the garden traditions of the East coast. When Church came upon the landscape scene in the 1920's, most of the Italian or Spanish style houses had an English landscape garden. Church found the answers to provide a usable garden space unique to the area. He took into consideration the unique climate of California, its landscape and lifestyle characteristics. The garden essentials were native trees for shade, a place to eat and basically live outdoors and enjoy the climate. Swimming pools were popular and gardens took advantage, where possible, of the fantastic views. Gardens were relatively compact, usually around half an acre. Church's approach was a symbolic lawn and simple planting plans using native and drought-tolerant plants alongside paved areas offering low-maintenance. Until the late 1930's, Church's work was conservative and based on traditional principles. After this time, he became more experimental, influenced by Cubism and Art Deco. He abandoned the central axis in favour of flowing lines. He incorporated new materials. This new style emerged as a solution to the needs of the smaller garden. In 1955 he wrote Gardens are for People. He designed and built more than 2,000 gardens. **Lakewold Gardens** is typical of his work as is the **Bloedel Reserve**, both in Washington State. His success was in combining the functional with form, creating landscapes in unison with their surroundings.

"Modern," said Church "was a battle cry that degenerated into a style and, finally, into a nasty word."

Essential elements of Thomas Church gardens are
Careful siting and orientation of house
Using existing topography
Native plants
Drive, parking area and front door to create a sense of arrival and entrance
Distinct connection between house and garden
The definition of the garden at once part of the surrounding landscape and yet separate from it
Functional space providing for the needs of the owner
Low maintenance
Plants that connected with the landscape

Dan Kiley (1912-2004)

Another master of the art, Kiley understood the relationship between who you are, what you do and the space you need. The **Kimmel Garden** is a landscape of exquisite contrasts – a soft meadow, geometric land form, lake, wide grass walks and rolling landscape into the hills. He also designed the Esplanade garden for the **Chicago Botanic Garden**, giving immense spirit to the entrance.

The Center for Medieval Studies, Pennsylvania State University, USA

The University has recreated an authentic medieval garden including a kitchen garden, a pleasure garden and a contemplation garden.

Agecroft Hall

A 15th century mansion was shipped from England to Richmond Virginia by Thomas C. Williams Jr. in 1925. The grounds, designed by Charles Gillette are intended to recreate the opulence of English gardens. A fragrance garden blooms with plants popular in the Elizabethan period and herbs grow in the knot. Annuals grow in the sunken garden based on the garden at **Hampton Court**.

Glebe House

This is the only extant garden in the USA planned by Gertrude Jekyll in 1926 consisting of 600ft of English-style border, a stone terrace and rose allée. The complete plan was never fully installed. The plans were discovered in the 1970's and carried out in their full splendour.

Hearst Castle

The house built in the Mediterranean Revival Style was the home of the famous newspaper owner. It is surrounded by an Italianate garden in lush greens on a series of terraces. Walls are decorated with bougainvillea, star jasmine and wisteria adapting the style to drought-stricken California. Along the Esplanade the azalea walk offers fine vistas. The design is more formal as one approaches the house. Imposing marble columns are interjected with Mexican fan palms and roses. Majestic native trees are carefully integrated into the design. The gardens were full of colourful flowers not associated with Italian gardens. Hearst lived here from the 1920's to late 1940's and the gardens are being restored.

The Lloyd Border, Whiteflower Farm

The Lloyd Border is in part a tribute to the great plantsman Christopher Lloyd and was designed by Fergus Garrett. The herbaceous border is 50m (280ft) long and full of dashing, daring and bold colour planted with 3,000 bulbs, shrubs, trees and perennials. In May tulips dominate, but the colour continues all season long. There are five acres of display gardens including a cottage garden, a tapestry hedge of dwarf evergreens and a display of Blackmore & Langdon's English begonias.

Tryon Palace and Gardens

14 acres offer three centuries of garden history. The 18th century wilderness garden shows plants that greeted the first European settlers. Lush displays from the Victorian era and the 20th century colonial revival are also represented. The current gardens were designed by Morley Williams at the time of the Palace restoration. None of the three historic plans recovered appear to have ever been implemented in their time.

Above: Hearst Castle
Below: Frank Lloyd Wright's Taliesin West Reflecting Pool; Left: Dumbarton Oaks

The Fort Worth Water Gardens in Texas were designed by architect, Philip Johnson from New York and amply display the incredible beauty and power of water. The park features three pools of water, the aerating pool with multiple sprays, the quiet pool with an expanse of flat water and the gushing fountains of the active pool. You can actually get down and stroll around the active pool, becoming part of the fountain.

Contemporary design in California is still very much inspired by the influential Thomas Church and the Californian School. Bruce Meeks, Russ Cletta and Dan Wheedon are three American designers showing clean contemporary lines.

Below: Bruce Meeks, Right: Russ Cletta, and
Top Right: Dan Wheedon's Infinity Pool

Garden design

Long Acre Design at Chelsea Flower Show

Visual tricks

There are several ways of employing visual tricks to make the garden appear larger than it is. The art of creating the illusion of space is employed to great advantage in small to medium-sized gardens.

By linking garden and house the total space appears larger. Create unity by keeping the same style, colours and spirit of the space. Employ some of the materials used in the construction of the house to build the garden. Marry colour schemes from the interior to the exterior. Employ natural continuity - a limestone house can be blended into the garden if limestone is used for surfacing and garden walls. Use flooring to link the two, tiles or wood.

Devote ground space to seating and walking areas and confine plants to raised beds. One focal point brings the garden together. Lead the eye to the farthest corner of the garden by planting a suitably sized tree with more than one season of interest, having beautiful bark as well as being pretty in flower or leaf. A flowering cherry will shine in spring and summer, then in autumn it will continue to catch your eye if lit up dramatically, and in winter you could even hang decorations from its boughs.

In tight spaces, a formal design with clean lines makes the space appear larger. Tall boundaries make the enclosed space seem smaller. Carefully judge the correct height of the boundary to provide privacy without plunging the garden into shadow. Disguising a boundary can make the garden appear infinite. This was the reasoning behind the ha-ha, to make the garden extend into the landscape so that they became one. Use evergreen shrubs of different plants to give an irregular appearance - the effect is one of a shrubbery not a boundary. Can you borrow from existing external features? If there is a handsome tree in the neighbour's garden, don't block it out, borrow the view, allow the top of the tree to be part of your own garden.

Small areas appear larger by the simple trick of employing a different level. Use shallow steps, diagonal or circular paving enhances the space. If the garden is long and narrow, create the illusion of space by having separate sections that prevent the whole garden being viewed at once. Small, partially hidden areas linked by a winding path, will make the garden appear larger than it is.

Employ light coloured materials to give the appearance of a larger space. If the garden appears dark, paint one or more boundary walls in a light colour to enhance the space. Carefully placed mirrors can make the garden appear larger too. These might be fixed to a wall or reflect the garden from a corner. Try mirror doors attached to a shed to reflect a much larger area of the garden. Position so that you are not reflected in the mirrors when you walk towards them and avoid catching the glare of the sun. *Trompe l'oeil* can be employed to give the illusion that the garden is larger. A reflective pool at ground level containing still water has the effect of making a space seem bigger. The combination of still water and a mirror doubles the effect of either one used singly. A mirror gateway is most effective in a small space. Secure mirror and gate surrounded by an arch of half-bricks. The reflection of path and plants creates a feeling of depth and the image of another garden in its reflection. Paths can disappear around corners and appear much longer than they are in reality.

Choose plants with more than one season of interest. Stick to light colours that are easy on the eye, limiting the palette to no more than three colours. Increase the surface area of the garden by growing climbers.

Gardens that employ visual tricks include **The Gardens of The Menagerie**, Horton, Northamptonshire, which appear to be fifty acres instead of only five. The imaginative layout and visual tricks are masterly. It is an elegant 18th century style garden with rustic houses, a shell grotto, fountains and statues. Designed by Thomas Wright it has all the ingredients of a fascinating garden.

Garden elements

*Above: The urn as a focal point amongst the informal
planting in the Dutch Garden at Hestercombe
Below: The pavilion as the focal point in the formal
style at Montacute*

Gardens are made up of a series of cohesive
components without hard and fast rules. These
elements are a combination of hardscaping – the
fixed elements and softscaping – the changeable
elements. The untrained designer might see nothing
more than pattern but it is more rhythm, colour, tonal
values and an awareness and organisation of space that
you must seek. The principles of design set out above and
the elements suggested here will help you to create a
harmonious whole. Most professional designers have a
preferred method of ordering the elements beginning with
the boundary, then working from the ground up. Whilst
you need not include all elements, those you do
incorporate should be in one style, bringing harmony to
the design.

Focal Point
Some of the elements within a garden play a supporting
role whilst others are the reason for creating a particular
scene. Focal points not only focus the eye, but also lead
the visitor on to the next part of the garden. They offer
drama, like the crescendo of a classical piece of music.

In a small garden, one focal point might be enough. The
idea is to lead the eye, not confuse the matter. Anything
can become a focal point. Focal points are found at the
end of lines, the culmination of a vista or at the cross
section of two axes. Generally speaking, focal points are
very noticeable. They contrast with the background and
often tower above everything else. Ensure that nothing
competes with the star performer. Think of the garden as
a series of pictures or scenes, like a stage. Imagine
entering the garden room, where will your eye settle,
what will attract your attention? Formal gardens often
have defined vistas where the eye is lead to the focal point
down a long avenue. In informal gardens it is necessary to
direct the eye with skill, using the natural line of plants,
shape and colour to guide the eye.

Hardscaping

Take great care and thought with regard to the hardscaping elements as they can be difficult and expensive to alter. They give the garden structure and bones whether it is straight lines or sinuous curves. This is the ground plan of the garden that is softened and enhanced by its counterpart the softscaping.

Hardscaping is the backbone of the garden - the permanent structure. It determines the tone of the garden and should be capable of standing alone. Some materials are unobtrusive, where others grab the eye. Gravel, concrete, grass, wood and water surfaces are neutral and undemanding. These materials allow the eye to rest on the feature you have positioned to take centre stage. Other materials such as coloured plastic and stainless steel are far more noticeable. If you opt for glass and steel, you have set the tone for a contemporary style. Natural materials set the tone for an Arts and Crafts garden. Regular, symmetrical shapes are restful on the eye and squares, circles and hexagons are a good choice for seating areas or for surrounding a focal point such as a fountain. Achieve harmony and balance by assessing the site and choosing what is right for each given area, linking to its surroundings. Think about colour, texture, pattern and the general ambience. Materials can be used in unexpected ways. Nothing adds softness like grass and when lush green it is so soothing. If you are using it, I wrote in my book 'Emeralds' that it is far better to use it as part of the design. Instead of flat rectangles or squares, design the area with fluid shapes or swirls as in landform. Lawn can be mown in interesting ways to provide texture; it can be shaped into mounds, anything that adds to the overall design.

Materials will be determined by your budget and there is a huge choice for all pockets. Try not to be negatively influenced by limitations. Seek alternatives that will make your garden work for you. Consider the hardscaping as the frame and the plants as the upholstery. Link hardscaping areas with paths. As a general rule, ensure that paths are winding and that not all parts of the garden are visible at once. Whether you design and build yourself or use a designer and contractor is entirely your choice but there are areas that are best left to professionals including any electrical installation. Consider a watering system as these are best laid at the initial stage.

Nowadays, it is easier than ever to colour-coordinate your garden. Colourful materials can match the colours of the plants chosen. Many gardeners choose to paint fences, gates and arches to complement the chosen plant scheme. Bear in mind, that anything painted will need maintenance, perhaps more so than surfaces left unpainted, above all in seaside gardens. Sometimes it is best to leave the garden understated, often by painting everything to colour-co-ordinate is saying just a little too much - less is more.

Whilst Jekyll brought co-ordinated colour to planting schemes, it is Luis Barragan who introduced colour to walls when in the 1960's he painted walls pink. The garden designer Martha Schwarz is much influenced by his work. Bold wall colours, whilst striking are hard to live with for any period of time and detract from the planting. Subtle colours are best as a background. In the last ten years the popularity of painted walls in a wide array of colours has increased in the average garden.

At Hestercombe the wall is clothed thickly and circular openings allow a view of the countryside

Gateways

Welcome home – make an impressive entrance that welcomes you when you return home. It will have an uplifting effect and revive you.

Entrances and exits mark the beginning and end of the garden and are part of the physical boundary or division of space. Their purpose is to let the visitor know that they are entering a very exciting space. They provide much-needed security but are also the first suggestion of what lies within. First impressions are lasting and so the visitors' first glimpse of the garden is important. Is its primary function to frame what lies within or exclude any view? Is it a welcome or a barrier? Is the gate to be purely functional or highly decorative?

Solid does not have to be boring; shape can still be imbued into a gateway by means of fluidity in solid structures or decorative in metal structures. A solid gateway reveals nothing until it is opened, thereby creating an air of mystery. Elaborate ironwork is best against a simple landscape where its ornate quality can be appreciated. Seeing just a glimpse of what lies beyond creates the urge for discovery. Give your gateway, no matter how humble, personality.

In the garden, a shut gate is uninviting, but an open gate invites the visitor to explore further. Partially hidden gateways and doorways impart an aura of mystery and are less obvious. Gateways can enclose an area or lead to another part of the garden. They can even be a part of the hedge itself, or created by two plants joining overhead. A gate can be imbued with symbolic meaning as in Japanese gardens. A moon gate is inviting, its circular shape welcoming. Rustic gates are enchanting in their simplicity. Ornamental gates can be adorned with a canopy. Ornate gates are best at the end of a grassed area, contrasting with its simplicity. Simple wooden gates suit a cottage garden with its frivolous planting. Contrast is always a good idea.

Gates can be made from almost any material and many are readily available. Choose materials in line with your boundary, wood or metal are obvious choices. If the entrance adjoins your patio, everything should tie in. Fixtures and fittings need to be sympathetic. Ensure that any exit or entrance is wide enough for its purpose. A frost pocket demands an open gate not a solid barrier that would serve to enclose the frost.

Gateways can also be used within the garden. Doorways can be false, leading to nowhere. The gateway is often an arch clothed in plants.

The door into the garden at Lytes Cary Manor

Surfacing

Quick Guide to Surfacing and its Uses

Timber decking: wears and mixes well with a natural look. Use for patio or over water.

Poured concrete: a cheap, versatile solution. Soften with planting when used for paths and terraces. It is used effectively for walls too, however think of the environmental consequences.

Crazy paving: informal, but out-of-date.

Reconstituted stone: cost-effective slabs are hardwearing and are more like the real thing than they used to be.

Natural stone or slate: ideal for formal or modern gardens.

Flint: highly suited to creating decorative patterns

Granite setts: hardwearing for paths offering a natural, rough and uneven look.

Cobblestones: charming and full of character yet slippery when wet and awkward to walk on. Good in combination with flags and pavers.

Stepping-stones: a way to cross shallow water or lawns.

Brick paving: highly suitable for making decorative pathways, especially in formal gardens. It is used as edging and also provides a link between house and garden for brick-built properties.

Bluestone paving: retains heat.

Terracotta tiles: good around pools and for formal gardens. They make an excellent transition from house to garden when used for a patio.

Timber sleepers: rustic for country or woodland gardens.

Gravel: good for introducing texture and ideal in awkward-shaped areas. Moves around and is not easy to walk on. Good in combination with concrete pavers, timber or stone. Better in modern, urban settings but can be used in traditional and rural gardens.

Grass: restful and functional in play areas but time-consuming to maintain a green sward.

Glass: ultra modern and adaptable.

Steel mesh: ultra modern, good for walkways.

Surfacing is a term used for paths, patios or terraces and areas of space or planting. Straight lines and geometric shapes signal a formal garden, whilst naturalistic curves are the identity of the informal garden space. The style of the house will give a starting point to opt for materials in sympathy with the house. Metal grille flooring would look ridiculous in an Elizabethan garden. It is best to restrict the number of materials to avoid a mismatched look. A maximum of two or three choices should suffice in one given area. Stone looks good with pebbles, red brick with quarry tiles. Smooth slabs with textured gravel look sympathetic together.

Some materials such as slate are offered as chips, pebbles, stones, paving slabs, topping stones and monoliths making it easy to tie all hardscaping together harmoniously. Slate can also be found in the form of tables and benches as well as pots. It can be used to create interesting, textural walls.

A simple yet effective use of gravel at Cothay Manor

Similarly, concrete can be laid as paving, used for walls, pots, seats and the supports of pergolas. Patterns are demanding on the eye and are best kept to the edges of an area only. Surfaces can blend in with planting or become a feature in their own right. A mosaic of bright tiles adds an artistic touch.

The garden floor with its paths, patios, grassed areas or play surfaces needs careful thought. Its purpose can be a quiet background or be a part of the design itself. Grass has begun to fall out of favour and will continue to do so. Whilst the immaculate sward had its heyday in the 18th century landscape garden, today's designers are faced with many alternatives. Surfacing is a decorative feature that helps ground the style of the garden. Knowing when to be highly decorative and when to have quiet flooring is one of the keys to good design. Allow the house and the garden to play its part in the chosen flooring schemes. If the planting is fussy, the paving needs to be quiet. It should look entirely natural.

Once the surfacing framework is decided upon, the design can progress to adornment. The hard surfacing is put in place first. Think of the flooring as a journey through the garden. You need to be able to walk through the garden easily, but also to have places to pause, linger and admire the view. You do not want to be hurried but need to be led through the garden at a gentle pace.

The first decision the gardener or designer needs to determine is the ratio of hard surfacing to plants. It all depends on how much maintenance and time you wish to give to softscaping.

If you are not fond of the newness of new materials, look for recycled ones that already look worn in and will make the garden look as if it has been there longer than it has. Natural materials are diminishing, but modern day simulated materials are getting better at imitating their natural counterparts. The modern garden can employ immensely different materials for flooring not found in the past. The materials can set the tone of the design and not the planting.

Give some thought to thorough preparation before laying any surface. Patios, paths, terraces, driveways as well as work and play areas all need to be surfaced in a harmonious way, fitting together like pieces of a jigsaw. Each area has different demands as they have a different purpose. For children's play areas, choose non-slip material that will cushion a fall. Wood bark is a good choice or cushioned rubber. Consider the wear and tear that each surface will receive and select materials according to their suitability and durability. Seating area surfaces need to be level, smooth and easy-to-clean. If next to the house, using a similar material will link the two. Small bricks and setts can look fussy and although suited to small spaces, consider using bigger slabs for effect. York stone slabs are best reserved for grand spaces. Terracotta and tiles give a warm feeling and can provide a pleasing link between house and garden. Make sure you purchase frost-proof tiles, preferably with a non-slip finish. The area also needs to be large enough to accommodate furniture and for your purposes. Give careful thought to the positioning of a main seating area for entertaining or eating. Once pavers are set in concrete, they are not easy to move. Draw several possible areas on paper and see which offers the best solution. Take a hosepipe or chalk and map out the area on the ground. Watch the area for a few days. Does it receive the required sun or shade? Is there enough privacy? Shade and privacy can be created but you need an area close enough to the house to be practical enough for serving food. Choose the site that offers the perfect solution for your needs.

Paths
The direction the visitor takes around the garden is determined by the pathways that enable movement from one area of the garden to another. This is achieved by means of paths, ramps or elevated walkways. Paths are the invitation to explore; a wide path invites the visitor to stroll whilst a narrow path leads to a more hurried pace. If narrow paths can widen at some point into a more open area, this offers welcome breathing space. Paths of all types contrast their harshness with the softness of plants and can be textured or coloured. Main service routes need to take the strain of wheelbarrows and lawnmowers. Check the suitability of the materials you buy with regards to frost-resistance, durability and if the surface will become slippery when wet.

For formal gardens, paths are usually straight whereas we find meandering paths in informal design. These curvaceous paths need to follow the lie of the land. Disguise the path with generous planting along its course. Gravel is a useful material for paths and is easy to lay and to fill difficult, serpentine curves and corners. Its recessive nature does not detract from the features of a garden as it forms a quiet background. Gravel was used in Elizabethan and in French gardens. It is available in various sizes from tiny pea gravel to large pieces of 2cm across (less than one inch). It is a good weed depressant but is sometimes difficult to walk on. Use gravel at a depth of at least 5cm (2"). The crunch of gravel underfoot can deter burglars. I like to use gravel on paths but deplore its other use as mulch for plants except tiny alpines. Gravel can be punctuated with railway sleepers on wide paths. It is a component of Japanese dry gardens in which it is raked to imitate seas. It has become part of the minimalist garden where it provides welcome texture. The only hue I would use is the golden yellow or grey, which looks great with marble type flagstones. The other colours are sickly; you do not want something that stands out, but a surface that blends. Remember that gravel will move and even gradually slide down on a slope; so retain with an edging strip or low wall. From time to time, the level needs topping up and an occasional raking will keep it tidy.

Slate chips have become very popular. In my garden a one stone high retaining boundary is complemented by slate chips laid on a fabric base to suppress weeds. These materials are fluid and highly suited to a town garden. Larger pebbles can create mosaics or cobbled paths. A pleasant effect can be achieved when using fine gravel with areas of larger pebbles in a sympathetic shade. Gone are the days of crazy paving, thankfully.

Bark chips are fluid too but I prefer these on the ground as mulch or on a woodland path than in the garden path proper. They are good for play areas. Use at a depth of at least 7cm (3") and replenish every year. Bark chips keep weeds at bay and reduce watering when used as mulch.

Grass is often used for paths in meadow areas where a mown path contrasts with the longer meadow grasses. It is largely unsuitable elsewhere as it needs regular cutting and maintenance and would need to take a lot of wear and tear.

Red bricks on end make attractive paths, as do stone. They can be interlocked whereas large slabs often need to be cut to size. Bricks are versatile and can make an individual path if you are feeling creative.

Below: a mixture of wood and slate
Left: a mixture of timber and brick

Pre-cast concrete slabs come in many colours and variations. They are easily available and are a cheaper option than stone but I shall say again, the much repeated advice through this book, that concrete is costly to the environment. Once wet, they usually have a different appearance. Good quality slabs are dense with well-machined edges. There are soft slabs on the market, which are more liable to cracking. Choose slabs that have been coloured all the way through. Natural colours have the advantage of not clashing with furniture and sitting comfortably with plants. Reconstituted stone slabs are more expensive and have a surface that resembles weather-worn stone. It is cheap, durable and fairly easy to lay. It is more or less permanent so thought should be given before covering large surfaces with concrete. Colour added when concrete is laid, will run evenly through the concrete. Colouring agents relieve the boredom and objects can be placed into concrete or patterns created upon its surface. I prefer mostly for this medium to be used for walls or division rather than flooring within the garden, but there is no denying that concrete has come a long way since the 1960's. Concrete can be poured on site, but a professional is best employed to do this. Areas should not exceed 5m (18ft) in any direction without thermal movement joints, which are necessary for the natural expansion and contraction of the substance. It is often better to employ a professional to lay concrete, particularly if you require surface treatments, some of which are only available to professionals. Tamped concrete has the roughest surface, creating a linear pattern, suitable for vehicles. Trowelled or brushed concrete provides a softer texture. Partially set concrete can be brushed, thereby exposing the aggregate. Concrete can be marked to make it look like flagstones. It can be mechanically impressed to imitate setts or bricks. A shiny but non-slip finish can be achieved by topping the surface with aggregate set in resin.

Resin bonding must be laid by a professional. The original surface can be concrete, asphalt or timber in excellent condition. All kinds of loose materials such as glass, rubber and gravel can be resin bonded. It takes wear and tear and is free-draining. It flows and can be used on steep areas or overhangs.

Granite setts are very urban and useful in areas where granite is local. Try breaking out of the conventional grid and employing interesting patterns. Set diagonally setts form a simple yet attractive pattern.

They can be used to edge a path. Set a circle into the centre of a broad path to add another dimension. If you can afford it York stone, limestone or granite has the advantage of instantly looking mellow. These materials suit old stone houses and I admit to a yearning for York stone slabs of immense size, thickness and quality. Second hand slabs can vary in size and thickness.

Cobbles are suitable for small, tricky areas where a path cannot be laid, but are generally not suitable for large paths as the surface becomes wet and slippery and they make an uneven surface that is uncomfortable to walk on. They can be used decoratively to break up paving or concrete with a design feature. Tiles need to be durable and as such, quarry tiles are attractive but hard to cut. They are useful for square patios or straight paths. Glazed tiles are fragile but can be very decorative and highly suited to Mediterranean, Spanish or Italian gardens. Slate tiles are handsome used on end at the edge of a path to create texture as Lutyens often did.

In a rustic setting, log sections make an attractive path, especially through woodland walks and much used in Scandinavia. Set them in a well-compacted mix of sand and gravel. The ideal size is between 8cm (3") and 15cm (6") thick. They must be pressure-treated and roughly sawn so that they are non-slip. The gaps in between can be filled with gravel or bark.

Non-traditional materials include Astroturf, glass beads, coloured sand, plastic and metal. Astroturf is ideal for modern gardens when used in shapes emerging from and just above the surface of ponds or anywhere that the gardener does not want the task of mowing grass. It can be taken with you when you move. It is an ideal surface for a low-maintenance garden. A smooth surface is needed for laying.

Sheet steel can look stunning, but beware the glare. Steel mesh is often used underfoot, but is best in minimalist, high tech, urban gardens as it is industrial in appearance. It provides both texture and contrast. Sturdy and waterproof, somehow, although I know it is, it never seems safe to me, I dislike looking down through holes of any kind when using walkways or steps. Aluminium foot-plates can be used for decks. They have a textured surface, providing a non-slip surface and look good with other modern materials and architectural plants.

Paths and patios need a solid foundation and good drainage. Remove topsoil and add a well-consolidated layer of hardcore covered with sand, ash or screened gravel especially in areas where the surface will take a lot of wear and tear. Bricks and pavers can be laid on a bed of sand for lightly used paths. Otherwise prepare as for driveways. Driveways need hard-wearing surfaces that can take the daily wear and tear. They require a strong foundation. Usually only one material with edging is used for a driveway. More would make the driveway into a feature and it is best to let the space recede rather than make it too noticeable. To lay a driveway, the foundation must be prepared thoroughly and it might be necessary to hire a compactor to prepare a level surface.

Ensure you have drainage to rid the site of excess rainwater. Surfaces that meet house walls need a fall of 1 in 40 away from the house to prevent water gathering at the base of the wall. Unevenness, sinking or breaking up of paths is a sign of poor foundations or bad drainage. Hardscaping usually requires edging. Edging defines the paths, driveways and wide, paved areas. Choose complementary or contrasting materials; they need to be sympathetic. With attention to detail, the hardscaping flows through the edging into the softscaping. Plants often overlap to soften the edge. Edging can contain loose materials such as gravel. In poor visibility, edging delineates the path, guiding you along. You might choose a low, physical barrier to finish off a driveway, or a small wattle fence edging for herbaceous borders. The edging does not have to be the same on both sides of the path - on one side, the barrier might be a one brick high wall retaining the border, but on the other side, the grass might come up to the path without a barrier of any kind. In this situation it is best to keep a narrow strip between the grass and path for ease of mowing. Edging is easy to buy in pre-formed bricks to set on edge, rocks, cast concrete edging, wooden stakes, terracotta, wattle or even plastic.

Decking

Timber decking has become increasingly popular for hard surfacing as we come to appreciate the outdoor lifestyle. Decking has a warm, relaxed, more modern style than most other surfaces without being harsh like concrete or plastic. It does not overheat like stone or concrete in hot weather. It creates superb level surfaces even over undulating sites and can be used imaginatively for curves and circles. It can follow the curves of a border. Lighting can be set into the surface creating instant atmosphere. Wood can be stained for decorative effect. Planks can be laid at different angles, diagonals or a V pattern to provide interest. Ribbed surfaces provide texture and are more non-slip. At the same time, it can be used for creating different levels easily.

Thomas Church floated decks amongst the treetops in California. Decking is a superb choice for roof gardens, easy to lay at a slight camber so that water can run off easily. Ensure there is an air-gap between each board for ventilation. On low decks spread fabric covered in gravel over the soil to prevent weed growth. Decking can be cut to any shape. It can be constructed at any height from ground to roof level. Used for steps, walkways and seating areas, it brings unity to the site. When used with other wooden materials for handrails, steps or bridges, decking provides a perfect, harmonious link. It looks right with most other materials too. Use its versatility to the full - try a viewing platform on high, or an extension over a pond. You can even cut around established trees or bushes.

However, it is not maintenance-free and needs to be power washed. Check that wood comes from a sustainable and renewable source. Oak or teak from renewable sources is the best choice. As long as it has been pressure treated and is good quality, with maintenance decking will last many years. The recommended thickness is at least 2.5cm (1"). Decks can be raised on low brick walls or concrete piers spaced at intervals of 1.2m (4ft). If attached to the wall of the house, decking needs to be at least 15cm (6") below the damp-proof course of the house and drainage channels are useful. Supports need a damp-proof course. Square or rectangular is fine, but do not overlook the possibilities of creating unique shapes that are impossible in stone or concrete.

Vertical Reality

Boundaries are part of the vertical element enhanced by divisions within the garden. Vertical accents, solid or open are needed in other areas of the garden. It is always useful to have different levels within a garden. Levels introduce a sense of surprise varying a flat, unstimulating landscape and creating an exciting environment. Vertical space is often sadly overlooked in a garden. Space has always been at a premium in cities and many gardens are small or long and narrow. Open space is always desirable; if there is not enough ground area, use vertical space to advantage. Go upwards. The sky is the limit and I believe this area of gardening will see more innovative ideas coming to the fore in the future.

Create Interest

The undulations of an English landscape garden offer a succession of different views of the garden. At Vaux-le-Vicomte, the levels provide an optical illusion. The element of surprise can be used dramatically. A whole garden can be hidden entirely from view, only to be revealed from a chosen spot. A small garden can be given a real lift with a change in level. In the landscape garden, landform creating smooth contours is favoured whereas in the small town garden it is usually steps that initiate the necessary change in level.

Chatsworth House

Levels

Steps along with terraces are employed to link and separate different areas of the garden. In this way, they might link upper and lower gardens. They are part of the principle of balance and symmetry. Just one step can signify a change in mood especially when ornament draws attention to the move from one space to another. This might be all that is needed especially in gardens for the elderly or infirm, where ramps might be preferential. Steps come in many forms; they can be purely functional or purely aesthetic. The classic balustrade steps of stately homes and châteaux are magnificent and can be imitated on relatively smaller scales. Rustic brick or stone are more humble whilst wooden steps and railway sleepers seem more at one with nature. Steps are simple and functional when used alone or more flamboyant when fringed by urns, finials and statues or softened by plants. A zigzagging or curving double staircase makes a real statement. However, in some situations, partially hidden steps are an advantage. Choose the style that fits in with the garden. Lutyens was master of this. Steps can be dramatic, set against the sky, or be quietly hidden amongst vegetation. They can be used to separate or to invite. When broad, they can have the function of a retaining wall. Broad steps make a bold statement and are best confined to no more than six steps.

When creating steps and ramps to move from one level to another, it is equally important that materials should blend readily thus forming a link to the different level. Wide, low steps are easiest for access. In small spaces, steps can even be cantilevered from a wall. Ramps are essential for disabled gardeners. A change in level with a platform offers a place to contemplate the garden, to pause and admire the view.

Think scale, location, flow and drama. Steps need to be constructed with solid foundation. Materials are chosen according to the design and its purpose. Brick, stone, concrete or wood can be used depending upon the style you have chosen for the garden. Grass steps are suitable for many gardens, especially with risers in wood, metal or stone. Railway risers look great with gravel treads. Remember in areas of high traffic, gravel will move around and it is not always user-friendly, being difficult to walk on with ease.

Steps can rise in a straight line up or down, be at right angles, a semi-circle or increase in size as they descend. With long slopes, it is a good idea to incorporate landings every 10 to 12 steps, this offers a breather and a viewing point over the garden. If the landing is a multiple of the tread, measured from front to back, it will be in line with natural gait when climbing the steps. 40 steps can look daunting, but when one or two landings are used, the steps look more inviting.

Steps can be integrated into the garden or free-standing. Make sure the risers are not too steep and that treads are wide enough to take a full adult foot comfortably. Risers are normally 15cm (6") deep whilst 35cm (14") is a good measure for treads from front to back. Do not change one without altering the other in relation to it. The riser should be pitched slightly to shed water. To work out the number of steps needed, plan the position on squared paper, measure the height and divide by the height of a single riser, for example 13cm (5") plus a single tread, 30cm (12"). On a terraced site, measure the height of the retaining wall. Matters become more complicated on a sloping site. Drive a peg into the top of the slope and a length of cane at the bottom. Tie a length of string between the cane and peg and establish the horizontal with a spirit level. Measure the distance from the base of the cane to the string for the vertical height of the slope. Divide this figure by the depth of the riser plus the tread to give the number of steps. Steps just 60cm (2ft) wide accommodate one person; two people walking comfortably side by side need a width of at least 1.5m (5ft). A good rule is that the steps should be at least as wide as any approaching path. Plants can soften the edges, and if wide enough, steps can take handsome containers; this would add at least another 60cm (2ft) to the width of the steps. Consider a handrail or balustrade for support. These often need to be added at construction stage, but you could always add a rope handrail afterwards. Lighting is useful especially at night when steps are plunged into the dark.

A major advantage of a slope is that it opens up the possibility of creating natural, cascading water features. The steeper the garden, the more dramatic the feature. Hide the edges with plants that enjoy moist conditions, avoiding anything that does not know its place such as the gorgeous *Gunnera*. Plants such as this can break through pond liners or even concrete and spread rapidly, knowing no bounds.

The curved steps at Chiffchaffs

When dealing with gardens on a slope remove the gradient and create two or three flat areas with steps in between. Is there scope for an upper terrace next to the house? A lower level could become a sunken or secret garden. When removing soil, take care to keep the topsoil separate. Tackling large areas by hand can be very demanding. Hire a self-drive digger to sculpt the land and replace the topsoil. Retaining walls might need to be created depending on the gradient of the slope. To create two flat areas, you need to build a wall between them. These walls have to withstand pressure and are often best created by a professional. For a small, 60cm (2ft) high wall, a foundation 35cm (14 inches) deep is required, consisting of 15cm (6 inch) concrete. Weep holes must be created for drainage. A garden sloping up from the house is more dominant. Irregular changes in level offer unique opportunities to create elements of surprise. Use a large hollow or mound to advantage by turning it into a feature - a sunken garden or pool, a circular feature of grass or a place for a folly.

Ramps are an alternative to steps or a necessity for wheelbarrows, lawnmowers and wheelchairs. They can run alongside steps. A gradient of 1:15 is fine for wheelbarrows, but 1:20 is better for wheelchairs. Whatever surface you use, ensure that it is non-slip.

Top left: Fontainebleau; top right and centre: Hestercombe; bottom right: Ham House; left: Chatsworth House

Plant Supports

Lighter structures act as plant supports. Obelisks are one of my favourite garden structures. These tall, needle-like structures add instant vertical impact in groups or used singly, used for pure decorative purposes, or as support for climbing plants. They can be temporary, adding height whilst the border gets into its stride or used in a more permanent fashion. Plant supports tend to be see-through, whereas purely decorative features tend to be solid, often in reflective materials. Ready-made obelisks abound in many materials; choose from timber, metal stone or glass. Timber and stone offer strong accent whereas metal and glass offer reflection in the sun and texture in the rain. Willow or hazel fits nicely into the natural garden; these supports are ideal for sweet peas and can even stand inside a pot. They are best cleaned and stored dry over winter. Metal obelisks look best in a formal garden. In its simplest form, three bamboo canes tied together to make a tripod, provide height and support for climbing plants. Chunky rustic poles could be used, driven firmly into place. Rusty metal is another option. Plain timber, nailed together makes a handsome structure that can be painted in any colour to suit the border. Obelisks also come in topiaries made from yew, holly, box, bay or shrubby honeysuckle. In 2003 at the Northwest Flower and Garden Show, Seattle, USA and at the San Francisco Flower Show the following month, I designed obelisks for my show gardens using succulents. They caused quite a stir. To punctuate the garden and create rhythm, use singly or in pairs at an entrance.

Pillars, reminiscent of Greece or Rome, can stand sentinel in stone or clipped plants such as *Sorbus*, beech or evergreens. They are most effective amongst the apparent disarray of a wildflower meadow or informal planting.

Plant supports can be decorative and portable. Swirling spirals in numerous materials such as iron, copper, steel or wood contrast dramatically when punctuating plantings in repetitive rhythm. Use them to add height to a border. The naturalistic garden and herbaceous border uses twiggy pea stick supports that are hidden as the plants grow. All supports must be in place whilst plants are young. Willow is best over-wintered under cover.

Buildings

Whether you go for DIY or a ready-made structure, the choices are almost unlimited from simple awnings to huge structures that are multi-functional. Many are assembled on site after preparing a suitable base. Terms have blurred in catalogues and in use but garden structures encompass summerhouses, cabins, sheds, pavilions and glasshouses. They can be open or enclosed. The modern trend is towards home offices. These structures are similar to much cheaper garden sheds but at a much higher price since they come complete with inner wall panels and electric lighting, much more an outdoor room. If you work from home, and have the garden space, it is worth investing in such an outdoor office. If you can afford one large enough, it can double as an outdoor entertaining space. Whilst the garden shed used for storage is traditionally tucked away, the garden office is a feature in itself and although there are some designs on the market that look just like an over-sized shed, the best garden offices are specifically designed for their purpose and most are very pleasing on the eye. These are one step up on the humble summerhouse

Arbours, gazebos and summerhouses do not necessarily need to be ornate. Unfussy is modern and the aim is to provide shelter and privacy. Arbours of woven branches readily fit into a rural setting. If you have a grand garden, be grand, but in a smaller space, be practical. Gazebos can be highly decorative and as such are usually purely ornamental. Allow them to frame parts of the garden and offer a view. A rotunda is any building with a circular ground plan often topped by a dome. Such buildings are majestic in a garden, particularly on the summit of a small hill or large mound. The folly was always found in grand gardens in Victorian times. The 19th century folly at **Elton Hall** in Shropshire is eccentric but exquisite. There is a wealth of unusual, eccentric buildings in English gardens. Sometimes garden buildings are just for fun and have little practical use.

Structures can be supported by walls in the corner of the garden or attached to a house or be free-standing. Use a look-out on stilts to give an elevated view of the garden, on land or over water.

Overleaf from top left: Lower Severals; Kew; Harlow Carr; Cothay Manor; Ham House; Wisley; Hestercombe

An awning is the answer to a less solid structure. Canopies can be made from translucent or opaque fabrics in canvas, flame-resist PVC-coated polyester or coated glass cloth. Muslin can be draped like blinds whilst silks add an exotic touch. Sail fabric can afford shade and provide a novel temporary structure. Awnings and canopies can transform a space quickly at minimal cost.

Taking this one step further, have you considered a tent? I'm not talking camping, although that can be fun in the garden but a canvas and wood tent. From traditional tents of the nomads, yurts to period tents, tipis to geodesic domes, you would probably have something the neighbours have not yet got. Tents in all shapes, styles and sizes provide a real outdoor experience. Kids love them. I used to drape a sheet over an old clothes-horse and my son used to play beneath it for hours, just as I had as a child. Tents tend not to allow heat to build up and are spacious enough to stretch and stand. Look for canvas and timber tents in circular structures. They can be fitted with wood-burning stoves, windows and jute carpets as well as a porch. They are a movable feature and something you can take with you when you go or move around the garden.

If the outdoor room is large, it then becomes a feature of the garden. However, do not let it become dominant. It is easy in spaces large or small to fill the available space too fully. The eye will be led directly to the room and so it must be positioned with care. Similarly, you want a room with a view. There are summerhouses that rotate on turntables to follow the sun. In the large garden room, think about ventilation, especially if there is a lot of glass - windows, doors or sliding doors are the options. You will probably need to use blinds too in summer. An opening roof might be desirable. Metal, wood, glass and perspex are materials used to build garden rooms.

Outdoor entertainment rooms are large enough to take a decent-sized dining table, entertainment centre, even a fireplace. Glass panels from floor to ceiling offer fantastic views of the garden. As we come to spend more time outdoors, we create a demand for larger structures in the garden. From a practical point of view, any outdoor garden buildings need to be waterproof.

Still pools tend to be algae-free when the water depth is more than 45cm (18"). It is best not to agitate it, but aerate it now and then to keep it clean. Install a pump for this purpose. Filters can help as can oxygenating plants. Water lilies are good for still pools, but choose the right water lily as some will outlive the given space quickly whilst others are tender and cannot withstand cold.

Site your water feature carefully. Do not place ponds in the shade or where deciduous trees overhang, as the pond will become full of leaves. Near buildings large pools can look dark and dull. Site them in the open where they can reflect the sky. Of course, you can use netting and this is a wise choice if you have fish and there are cats in the neighbourhood and is also necessary where there are young children. Avoid slippery surfaces around pools. Willow, ash and aspen all have deep, water-seeking roots that can puncture pond liners. Try to avoid windy sites that blow water where you don't want it to go. Plan areas adjacent to large water features such as pools or ponds at the same time.

Consider the scale. If the garden is no more than decking and a few plants confined to the perimeter, then a large surface of water can work well reflecting the skies. However, as with everything else in the garden, the water feature has to fit in. You don't want a huge oversized canal. If you have the space go big, but don't let a large water feature dominate a garden. Vertical water features are dramatic and unexpected. If your space is small, don't overlook a bowl, trough or barrel filled almost to the brim with clean water or a simple pebble pool. Reflections are fantastic.

Static expanses of water can be turned into dramatic features by the addition of a vertical sculpture. I recently came across a surprising element at the **Luxembourg gardens** in France, where a face floated just on the surface. Similarly, a person is glimpsed swimming or drowning in a feature at **Corpusty Mill**, Norfolk. Comical, whimsical and definitely eye-catching.

If you have naturally damp soil, use it to advantage to create a bog garden. There is no point in fighting the elements. Make it a feature of the garden. If you are lucky enough to have a natural source of water on your land, use it to its full potential.

Previous page: Grand Cascade, Chatsworth
Above: Revelation by Angela Conner at Chatsworth
Below: The fountain at Montacute

Above: Emperor Fountain, Chatsworth; Below: Hester-combe; Left bottom: Plas Newydd; Top: Kew

Lighting

Forget the security light keeping the neighbours awake with its wattage, enough to scare away Dracula himself. Artificial lighting can be dramatic without looking like a floodlit football ground. Consider your neighbour. Think subtle, unobtrusive, glimmering not glaring. Lighting can offer altered images, a different way of seeing your garden. It can create moods and drama. Shadows and silhouettes, highlights and spotlights are effective. Soft, diffused lighting creates a relaxed atmosphere. Lights in pools can add a mysterious glow. Uplights and downlights can outline architecture or garden features as can directional lighting. There are lights for paths, water features, decking and for walls.

Lighting makes the garden accessible at night in warm weather or for those with an outdoor room. Steps and paths need to be illuminated and low-level units with downward-cast beams avoid any unnecessary glare. Floating or submersible lighting is best in swimming pools or ponds. Light fixtures can be decorative or purely functional. Power supplies need to be a part of the construction process and should be fitted by a qualified electrician. If you spend most of your evenings outdoors, consider a fragrant evening garden or moon garden. Trees can be lit by a single spotlight from the ground, or by soft lights concealed amongst the branches.

Apart from electricity, candles, torches, night-lights, lanterns and oil lamps can be used. The slightest breeze can extinguish flames, so protect from wind and place in specially made glass lanterns. These can be hung from poles or brackets or in trees. Oil and natural flame torches are hazardous and need to be used with care. Solar power is good to use in the garden.

Above: a water feature in Sheffield

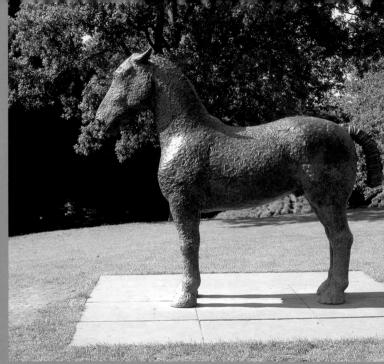

All statues as part of the exhibition at Chatsworth House, the Horse is a permanent statue on the lawn beyond the Emperor Fountain

Different sculptures can be used in different parts of the garden to evoke a different mood.

Cast concrete was once the domain of the unimaginative, but now more adventurous and modern pieces are being produced. It can be moulded into unusual shapes. Mosaics can easily be applied to alter the look dramatically. You can also embed glass and other materials into concrete. It is quite versatile. The renowned landscaper, Dame Sylvia Crowe was the first to use large concrete containers at the Chelsea Flower Show. Unfortunately, we need to seek other alternatives to cast concrete because of its effect on the environment.

Terracotta is another natural for the garden and it is not just for pots. Stakes can be enhanced with terracotta shapes, finials or whatever you can imagine. Coloured glazes can be added to match objects to the predominant colour in your garden. Remember all outdoor terracotta must be frost-proof.

Stone appears natural in the garden too. There is a huge trend for monoliths at the moment. I placed three purple slate monoliths in my garden amongst my golden border. In winter they stand alone; in summer they are partially hidden from view by the growing plants. Even rocks, large or small make a statement. Rough-hewn, stone adds texture to the garden whilst beautiful smooth pieces offer calm and serenity.

Metal suits the modern urban garden space. Aluminium plant supports come in spiral shapes that punctuate plants or can be used in groups in their own right. Metals weather appealingly, but if you hate the rust effect, then avoid any metal other than stainless steel. If you still have a local blacksmith, pay a visit for interesting sculpture, plant supports, gates and arbours in simple or ornate forms. I had three plant supports made imitating plant forms. Large ornament is available in a variety of metals including stainless steel and iron.

Ornaments can hide deficiencies or an ugly but necessary item in the garden such as manhole covers. Disguise walls with trellis or trompe l'oeil or the two combined. A trellis arch can house a trompe l'oeil open door, giving the illusion that the garden continues where it actually ends.

Trompe l'oeil meaning to trick the eye was practiced by the Ancient Greeks who tapered the top of columns to make their temples appear higher. A trick often employed in the garden is to narrow a path or border as it recedes, suggesting a greater distance. All uprights in the garden must obey the same rule. Transform a utility shed into a folly, or pretty summerhouse by creating a home for climbers on trellis-work.

Other ornaments include sundials, armillary spheres, bird boxes and baths. Particular themes will often denote certain ornaments to be included in the garden. Driftwood is at home in the seaside garden.

Plants themselves are a form of ornamentation; I feel very strongly that plants are essential to gardens. It is possible, but not wise to create a garden without any other ornamentation. However a space without plants is not a garden. Plants alone soften the hardscaping. They can be used to add a focal impact and act as ornaments. Plants are the soul, ornament the mind or spirit of the garden. To become a focal point, plants need strong visual impact. Some plants are naturally architectural in shape such as *yuccas, phormiums* or *agaves*. Grown in an urn against a dark hedge, they have as much impact as a statue. Plants can achieve focal point status through size, shape or colour in contrast to the surroundings. When isolated from its neighbours, or framed, the effect of a structural plant is enhanced. Topiary is a sculptural art form used to great effect at **Levens Hall**. Fern tree trunks can be carved making a most decorative feature as seen at **Heligan**.

Grass carvings or sculptures that emerge from the earth are fun and seem to break from the earth as if alive. Ancient land carvings influence them. The most effective example is perhaps the water-spouting face at the Swarovski Crystal World, Austria designed by Andre Heller. It conceals three storeys within the carving and covers 2000m2. Heller has also made a floral picture for the World Garden Show in Berlin, 1995 as well as a sinking giant in the Baroque garden at Schoenbrunn Palace in Vienna, both with textured plants. I also like Eve, created by Sue and Pete Hill, first seen at Eden but then replicated for the Chelsea Flower Show 2006. Grass can simply be manipulated into hills, cones, spirals and swirling, organic shapes known as landform, inspired by the landscape era and with its origins in the Mount.

Some plants are architectural such as *Melianthus major* and *Agave* and can be used in a sculptural way. Topiary can be made from box, bay or yew and trained and clipped into sculptural shapes such as cones, balls, spirals or even animals. Claudia's Garden at **Bonfante Gardens**, a horticultural theme park in the USA is one place to see unusual topiary. Conifers and hollies have been trained in amazing shapes. Parts of this theme park are like Legoland for gardeners. Topiary was first used by the Romans. A visit to **Tatton Park** or **Levens Hall** shows good use of topiary. Living willow is much used nowadays and is useful in the garden for arbours and seats. Chamomile seats are scented and attractive and once a feature of the Elizabethan garden – they retain their charm.

Sculpture gardens:
Barbara Hepworth (1903-1975)
Born in West Yorkshire, Hepworth was one of the greatest sculptors of the 20th century. Barbara Hepworth Museum and Sculpture Garden, Cornwall, England offers a unique insight into the artist, her work and private garden. Sculptures stand alone or blend into the subtropical gardens perfectly. Abstract sculptures large and small, solid and see-through have immense presence. The sculptures are not only well-sited given the small space, but exquisite in shape and form. These bold sculptures frame the plants yet would stand perfectly well alone. Some of the sculptures have windows through which to catch glimpses of the garden. The sculptures interplay. They are perfect for the modern garden, but they transcend time and would not look out of place at the end of a formal vista. The garden, though tiny, is a fitting tribute to the work of this talented artist. The Tate Gallery have owned the half acre garden since 1980, five years after the death of the sculptor.

The Cass Sculpture Foundation
Here is a changing display of seventy specially commissioned pieces. The Foundation charts the development of 21st century British sculpture. Most of the sculptures are large and all are for sale.

Chatsworth House
Chatsworth is resplendent. If I could have my choice of stately homes, this one would be top of my list. I love the approach, that moment when the house first comes into view. The garden has many new features but many old ones too.

The house has been the home of the Cavendish family, later the Dukes of Devonshire, since the 16th century. There is a 16th century banqueting house. The first garden was created in 1617. There has always been a kitchen garden although the site has often changed. The present day kitchen garden is sited nearer the house and is aesthetically pleasing in every way. The landscape garden was designed by Brown in the 1760's to 70's by destroying the fabulous formal gardens with terraces, parterres and fountains designed in 1699 and replacing them with five acres of grass known as the Great Slope. Despite many additions to the garden since that time, Brown's landscape remains largely intact.

It is perhaps the water features one remembers most vividly. They reflect the use of hydraulics in England in the 17th century. I think what is most remarkable is that they appear new and modern. The copper willow is a Victorian copy of the original, set to shower the unsuspecting visitor. There has been a 'joke tree' in the garden for over 300 years. The cascade is the only remaining original of its kind in England. Created in 1696 and restored in 1994-6 it is a magnificent feature with the gentle ripple, playful splash and forceful torrent of water all at once tumbling down. Water pours down 24 sets of stone steps arranged to make different sounds. The magnificent canal pond is a sheet of water some 287m (314 yards) long. From the far end the house seems to float on the water as the south lawn is set a few inches below the pond. The Emperor Fountain built in 1843 sits within the canal pond and has reached a height of 90m (296ft). It shows Paxton's engineering skills. The gravity fed fountains are supplied by lakes high above the gardens. The lakes are filled with rainwater. Hidden away in the Jack Pond is Angela Connor's Revelation sculpture added in 1999. Relying on water and gravity, the petals of a flower open up to reveal a golden interior.

The Conservative wall was created before 1842 by Paxton. Chatsworth is equally known for its sculpture from Flora's Temple and the classical figures to the modern bronzes such as Drummer by Barry Flanagan and the War Horse sculpture by Dame Elisabeth Frink. In summer the outdoor exhibition features sculpture from classical to modern in the grounds.

Gibberd Garden

The 16 acre garden was built by Frederick Gibberd from 1956 when he was working as master planner of Harlow New Town. The garden of this modernist architect seems to look to the past with Corinthian columns, however many pieces of 20th century sculpture decorate the garden or rooms. It is now owned by the Gibberd Garden Trust.

Newby Hall

Built in the 1690's and added to by Robert Adam in 1767. The garden was designed by George London and had a patte d'oie of avenues leading to an entrance forecourt with topiary. Formal groves of trees surrounded beds and lawns. Little survives; the Compton family have devised a bold axis with fine herbaceous borders and use tender plants. There is an unusual curved pergola supporting the weight of *Laburnum*. Newby paved the way in the 20th century for a quintessential style. The autumn garden is colourful and well-structured with an urn fountain as its focal point. Each year, Newby displays a unique selection of sculpture, between fifty and sixty contemporary works from new and known sculptors. All the sculptures are for sale and the display is open from June each year.

Portrack House

Charles Jencks (b. 1939) and his late wife Maggie, Lady Keswick created an amazing, sculptural garden. Jencks was an American architect often described as defining the postmodern school. He has become a leading figure in British landscape architecture. He designed the landform for the Scottish National Gallery of Modern Art in Edinburgh. Between 1990 and 2000 he expanded upon his garden theories in his own garden at Portrack House, the result is known as the 'Garden of Cosmic Speculation'. The garden is divided into very different areas. The Garden of Physics is dominated by the sculptures representing DNA. The garden has great movement, the mounds of land, curving water and organic sculpture amaze.

The Yorkshire Sculpture Park

Set in 500 acres of 18th century parkland, sculpture is shown off to advantage in this fine setting. Permanent sculptures and exhibitions take place here. In addition to the open-air galleries, there are four indoor galleries. It was Henry Moore who pioneered the outdoor siting of sculpture in the 1930's and his pieces are represented in the park.

Nicki Saint Phalle was a French sculptor who created many larger than life and colourful mosaic figures that make fascinating ornaments for the garden. The huge Cyclops stands in the forest at **Fontainbleau**. The **Tarot garden** in Italy is testimony to her genius. The garden, in Tuscany, near Capalbio, opened in 1998. Here one can see the influence of Gaudi. **Nek Chand's rock garden** in Chandigarth, northern India features hundreds of mosaic standing figures. The **mosaic gardens of Happonvilliers**, near Chartres, France are supreme. The pink and the blue garden are superb examples of modern mosaics created in recent years. **Claire Dohna's garden** on Vashon Island in the Pacific Northwest of America is a kaleidoscope of mosaics and plants. The beautifully colour-co-ordinated mosaics set the tones for the plants. The deck overlooking the back garden focuses the eye on the 18m (60ft) long snake decorated with a diamond-pattern of exquisite blues and greens, the colours echoed in the blue *Ceanothus* and yellow *Spiraeas*. Dohna is also known for her ornamental pieces, balls, eggs, birdbaths, pavers or frogs. All these artists show the diversity of mosaic.

Nicki Saint Phalle sculpture at Chatsworth

Containers

Pots are the ultimate mobile accessory to the garden. Easily moved to where they are needed, containers are flexible, changing a given area quickly and providing seasonal displays. On the patio, pots can be too heavy to move around. If you are planting large pots, or have difficulty lifting, prepare in advance, and get a pot holder on wheels. Use pots as a fail-safe to hold up an area where early plants have left bare soil, injecting new life and colour when needed. Always keep some pots planted up for this reason.

Since many flowering plants only put on a brief show, it is a good idea to plan spring containers featuring spring bulbs, summer displays, autumn displays and finally a winter foliage display. Tulips are suited to growing in a variety of containers.

Containers look good together and can be grouped by colour, type or theme. You can easily group a selection of pots for a party or entertaining on the patio. Attract attention by grouping similar containers together. Space them apart on a patio to give rhythm and lead the eye through an area. Two containers can frame an entrance. Elevating the containers on plinths makes them more immediately noticeable. Small, low containers are suitable for low-growing plants such as succulents. Tall pots look perfect by an entry to the garden or by the door. The modern trend is to repeat the theme. Fragrant pots will put you in the mood for a quiet, romantic evening. Terracotta pots on windowsills look inviting. You have the option to plant a wider range of plants than your climate allows for, simply by having tender plants in pots and bringing them under cover before the first frosts. Add seasonal interest and dress the terrace with pots to add vital colour.

Most gardeners use pots of some kind, but when used correctly they add so much to the garden. The mistake that most gardeners make is to use pots that are too small. Try a bigger pot and see the effect it has. When walking around a garden, I have often been stopped dead by the singular use of a large pot. Use pots to define space, as a focus or to enliven a dead area.

Containers with box topiary in many shapes or standard bay make a good focal point for an entrance. Containers can blend in, be entirely functional or be used as dramatic ornamentation. Unity and balance can come into play when pots are used in symmetry.

Containers require real input and maintenance to look good. Large pots brimming full of plants is real eye-candy If you wish to minimize your workload in the garden, go for the empty container. Choose interesting, medium sized urns for this purpose, one amongst the border plants, or a series on top of a wall. Use large urns as a piece of sculpture; they are fine standing alone without plants. Often they are seen to great effect, turned on their side. Containers are available in many shapes, sizes and materials. Choose a pot that will stand out in the border and not be smothered by the surrounding planting.

Pots do not need to be confined to the ground. Wall-mounted pots add interest to plain walls and lift the eye. Window boxes can adorn sills or be mounted. Hanging baskets full of trailing plants add further interest. Change plants for winter interest instead of leaving the basket empty. When planting any container be sure to match plant and container. Special plants deserve a tiered display to show them to their advantage. These are especially useful where space is at a premium.

There is a huge choice of containers both traditional, modern and unusual objects that can be cajoled into a role as container. One of the best I have seen was a small, French mailing box filled with black pansies. As long as it holds compost and has drainage holes, it can hold plants. Choose whatever fits into your garden style. Stainless steel is the height of fashion and suits the modern, minimalist garden whereas terracotta or wood still reign in the formal garden. Ensure that terracotta containers are frost-proof or they will need to be brought under cover. I adore the new oversized, glazed pots in stunning colours brimming with plants. Stone sinks, trough, tufa and chimney pots all make handsome containers but I deplore the use of twee wheelbarrows and other objects. Succulents look good in shallow pipes or dishes but must have drainage. Surfaces of pots can be painted, sprayed, covered with mosaics, aged or have texture added in the form of shells or rope but these surfaces add to maintenance of the pot.

Some types of plant suit certain containers. Plants with long roots such as poppies need deep containers. Those with excessively vigorous roots are not always suited to containers at all such as *Leymus arenarius*, which quickly breaks through pots. If plants are exceptionally vigorous in pots, they will run riot if let loose in the garden. Try to contrast the shape of the pot with the shape of the plant. Long tall plants look good in square containers. Modern containers do not always offer the same insulation as good old terracotta. In stainless steel containers for instance, try a layer of insulating bubble wrap around the inside, avoiding the base so that plants do not bake in summer and freeze in winter.

Hanging baskets are perfect for summer annuals, but can also be used for herbs and for winter foliage. They do have the disadvantage of drying out very quickly and need to be watered sometimes twice a day in very hot weather. Add slow-release fertilizer and water retaining gel when preparing. Water slowly and a little at a time.

Raised beds

Raised beds are ideal for people who have difficulty bending or kneeling. They are also ideal for alpine plants. A raised bed is simply a border, raised above ground level and contained by walls constructed from any suitable material. The wall can be wide enough to double as seating. The chosen material should fit in with other materials in the garden. Railway sleepers are often used in informal gardens; simple planks of wood joined together to the necessary height, bricks or paving slabs are other options to consider. If the raised beds are against a wall or fence, make them only as wide as you can comfortably reach. If they are free standing, you can easily move around all sides and the beds can be wider. Insert weep holes around the base to allow for drainage.

Brian Makin's terrific Tangerine Diva urns provide balance in this private residence

Furniture

Gardens are hard work, and once the tasks are finished you need somewhere to sit, relax, entertain or simply enjoy the garden. This is another area where new designers are becoming increasingly creative and imaginative. From traditional to ultra modern, in every conceivable material, furniture can be found to adorn any style. Strong ornate style can perform the task of a focal point. Furniture is a movable or fixed asset. Simple or complex, free-standing or built-in, the choices are almost unlimited from a simple tree branch to state-of-the-art designer seats. Ensure those eye-catching, futuristic shapes or unusual materials are comfortable to use. From traditional materials of wood or stone to newer materials of perspex and concrete, from benches to hammocks, there is something to suit all budgets, tastes and gardens. Explore the choices and think of the use, durability, comfort and suitability. Some seating will not withstand extremes of heat and cold. Others may get too hot to sit on. The most comfortable width is 45cm (18"). If you use your garden every day as an outdoor room, you will probably opt for permanent seating, but if, on the other hand, it is an occasional hour spent in the garden, you might go for more temporary options.

Seating does not have to be furniture though, especially in small spaces, you can make use of steps, low walls or wood stumps. If space is tight, hang a seat from a tree, or sling a hammock between two trees. In the small garden, moveable seats such as a folding chair are a bonus. Siting is important; a seat around a tree will usually be in shade. Seated areas or one chair can be used to punctuate a walk, or to view a vista. Any form of seating should be sited where there is something to look at. A meandering path can lead to a place to rest. Visible or hidden away, a seat within the garden is best with something behind it. Use seating to advantage in fragrant areas of the garden. Planters and seats can be combined and are refreshing when planted up with fragrant flowers. I prefer seating to play a supporting role and not be the dominant feature of a garden. Apart from the dining table and chairs, benches and seats, you might also wish to consider a lounger. Heavy furniture is best suited to spacious areas whilst in the small garden something lightweight works well such as wirework or cane. Simple style is best.

I have mentioned elsewhere the effects on the environment when making concrete. Cast concrete can look like stone when finely ground stone filler is used in construction. Concrete seats can be softened with cushions and pads. In this way the concrete can be kept in a neutral colour, and the soft furnishings can easily be changed for different colour effects. Concrete is flexible as shape can be formed by moulds into which the concrete is poured.

Metal is most suited to the modern garden with wide and varied styles. Modern steel uses a slim framework, elegant and sleek. Pieces are available in solid metal or mesh, linear in shape. Galvanized metals with brass or chrome fixings will not rust. Metal pieces can be intricate or plain. Timber from renewable sources is always attractive. Enjoy the grain of hardwoods or pressure-treated softwoods in the garden and the natural, warm tones of wood. Timber, though often the domain of the formal garden suits most types of gardens, depending on the chosen piece. Wood requires maintenance and treating with preservative, although for cedar and oak this is usually unnecessary. Wood pieces vary from ready-made, straightforward outdoor dining sets, to innovative style commissioned from a craftsman or designer. Sleek and modern to chunky and rustic, wood offers many solutions.

Plastics are enjoying a revival, especially sturdy pieces at the higher end of the market. The bright colours are in tune with the ultra modern garden.

The outdoor cook

The outdoor kitchen takes furniture to the extreme. If you enjoy eating outdoors or entertaining, an area close to the house, especially in south-facing gardens, will provide much enjoyment. In north-facing gardens, the sunny area will be at the end of the garden. As we become more and more embedded in the outdoor lifestyle, the outdoor kitchen is upstaging the small barbecue. Barbecues can be mobile or fixed and are relatively humble compared to the outdoor kitchen that has everything including grill, sink, fridge and cupboards. You no longer need to go back and forth into the kitchen to cook outdoors. Fleming's Nurseries and Trailfinders in Australia created an outdoor kitchen in their garden for Chelsea 2006, which won a gold medal. Dean Herald designed the garden in which the kitchen space included electric grill, sink and fridge.

The novelty did not stop there as the dining table included a water feature cascading between the glass top and flowing out into a pond. This exciting rendition of an outdoor lifestyle is one that many of us yearn for as we emulate the outdoor living styles of the Mediterranean and Australia. A covered area is practical in unpredictable climates such as England. Lighting and plants can help to create a romantic atmosphere for evening entertaining. Any barbecue and outdoor heating needs to be environmentally friendly.

The children's area does not have to take up the whole garden, children love a secret hideaway.
Below: The treehouse at Plas Newydd.

Children's area

Gardens can be great fun for adults but for children it is essential to have somewhere to play, invent, discover and let off steam. Not only do children need a space to have fun, they also need an area to garden in their own right. Open spaces are fine for games, but children also love hideaways. The space will dictate the games that children can play.

The space you allot depends on the space you have to start with in the beginning. A small sandpit would suffice in a tiny garden. Sandpits need to be covered. A medium sized garden would allow for a lawn to play games and if space allows a den. A larger space could allow for a children's garden where sunflowers and easy plants can be grown. A play system with swing, slide and covered area or playhouse is ideal. If you have space, allow for a maze, jungle or tunnel. A trampoline is fun and helps work off extra energy. Tree houses are imaginative, in construction and in their use - allowing children to escape reality. A splash pool or small, bubble fountain will attract children, but be aware of the dangers of water features, especially to toddlers. A Wendy house is another space where children can let their imagination run riot.

Informal gardens are best for children. If you are planning a football area, ensure that planting is minimal otherwise you are going to constantly worry about your plants being bombarded by footballs. If children are small, you need to be able to see them from wherever you are, so siting of the area will need to be by the house. Make allowances for the area to be converted into useful space when the children have outgrown it.

Encourage children to grow easy plants such as sunflowers and cornflowers and vegetables like lettuce and radish. It's not a bad idea to let them have a go at something a little more challenging and to explain that not everything is instant, and that nature rules.

Few public gardens make any consideration for children. The structure at **Glendurgan**, the 'Giant's Stride' maypole built for the Fox family takes up space, but is magnificent. At **Alnwick**, children can use trucks to move water, allow plenty of time for your visit, kids love this activity.

Softscaping

The hardscaping is the backbone of the garden, the softscaping its living flesh. Clothe the garden with an eye on the existing natural surroundings using native plants where necessary. Trees and hedges are part of the structure followed by the embellishments, jewels and refinery. The gardener has a wonderful palette to create colour themes to suit the site.

Gardens can be made through an over-riding passion for plants and it is so easy to get carried away. However, don't be tempted to go to the nearest garden centre and fill the trolley willy-nilly. Careful thought must be given to the selection of plants. They can be chosen according to your skill as well as their requirements and maintenance.

The huge diversity of plants available to us is not a problem in itself. Carefully select those plants, perhaps in limited number that suit the design, enhance the landscape and express the original style of the garden. Few are naturals at putting great plants together automatically. Practice makes perfect. Gardens are forgiving; plants can be moved around and changed until you get it right.

Get to know and understand the individual characteristics of each plant. Some are fussier than others. Think about the plant's natural habitat and whether you can provide similar conditions. Plants have a job to perform. Do you need a screen, scented plants around a seating area, plants to eat? What will grow in that shady spot? What thrives in chalk soil? Trees provide structure and shade, shrubs can hide ugly boundaries and hedges define space. Some plants suit large spaces, others small spaces. Indeed space can be made to look smaller or larger by the choice of plants. Plants need to be in keeping with the scale of the garden and house. Use the eventual size of the plants to determine the correct scale. Balance a flat horizontal of paving or water with a rounded shrub and a tall spire. Contrast a strong pattern of foreground planting against a solid hedge of yew. Does the plant stand best as a single specimen or as a group?

Next page: Cotinus and Foeniculum; the black palette; Euphorbia, Dicentra and Ballota; Tulipa; the golden border; conifers; lavender; Molucella laevis

A mistake often made is a mish-mash of too many plants, especially when species or hybrids are planted singly. A far stronger impression is given by a greater number of fewer types of plants. Simplify by limiting plant material. If space permits, plant in large groups of a single plant and repeat plant to tie areas together. The aim is to create pleasing and lasting groups of plants that grow together in the same situation and soil. Each planting group should create a vignette of scale, form, shape, texture and colour according to preferred habitat. Upright, recumbent and prostrate forms, as often seen in Japanese gardens are a key to combining plants successfully. A relationship must exist between plants within a group at the same time there must also be a connection to the next group of plants. Texture or colour offers a means of unification. Look at natural plant groups. Ask yourself why you find a particular association in a garden effective. Select plants for their contribution to the overall composition.

Contrast textures and leaf form for added interest. Use glossy leaves to enliven a dull area. Complete contrast in all plants would make a restless not harmonious composition. Aim for some similarity that offers the desired link. Choose one quiet player and the other more flamboyant to balance the effect. Build up from this, making sure to link each group. Varied height adds interest. Accent plants and drifts bring unity, rhythm and cohesion. Texture is also solid or see-through. A solid plant with close leaves makes a good backdrop. Dixter is an example of the beauty of layered planting. Broad borders allow for layered planting. To create a similar effect in a narrow border, layer vertically. This is what nature herself does in woodland. Plant spring bulbs, herbaceous plants, shrubs and a small tree. The backbone of all planting should be foliage; flowers are the icing on the cake. The planting needs fillers and focus, quiet areas and drama. The easiest way to achieve harmonious planting is to plant in large drifts.

Strong outlines make perfect specimen plants, try *Yucca, Phormium, Agave.* Open textured plants can be used in the foreground whilst denser plants are best in the background. Consider the outline of the plants and aim for contrasting forms such as spiky and round or spiky and lacy to achieve a whole that looks balanced and interesting. You might wish to echo the distant hills in a countryside garden or the shapes of surrounding buildings in a town garden.

Colour

Colour is often the only consideration given when choosing plants. In modern gardens colour can come from hardscaping just as much as from plants. The plants and hardscaping are two halves of a coin and must flow and fit together. If you have a favourite colour scheme, you will have opted for tones, which complement each other in both hard and soft landscaping. The Italian gardens were almost designed in monotone, dark greens embracing the garden with only a few high notes of colour. The colouring of the house affects the tones and colours used in the garden. Cotswold stone or sandstone is admirable with yellow, yellowish greens and blue-green foliage and flowers in a range of yellows and oranges. A red brick wall is suited to a purple scheme enhanced by red flowers. It also looks good with grey-green foliage and dark greens. A white house is set off by a dark background with white flowers and grey foliage. The pink thatched cottage is at home with the summer colours of the cottage garden – pinks, purples, blues, whites and yellows. Perspex forms a decent background to pastel or purple flowers.

To design with colour, you need the eye of a painter and the knowledge of a plantsman or woman. You must understand colour, its effect and interaction as well as the behaviour of plants. Colour in the garden interacts with light, surroundings and neighbouring plants. Knowing how to balance colour is an art. Colour can be used effectively to affect the mood of a place. Sunlight can dilute colour and pale yellows and whites often look better in shade. Yellow is always sunny even when planted in a dismal spot. Nature is an easier act to imitate. In itself, it provides interesting colour schemes. One colour often dominates the landscape and nature always appears to know the trick of colour harmony. Think of a bluebell wood or poppies on the edge of the hayfield. Colours influence perspective. A cool spectrum such as pale blues and pastels has the effect of lengthening perspective, making a border look longer when planted at the far end. Hot colours such as reds are eye-catching and advance towards us; they can be used to detract from an unsightly scene. Background and foreground must harmonize. Dark foliage provides the perfect backdrop for paler plants. Strong 'hot' colours look best against a plain, unfussy, dark background. Busy areas need to be balanced by areas planted with nothing but green.

I prefer tonal shades together rather than contrasts of red and green, yellow and blue. It makes you think more about each plant and its role in the garden. Blue-green foliage combined with silver foliage is a wonderful foil for pink flowers. Green and white are calming and neutral, a classic. Yellow works well in spring and in a yellow border as long as there are not too many daisies. I can take red, although many people are afraid of it. It can work at the end of the season with orange and russet tones in a sunset border or autumn border. These tones are handsome in the spring flowers of *Hamamelis*, witch hazels too.

You can play on the safe side of colour or go bold. By and large, I find colour is misused in most gardens. Colour schemes have to hang together completely. Colour in England is still largely safe pastels. For me the most dramatic colour in the garden is black, but colour preferences are very personal.

Use plants to create structure – hedges and specimen trees will do this job admirably. Structural planting is really a form of hardscaping and is one of the decisions you will have made initially with regard to your plans. Shrubs provide bulk and large herbaceous perennials such as *Cynara* (artichoke) are dramatic enough to have a structural effect. Is there enough structure to give the garden good bones in winter? Seasons affect the look of the planting, so plan for successional interest. It is far better to designate different areas of the garden to seasonal interest than to have something in flower at different times of the year in every area of the garden. Create a winter garden that really shines whilst the rest of the garden goes quietly to sleep. A spring garden to let you know that life has come back to the garden.

Lonicera nitida 'Baggensen's Gold' and Geranium 'Anne Folkard'

Will it Grow?

The physical conditions of the garden determine what you can grow. Put your plants in the wrong place and they curl up their toes and die.

First, test your soil in different parts of the garden as it can vary. You can use a simple testing kit, which is readily available. It is also quite easy to determine your soil type by taking a small amount of soil and rubbing it between your fingertips. Clay sticks together easily and forms lumps. If the soil falls apart, it is sandy. In between means it is loam, the gardener's gift. Make the best of your type of soil whatever it is. If you have soggy ground, don't fight it, make a bog garden. If you have poor soil, there are plants that will grow in it, but you might wish to enhance your soil to grow a wider variety of plants. You need to know if your soil is clay, loam or sandy and also if it is alkaline or acidic.

Some plants will only grow in acid (ericaceous) soil, *Rhododendron, Camellia, Pieris, Crinodendron, Erica* (heather), *Hamamelis* (witchhazel), Viburnum (blueberry) and Ilex (holly). Acid soils are usually peaty and have a pH between 1 and 7. They are sometimes referred to as lime-free. The majority of plants grow in pH 6.5-7. *Saxifragas, Syringas* (lilac), *Weigela, Lilium* (lily), *Dianthus* (pinks) and *Philadelphus* (mock orange) like alkaline (lime) soil. Most lime soils are chalky and have a pH of 7 to 14.

Aspect can determine the kind of plants you grow. In windy sites, establish a shelter belt before you think of anything else. Privet, sea-buckthorn, gorse, sycamore and Austrian pine can cope with cold, coastal districts. Facing north in temperate climates means the garden can be quite inhospitable to many plants. The garden will be cold in winter, cool in summer and shady. Use hardy, shade-loving plant such as ferns, hostas, foxgloves and *Cotoneaster* or *Pyracantha*. You will probably need to protect plants in winter. Facing south means warmer winters and hot summers will grace your space. Here you might need to watch out for drought and plant scorch, especially with gold-leaved plants. You are faced with a wide choice of sun worshippers. Incorporate humus to retain moisture and mulch well. *Abutilon* will do well and South African plants such as *Agapanthus* or drought tolerant plants like *Artemisia* and other grey-leaved plants.

Facing east can mean a cool garden with bitter winds in winter and warm, dry summers. Evergreen conifers or *Acers* might suffer windburn and frost damage. If growing *Magnolias* or *Camellias*, shade them from early morning sun. Use plants recommended for a north-facing garden. West-facing gardens are often considered the best. They are similar to south-facing but without the extremes. Most plants will do well, especially border hardy plants such as *Salvia, Akebia, Jasminum, Leptospermum* and *Actinidia*. Even gardens on opposite sides of the street differ greatly in the amount of sun they receive.

Each country has its own climatic problems from torrential downpours to blazing sun with little rain. Native plants adapt to the local conditions. The number of plants you can grow is usually affected by the amount of frost your garden gets. Conversely some plants are heat-sensitive. Coastal regions have special requirements, not only because of wind but the salt-laden winds. There are plants aplenty to suit every aspect and soil condition nature has provided. Your garden will look more natural and be easier to cope with if you select the right plants in the first place. Sloping sites drain easily, a flat site will take longer and sites with undulations may have pockets where water sits. Some plants might look just the thing, but they are badly behaved. Both bamboo and *Gunnera manicata* are widely used at present and I love both, but they gobble space. There are ways of containing the tendency of bamboo when initially planted, but *Gunnera* is difficult to contain. Some plants are also very difficult to eradicate, so give some thought to the anti-social behaviour of some plants. It's easy to make the wrong choices.

Crinodendron hookerianum

Plant Selection

Core plant lists or best plant lists are to be avoided. Look instead at planting for particular situations, dry, shady, sunny and by aspect such as west-facing and find plants that suit the soil be it loam or clay.

Assessing plant suitability is a skill. There are key factors to follow to help you decide which plants suit your garden and lifestyle. Plant preferences can be exercised but not to the point where you can just have all the plants you really like because chances are they will not all grow in your soil. If you cannot live without a particular plant unsuited to your soil, plant it in a container.

Choose:
Strong lines for rhythm and structure
Architectural plants for accent
Foliage for continued interest
Seasonal colour
Choose plants with more than one season of interest
Choose plants according to your soil type
Select plants that suit the aspect, shady, sunny, dry, wet
Opt for plants that look good together
Look for different types of plants

Choosing Plants
What are you looking for from the plants in your garden? Think of plants as a blue-grey strappy plant, a tall green spire, a rounded silvery-green, a silvery fountain of airy leaves. Choose plants suited to the climate, soil and exposure. Look at what other people are growing in your area. Consider the site, soil and aspect and select plants according to colour for a specific function, such as:

An evergreen tree to 3m (10ft)
A mixed colour dense, evergreen hedge to 1.8m (6ft)
A green, bold accent plant to 1.5m (5ft)
Summer-long flowering plants in blue
Autumn colour border in red, orange and yellow
Spring flowering bulbs in yellow and blue
Pink, fragrant climbers for a sunny wall

The Sensory Garden

Tantalize with plants and materials that appeal to all senses.

Touch: Sensory plants have touch-me, soft, furry or textured foliage. Hard landscaping can use rubber, wood, concrete and other textured materials. Soft cushions and fabrics can soften hard surfaces. A simple bench can look much more homely dressed with cushions that echo the colours of the plants around it.

Sight: Most plants appeal to the eye, but try to find something that does so in more than one season with the added interest of decorative bark, colourful berries or dried seedheads that remain visually stunning on the plant. A cutting garden is attractive as garden produce can be used to decorate the home. Drifts of colour have more effect than bitty planting since the eye is led along seas of colour. Likewise, hardscaping again greatly adds to the effect and is a real feast for the eyes when done well.

Smell: Fragrance is found in flower and foliage and can easily arouse the senses. Not all scents are pleasant. Some scents are much stronger than others and it is unwise to mix too many scents in one area. I love Jasmine, Lavender and *Stephanotis*, and most of the roses. Some foliage only releases its scent on touch. Some bark is fragrant too,

Sound: Water, music and plants such as ornamental grasses and bamboo add sound to the garden. One of the finest examples of the effects of water is found at the **Alnwick Garden**, in Northumberland but I believe the cascade itself was better done at **Chatsworth**. A single jet of water or a bubble pond can be effective where space is lacking. The pond at **Kiftsgate Court** is enchanting with its use of sculpture. Water trickles from the 24 gilded bronze *Philodendron* leaves - it's magic. The golden leaves are reflected in the dark depths of the water. It is a wonderful use of space, scale and geometry. Rectangles of grass, water and paving are in harmony with the rising stalks of the sculpture.

Taste: Many flowers are edible and gardeners can choose from a small herb container to a large vegetable plot. Even tomatoes can be grown in a hanging basket and courgettes are decorative enough to grow in the border.

To be aesthetically pleasing, all elements have to marry. Space has to be used effectively, both horizontal and vertical space and linked to the landscape beyond the garden if there is a view or in the case of city gardens, enclosed in privacy

Perennials

The mainstay of the flower border, handsome perennials are reliable, prolific blooming and live for a long time. There is a large selection of hardy or tender perennials available. Plan for all seasons, after the first show, the garden can look empty. *Asters, Hemerocallis, Helenium, Rudbeckias* and *Sedum* are all good late perennials.

Acanthus

Tall spikes of purple and white hooded flowers with glossy, thick large leaves are bold and attractive. They come into flower through July and August. **A. 'Hollard's Gold'** has almost entire yellow leaves that fit nicely in the golden garden. In contrast the leaves of **A. spinosus 'Royal Haughty'** are extremely cut and spiny. Somewhere in between is **A. mollis 'Summer Beauty'** with its attractive cut foliage and taller growth to 75cm (30"). *Acanthus* needs space and is difficult to dig up if you have put it in the wrong place. It's good for the edge of a wildlife garden and is best grown in sun in soil that does not completely dry out. These Mediterranean plants are also known for their symbolic leaves used in classical architecture, especially on Corinthian columns. Z6.

Achillea

Providing interest all summer with their flat, plate-like heads, *Achillea* flowers often change colour throughout the season. Strong and bold is found in full force in the tall and commanding **A. filipendula 'Gold Plate'** with its saturated yellow blooms or the even taller **A. 'Cloth of Gold'** up to 1.8m (6ft). However, easy on the eye pastels make their gentle statement. 1.5m (5ft). **A. 'Lachsschonheit'** (Salmon Beauty) has beautiful salmon-pink tones. 95cm (38"). **A 'Moonshine'** is a lovely yellow although it appears inconsistent. **A. Summer Pastels Group** is quick into flower and very gratifying. Achilleas suit dry, light or sandy soils and some have lovely silvery leaves. These excellent perennials for the beginner are found in flower from June to July and again in August to September if deadheaded. New cultivars have been bred in Germany by Ernst Pagels to withstand cold winters, but plants, although hardy throughout Great Britain can die in moist or clay soils over winter. For a better chance of survival, cut plants back hard after flowering. Tall varieties will need staking. They associate well with *Salvias* (sage) and *Verbascums* (mullein). Z4.

Alchemilla

Fabulous green foliage, the best known being **A. mollis** for its soft leaves and mass of chartreuse flowers. If it has a fault, it's that it can seed around too much, but many welcome it for such a handsome plant rarely seems out of place. Like hostas, it has that amazing ability to catch rain droplets like mercury rolling on the surface of its leaves. Use it to soften the edge of a path or for groundcover. This easy to grow plant is even tolerant of heavy clay and once established, it takes drought too. It enjoys humus-rich soil in a sunny to part shady position. Cut back fading flowers in August and you might well be rewarded with a second flush. Ladies mantle is a good mixer with other cottage garden plants such as *Geranium, Campanula* and *Hosta*. (60cm). Z4.

Campanula

Bellflowers come in many shapes and sizes, some suitable for borders others for rock gardens. **C. cochlearifolia 'Elizabeth Oliver'** bears dainty, double-flowered blue bells on slender stems on compact plants whose roots will spread to form a carpet. Try it in cracks in paving or the edge of gravel paths. **C. 'Sarastro'** is a personal favourite for its hanging bells to 5cm (2") long in deep purple-blue. The classic Canterbury bell is **C. medium** which is available in shades of white, pink and blue. They look spectacular all summer in sun or a little shade grown in well-drained soil. Good companion plants are geraniums, roses and delphiniums.

Delphinium

Blue summer skies are reflected in the flowers of this cottage garden standby. Spires of various blues provide a focal point adding much needed height to the border. These are heavy feeders and need staking so are not as popular with modern gardeners. The species **D. belladonna** has bright, sky blue flowers and is easy to grow. Jekyll might add a touch of these to a yellow scheme, to add zest to the planting. Another strong colour is purple and I like these too. Z5.

Previous page: Acanthus; next page clockwise from top left: Achillea Lasschonheit, Tulipa, Echinacea, Dianthus, Lilium longiflorum, Campanula 'Sarastro', Scabiosa 'Blue Butterfly', Delphinium 'Bruce'

Dianthus

Pinks are great at the front of a border and their silvery-blue foliage is useful too. **D. 'Mrs. Sinkins'** has fussy, laciniated petals that are more suited to a larger flower such as the poppies. **D. 'Doris'** is a lovely pink with a carmine circle around its semi-double flowers. This was developed by Allwoods nursery and is a repeat-flowerer. **D. 'Letitia Wyatt'** is probably my favourite for its large, soft pink blooms keep coming and it is quite robust. The Cheddar pinks, **D. gratianopolitanus** can be useful for mass planting and display the best qualities of these plants, pink blooms, bluish foliage and clove scent. Many are scented. They have an old-fashioned charm and are easy plants to grow. Plants of **D. plumarius** were brought to England by Norman monks. *Dianthus* do best in full sun in well-drained soil. Z3-9.

Dicentra

One of the most charming perennials in all its forms. Ferny foliage and delicate dangling flowers are usually in shades of pink or white. **D. spectabilis** is the most widley grown and is excellent in good humus in light shade.

Digitalis

Another flower that makes attractive spires in the garden. The English native since the 15th century, **D. purpurea** is biennial and will self-seed. The soft, felt-like leaves rise to many tubular flowers held on strong stalks. From white buds, rosy-pink flowers open with spots on the inner tube. **D. 'Sutton's Apricot'** is a soft colour. Foxgloves attract bees into the garden. They are suitable for part shade or sun. All parts are poisonous if eaten. 1.5m (5ft). Z3.

Echinacea

These North American natives have real flower power. Big, bold daisies have migrated from the Prairies to grace our borders. There is a limited number of around nine species, but breeders have been doing their thing with the coneflowers, yet the simple species or cultivars are still the best. **E. purpurea 'Magnus'** has horizontal purple pink petals as opposed to the drooping petals of the species itself. It has a dark orange cone. **E. purpurea 'Rubinstern'** has large ruby-red flowers. **E. 'White Swan'** is a lovely addition with its white flowers contrasting with the dark cone. It is a small grower to just 60cm (2ft). One of the best recent introductions is **E. 'Art's Pride'** which heralded a new colour break on the orange side.

Along with **E. 'Harvest Moon'** in yellow tones and **E. 'Sundown'** in orange, the coneflowers are now a valuable part of any sunset garden. They bloom for weeks on end and are fragrant. Echinaceas need full sun and although they appreciate good loam, any decent soil will suffice. These sturdy plants do not need staking. Plants are usually propagated by division but you can take cuttings of young shoots in spring or grow from seed which usually comes true to the parent. Z4.

Euphorbia

Hard to live without but most need room to grow. The smallest growing are **E. dulcis 'Chameleon'**, not as weedy as often purported, for me at least or try **E. amygdaloides** cultivars for red foliage in spring.

Geranium

Easy enough for beginners yet floriferous and handsome in leaf too. They often produce a second flush of flowers if cut back after flowering. Many species grow on clay, chalk and just about any soils and are suitable for full sun to shade. Border types come in a range of colours from blue through purple to pink with the occasional white. Leaves are textured or coloured, many plain green. Many form large clumps easily; some outrun their space quickly like **G. pratense** and its offspring. My favourite species is **G. renardii** for its crinkled leaves. In flower, **G. magnificum** is attractive and makes large clumps quickly if you have the space. **G. 'Khan'** has large magenta-purple flowers from May to November. **G. 'Ivan'** is a striking pink with deeper magenta veins. **G. 'Rozanne'** is splendid in its pretty blue flowers, deeply cut leaves and spreading but not untidy habit. **G. 'Dusky Crug'** has milk chocolate foliage contrasting with the soft pink flowers from May to November. If you like plants that get noticed, employ **G. 'Anne Folkard'** with abandon for its golden foliage in spring and its heart-stopping magenta flowers with a black centre. It is not the tidiest *Geranium*, but I would not be without it. I grow it with **Lonicera nitida 'Baggensen's Gold'**, **Sambucus racemosa 'Sutherland Gold'** and a few other golden counterparts such as **Cotinus 'Golden Spirit'**, **Centaurea 'Gold Bullion'** and **Spiraea 'Golden Princess'** with a good clump of bronze fennel, **Foeniculum**. Most Z5.

Next page clockwise from top left: Alchemilla mollis; Hosta 'Sagae'; Lavandula; Euphorbia; Perovskia and Verbena bonariensis; Pulmonaria; Geranium 'Dusky Crug; Dicentra spectabilis

Hemerocallis

Only lasting a day but with an endless succession of summer blooms, daylilies suit well-drained, sunny sites with attention to afternoon shade for dark varieties that tend to fade. They come in evergreen and semi-evergreen varieties. Plant at any time from spring to early autumn and mulch to conserve moisture in spring. These sturdy plants are heat and drought resistant. The peak flowering period is July, fading flowers must be removed. Divide every three to four years in spring. Easy plants for beginners with a bonus of edible flowers. My particular favourites are the darkest reds with black in them and I am also partial to the plums, peach shades and pale pinks. I prefer singles by far and also like the spider types. There are many hybridizers in the U.S and thousands of cultivars have been registered. **H. fulva** and **H. lilioasphodelus** (flava) are two species that are commonly grown. **H. 'Gentle Shepherd'** is to be recommended for its delicate pale pink wide-open blooms. I love **H. 'Africa'** for its darkest flowers but it is a weak grower, so opt for **H. 'Chicago Royal Robe'** instead.

Hosta (funkia)

A favourite of Miss Jekyll, *Hostas* are the Queen of shade plants in green, gold and blue foliage, some have red stems. Most have white or lavender flowers, some being scented. They come with rounded or pointed leaves and many have superb texture; in tiny forms to great big guys. One down side, is slugs, so be prepared to control these. Hostas make good clumps and should be allowed to do so for five years before you think of dividing them. My favourite is **H. 'Krossa Regal'** for its vase-shaped foliage is tinted in a glorious blue and **H. 'Sagae'** is fantastic.

Lavandula

Lavender is another scented beauty that graces the garden. It is also visually pleasing with its varying hues of mainly purple flowers. I like the white varieties, but the pinkish reds do nothing for me. Some are hardier than others. My favourite of all is the French lavender, **L. stoechas.** It's the bunny ears. Z7.

Nepeta

I can understand why people like catmint, especially when used en masse, this purple perennial is handsome. However, be aware that this plant is beloved by cats, attracted by its scent, they often roll around in it. I think that's the problem.

Perovskia

Known as Russian Sage, many think this is lavender when they first see it yet it smells of sage when bruised. **P. 'Blue Spire'** is a sub-shrub that produces blue-grey foliage topped by blue flowers in summer. It suits a dry, sandy soil or very well drained soil in full sun. It associates well with *Echinops, Lavandula* and *Verbena*.

Pulmonaria

The spring lungworts are one of the first flowers to get the season on its way. Mainly blue or pink, I love their clear little flowers against the spotted or silver foliage. Plain green foliaged ones do not have quite the same charm for me. They are good front of border plants that are best in some shade in humus-rich, well-drained soil. **P. 'Bertram Anderson'** is happy even in clay. It has nicely spotted foliage with heavenly blue flowers. **P. saccarata** is well-spotted and in some forms wholly silver. **P. 'Majeste'** is recommended by many, but out of all the ones I have grown, this is the only one I have had problems with – the leaves are fantastically silver yet it suffers from mildew. There are many hybrids, so I would opt to leave this one alone. Z4.

Salvia

I cannot hope to do justice to the many sages I love here. They are excellent late flowerers suited to warm, sunny climates. Many of the best do not perform well in the north of England. **S. guaranitica** is handsome, I like **'Black and Blue'** for its dark calyces holding deep blue flowers. The best known is **S. patens** which grows here and is famous for its blue flowers, **'Cambridge Blue'** and others.

Scabiosa

I have been in love with these humble flowers for many a year. They are a mainstay of a summer garden. You can opt for pastels found in the pale primrose yellow of **S. ochroleuca** or the deepish lilac of **S. caucasica 'Fama'** or you can go all out for devilishly dark scabious. I first grew this as **S. 'Saatchmo'** in 1994, now it is found in several forms, some better than others, some annual, others biennial and yet others seeming more perennial in dryish winter conditions. **S. 'Ace of Spades'** and **S. 'Chile Black'** add another dimension to the usual 'pretty' colours of the cottage garden style.

Next page clockwise from left: Calamagrostis; Berberis and Stipa; mixed grasses (2); Stipa arundinace; Carex

Stachys

Grown for its furry leaves, stachys is a classic sensory plant. Its only downfall is a downpour as the wet leaves really look bedraggled. It makes a nice front-of-border plant. I like the classic silver type, but I am also enamoured with yellow-leaved **S. 'Primrose Heron'** and the lime **S. 'Limelight'**. It is easy to grow in well-drained soil.

Verbena

V. bonariensis has become a favourite with many gardeners. It is a short-lived perennial and is half hardy, needing protection from frosts. Its tall stems hold heads of purple flowers that are a delight. They will self-seed where happy. Grow in moist but well-drained soil in full sun. Sown in March to April, it associates well with ornamental grasses and *Perovskia*.

Viola

Pansies, violets and violas can all be grown in the cottage garden adding sumptuous colour at the front of borders and along edges of paths. Violas are smaller than pansies and look wonderful en masse. **Viola 'Molly Sanderson'** is a favourite, easy to grow providing flowers all season given a little shade. The matt black flowers are astonishing and very sexy. **Viola 'Boughton Blue'** has pale blue flowers. Propagation is by cuttings. Grow in any well-drained soil. Z3.

Yucca

One of the staples of Jekyll's planting schemes. She would use them at the edge of borders, usually at a corner to focus the eye. Their architectural foliage is best seen against a backdrop. The flowers are fantastic off-white candles. Z7, some to Z5.

Grasses

Ornamental grasses are being used to add architectural form to new herbaceous borders. Most grasses are adaptable and grow in poorer soils than many garden perennials. Some are much more vigorous than others and they have different water requirements. The correct grasses form impressive prairie plantings.

Carex

There are many species of *Carex*, some hailing from New Zealand. The best sedges have variegated or bronze foliage and add interesting colour to the garden. **C. elata 'Aurea'** is often known as Bowles' Golden Grass. It really does add that Midas Touch to the spring garden with its arching leaves that are best in part shade to sun in average to damp soil. This semi-evergreen native is happy near water. **C. buchananii** has striking coppery bronze foliage with characteristically curled leaf tips. This evergreen is stunning in a sunny, well-drained spot. 50-60cm (20-24"). **C. comans bronze form** is an evergreen bronzed sedge happy in sun or part shade making elegant mounds at the front of the border. 40-50cm (16-20"). The taller, evergreen **C. tenuiculmis** also exhibits bronze foliage in sun or light shade. 50-60cm (20-24"). Z5.

Deschampsia

D. cespitosa 'Goldtau' and other gold forms make clumps of airy, golden leaves to 60cm (2ft). Z4.

Hakonechloa

H. macra 'Aureola' is a favourite for its variegated foliage combined with a fountain habit. This small grass, shade-tolerant and a bamboo look-alike is lovely by the edge of a path. 45cm (18"). Z6 with protection.

Festuca

This species is invaluable in the blue-themed garden and makes a good contrast in the golden garden too. Fescues are drought proof once established. **F. 'Elijah Blue'** is one of the best with its thread-like foliage. Grow in well-drained soil in full sun. They can look dead in winter. Z4.

Miscanthus

This can be rather domineering in the loveliest of ways. These tall grasses need space, not only to grow but to admire. **M. 'Silberfeder'** is attractive. Z5.

Rudbeckia

Stipa

S. gigantea, the golden oats is striking and tall but airy making a fountain shape with the best colour in summer. Use it instead of the ubiquitous pampas grass. It is good in the border or gravel garden. It likes full sun in well-drained soil. 1.8m (6ft). Z5.

S. tenuissima is a compact perennial with thread-like stems covered by masses of pale seedheads in summer with a feathery appearance. It appreciates well-drained soil in full sun. 60cm (2ft). Z7.

Below: Grasses at Queen Mary Gardens in Falmouth, Cornwall include Festuca, Pennisetum and Arundo
Below Right: Epimedium skirts the rustic steps at Keukenhof providing foolproof ground cover

Groundcover Plants

Both foliage and flowering varieties provide great texture whilst doing a great job at suppressing weeds. Ensure that the area is weed-free for the first year; the plants should then be able to more or less look after themselves. Traditional groundcover is seen in swathes on slopes and under shrubs but groundcovers that take foot traffic can make an excellent alternative to lawns. Try *Dichondra*, *Leptinella* or *Chamaemelum* (lawn chamomile). Some low-growing grasses can also be used as lawn alternatives such as *Festuca*. These can provide an alternative foreground to a green border. Imagine *Acaena* 'Blue Haze' and *A. purpurea* mixed for a stunning landscape. One word of warning, many plants now being sold as groundcover are real runners that don't know when to stop. Some gardeners have encountered problems with *Leptinella*, *Lysimachia*, *Acaena*, *Sagina* (Scotch Moss) and *Soleirolia*, the latter also known as Baby's Tears is exceptionally difficult to eradicate. People fall in love with it, but I believe it is best kept as an indoor plant if you really want to grow it. It appeared voluntarily in my last garden, and I thought it pretty at first, but when it ran into the vegetable plot and lawn (yes I had one then) I tried to take it out. Any tiny piece left behind regenerates ad infinitum. *Hedera* (ivy) used to be the classic groundcover and has been ostracized in America as invasive. Here in England it is native and I have never encountered problems with it. There are some superbly variegated ivies that can brighten shady spots, the colour range is fantastic from grey to black, dark to light green and gold to cream. Herbs such as *Thymus* make attractive creeping scented mats. One of my favourites is blue *Juniperus* (juniper) in sun and *Hostas* in shade. Groundcover can help to reduce soil erosion. It will really cut down on maintenance.

Shrubs

Shrubs are woody plants that have more than one stem from the base and can be quite small and up to 3m (10ft) high. They are useful for both flower and foliage and are often low maintenance. Shrubs can contribute to the backbone of the garden. In small gardens they can be used almost like trees – singly as a focal point or in groups. They can divide, enclose, screen or shelter. On contoured ground on a small scale garden, shrubs can have the same effect as tree groupings in the larger scale landscape. Their ability to grow almost to ground level, without a clean trunk offers the advantage of their use as division. They can be part of the structure as *Acers* are in the Japanese garden, merely decorative or a focal point. My most dependable shrubs include *Acer, Berberis* (barberry), *Mahonia, Elaeagnus, Fatsia* (does not like too much cold). Roses are some of the most planted shrubs; try to select those that are fragrant, repeat flowering and disease free. If overwhelmed by choice, look at your site for aspect then decide on the required height and flowering season. Allow enough space for shrubs to develop their natural form; don't hem them in.

Shrubs are beginning to lose their tawdy image and are once again being appreciated for their contribution to the garden. I like small hebes for their rounded, sculptural qualities. I also love floriferous shrubs such as *Hydrangeas* and have a passion for species *Ribes* and golden *Rubus*. Make the most of a shrubs unique character. Silver, gold and purple can relieve the background of green. *Berberis* are useful easy growers for they come in rounded forms as well as pencil thin, in green, gold and purple. *Rhododendrons* and *Camellias* are favoured in many Cornish gardens and in the Pacific Northwest. Shrubs are particularly useful to provide winter colour. *Deutzia, Hamamelis* and *Chimonanthus* are all useful as well as the ubiquitous *Jasminum nudiflorum*. Whilst shrubs are often used in a mixed border; they can contribute to the garden in other ways. Employ repeat lines of a given shrub to make a strong statement.

Choose shrubs appropriate for your style and period. Tropicals were favoured in Victorian times and have made a recent comeback. Flowers are favoured in cottage gardens and the herbaceous border. Foliage is featured in many contemporary styles.

The circular herbaceous borders at Pine Lodge, Cornwall are given a backbone of shrubs and trees

Cornus

As large shrubs, these take some beating. Fabulous foliage, great flowers and stems are found on these shrubs, but not always on the same plant, so decide what your main focus is. For red stems try, **C. 'Kesselringii'**, **C. florida 'First Lady'** for its golden leaves.

Rosa

True cottage gardens grow old roses. I admit to a weakness for roses, my favourites being the darkest reds, bordering on black and the apricots plus a passion for a few pinks. I have no desires to see a blue rose. My favourites are hybrid teas and David Austin Roses. I walked in circles round and round the rose garden at **Alnwick**, until I knew not if I were dizzy from circling or from the heady perfume that draws you in so you need to linger. Hard to choose favourites as there are few I dislike. Roses tend to be the only plants where I go for so many doubles, normally much preferring single flowers. Roses remain the most romantic flower of all. There are roses for arbours, swags and hedges, for sun or shady spots. Choose disease resistant roses for a head start. **R. 'Pat Austin'** is a classic with sumptuous amber colouring and a delicious tea fragrance, **R. 'Ambridge Rose'** a delicate beauty, **R. 'Constance Spry'** incredibly feminine pink whilst **R. 'Jude The Obscure'** is deliciously, fruitily fragrant. Z5.

Trees

Trees are invaluable in any garden as long as you choose the correct one with regard to size and performance. So many trees are planted that are far too big for their allotted space. Ensure that you have the space to accommodate the tree in ten years' time when it has matured. Much has been written about trees in small gardens, but it depends on just how small the garden is. The best small tree for gardens is an *Acer*, Japanese maple and they can be grown successfully in pots. Try *Sambucus*, elder the golden and black forms are truly wonderful and can be cut hard back each year and kept as a large shrub that makes good growth to 3m (10ft) in one season. Fastigiate trees are slim and can fit into smaller gardens, try *Fagus sylvatica* 'Black Swan'. Trees such as *Betula* (birch) provide great silhouettes and many have interesting bark. Some trees must not be planted near drains, ponds, paved areas or decking, especially *Salix* (willow) but also *Tilia* (lime) *Populus* (poplar) and *Eucalyptus* have invasive roots, although these can be controlled by digging a trench with a barrier around the tree. For a tiered effect choose *Cornus controversa* 'Variegata' or *Viburnum plicatum* 'Mariesii' both of which are gorgeous. Larger spaces have a vast choice, including the King of all trees, needing a veritable Kingdom to grow in, the majestic *Cedrus deodar*, the Cedar of Lebanon.

Trees can be planted singly as a focal point or in majestic groups; used to provide division or visual excitement when used in a circle or to obscure the view. Groups of *Sequiadendron* are incredible in their natural setting along the Californian coast. *Cypresses* conjure up Italian gardens just as majestic oaks are essentially English. A single line leads the eye such as the lines of *Robinia pseudoacacia* 'Frisia' the brightest of golden trees, on the approach to Renishaw Hall.

Some plants are naturally graceful such as willow and silver birch whilst beech and ash can sweep to the ground. Other trees have different effects poplar being narrow, chestnut broad, pines can be chosen for interesting bark. In general, upright trees are suited to the formal garden and those with broader canopies to informal design. Olive trees are handsome in a formal setting. Palms are strikingly architectural. Trees can be enhanced by planting bulbs at their feet in a natural setting and by rising from box topiary in a formal setting.

Some trees have spectacular qualities; *Populus candicans* is remarkable for its silver leaves, *Betula utilis v jacquemontii* for its white bark, *Fagus sylvatica* 'Dawyck Purple' for its purple foliage, *Davidia involucrata* for its white handkerchiefs, *Magnolias* for their incredible flowers, *Prunus* for their frothy spring blossoms and *Acers* for their autumn foliage.

Robinias make a transition from the lawn to the kitchen garden at Chatsworth

Spring onions are tasty and their linear foliage handsome. I grew mustard leaf one year, very attractive with its red veining, but it was too hot for me to eat. Rocket is easy and nutritious.

I love growing tomatoes and they are not at all difficult. Choose bush types or small tumbling varieties to grow in baskets. The tip here is not to damage the stem. Feed them with a specialist tomato fertilizer. Potatoes are easy too but do need space to grow.

Vegetables can add height to the garden; with wigwams you can grow climbing beans, gourds or cucumbers. Many vegetables can grow on the patio in containers in a sunny spot. There are even mini vegetables offered by seed companies for this reason. From pot to potager you can grow your own delicious food.

Below: Structure in the kitchen garden at Chatsworth with apples on arches; Top Right; Swiss chard; Centre: Herb garden at RHS Harlow Carr; Bottom: Origanum 'Kent Beauty'

Foliage Garden

In recent years much emphasis has been put on foliage. In many ways foliage is just as colourful as flowers and yet it gives a longer season forming the backbone of the garden. Foliage gardens can be colour-themed with green the obvious choice. Yet there is also a vast range of colourful foliage in tones from bronze, through red to purple and even approaching black; gold, silver and blue, not to mention variegated leaves. Many gardeners are unaware of the enormous number of plants that have coloured foliage. This has become my domain; see the books 'Black Magic and Purple Passion', 'Gold Fever', 'Silver Lining' and 'Emeralds' for the huge range of plants available. More are on the way. Foliage plants not only offer colour but also texture in their glossy or dull leaves, the texture of their surface like a mirror or as soft as velvet. Choose contrasting leaf shapes for interest, juxtaposing sword-like leaves of **Phormium** (New Zealand flax) with the palmate leaves of **Melianthus major**. The tiny, rounded leaves of **Ballota** look good beside the lance-shaped leaves of **Euphorbia**. Contrast makes for interesting compositions. Grasses and bamboos have movement and contribute sound to the garden. Large-leaved plants have their own architectural status.

Foliage is low-maintenance. A covering of leaves means little room for weeds. Suitable foliage plants exist for every aspect; ferns and hostas are suited to shade, tropical type plants to sun, Rheums for damp soil.

Great foliage plants

Acer
Berberis
Cordyline
Cotinus
Epimedium
Fatsia
Hosta
Melianthus
Phormium
Ricinus
Solenostemon (Coleus)

Above: Fatsia japonica
Below: Melianthus villosus

Great Plants for the Small Garden

There are many dwarf plants available which might suit your purpose, but you also need spires and groundcovers as well as something that makes a statement. The narrow plants in the vertical reality section are a good start. Blue and purple can make a small space seem larger. Many conifers are suitable for small spaces. Add colour with seasonal containers. Manipulate the space with visual tricks, see this section. Colour repetition provides harmony. Avoid space-hugging beasts.

Ajuga
Azalea
Berberis 'Helmond Pillar'
Dianthus
Hebe
Heuchera
Juniperus 'Sky Rocket'
Ophiopogon
Phormium
Spiraea
Viola

Top right: Hebe; Centre: Ophiopogon; Bottom: Spiraea;
Below: Azalea Koster's Red; Heuchera

Maintenance

Garden basics are important. How long you have to spend on keeping the garden looking neat and trim depends on a variety of factors. Get the basics of soil, aspect, watering; plant selection and maintenance right in the beginning and you cannot go far wrong. The same principles apply to an established or new plot. Without these basics your beautiful garden will deteriorate rapidly.

Ensure that your soil is good by working in humus. Many plants die through over-watering, and just as many die from being in the wrong place or in the wrong soil. Even experts kill plants from time to time - it's part of the process of being a gardener.

Position is important, late frosts can ruin a display of *Rhododendron* or *Magnolia* whilst winds play havoc with bamboos and maples. Give plants a good start. Like humans, plants can suffer stress - if they do not receive enough water they wilt. All plants require more water when first planted, until established. When planting, always dig a hole big enough for the plant. Water until it has made a mini moat around the plant. Come back after a few minutes and do the same again. Water regularly until established, even if it rains, only heavy downpours soak right down to the roots.

Which plants are best for your lifestyle? If you lead a busy lifestyle yet wish to keep a tidy garden you need to know the requirements and maintenance of each plant. Wherever you garden, your experience and choice of plants should be suited to your soil and your first choice should be natives. I have selected principally easy to grow and low-maintenance plants.

According to Dame Sylvia Crowe one person can look after three acres of average garden. This is not quantified as regarding a working person or not, nor by how many hours you are expected to work in the garden. Many find it difficult to cope with the average English town garden and many more pave over the lawn or the front garden, thereby losing the very area guaranteed to give some pleasure and to enhance the house. You need to decide at the beginning how much time you have to spend on maintenance for it determines not only the kind of plants but other elements of the garden. Absolutely no garden is maintenance free.

After planting it takes two to three years for plants to establish and during this initial period maintenance is at an all-time high. Watering, weeding and pruning are all demanding. It is true that most plants die within the first few weeks of being planted owing to lack of or the wrong maintenance, especially too much or too little water. You might wish to employ someone to help with maintenance until the garden is established and tasks diminish and you feel you can handle it alone. Keep notes and a photographic record to spot any weaknesses or any improvements you can make in plantings.

Some tasks are far more time-consuming than others and unless you know, it's easy to opt for what you like without thinking about maintenance. Gardens soon begin to look untidy and lose that dreamed for serenity. Think ahead. Let's take a look at all those time-consuming areas of the garden and how to make them into pleasure zones. You need to pare the garden down to minimal in terms of doing but maximum in terms of enjoyment. If you fear this means concrete and no plants, I'm a plantswoman first and foremost and for me plants make the garden.

Hardscaping

Opt for surfaces that are easy to keep clean and furniture that looks good without too much maintenance. Remember any painted surfaces will need frequent maintenance. Select features for their durability. Choose a simple water feature. Ensure the garden is functional and practical, meeting your needs but with individual and artistic flair. In minimalist gardens maintenance exists in the clearance of algae, dirt and moss, brushing, painting and scrubbing. Instant gardens still need maintenance too, so again give thought to whether you understand the garden and what it needs to keep it looking good. Gardens can be just as difficult to keep in shape as bodies.

Routine mainenance at Het Loo Palace, Holland

Low maintenance plants

If you have opted for walls or concrete boundaries, these are relatively maintenance free unless painted. They might need painting every year or two. They benefit from the softening effect of plants growing on them, which need annual trimming and can leave unsightly marks.

For today's lifestyle, low maintenance is the buzz-word. Choose shrubs and trees, ground covers and add seasonal colour with large pots. Underplant with bulbs that can be left in the ground. Give careful thought to the softscaping especially- by choosing the right plants, you can minimise maintenance. Plants sold as low-maintenance are often topiaries. Topiaries need clipping and take some skill to keep their shape.

Are you growing time-consuming plants that can be changed to lower maintenance whilst retaining the pleasant aspect of plantlife? You cannot possibly select plants for a garden unless you understand which plants will grow where, and which look best together. You need to know the eventual height, width and behaviour of the plants as well as their individual maintenance requirements. Grow the right plants for your lifestyle.

Easier options:
Change bedding plants and annuals for perennials
Beds cut in lawns to borders
Herbaceous plants that need staking to those that hold their heads high
Herbaceous borders to shrubbery
Grass to groundcover
Make the best use of space
Long borders to raised beds

Low maintenance garden styles
Some garden types are easier to maintain than others. Woodland is the easiest. Simplify in order to reduce upkeep. Make life easier by choosing the right style of garden for you. You might love flowers and long for a 200ft herbaceous border but if you only have an hour or two at the weekends, this is not the way you want to go. Foliage is easier in general to look after than flowers. Maintenance is lessened when you garden with the local flora and fauna in mind.

Time matters. The most time-consuming tasks in the garden include
Lawn - keeping a lawn trimmed, mown and weed-free is high maintenance. If you must have a lawn think carefully about its size in the garden. Choose the most appropriate grass type for its intended use. Lawns need to be cut every week in summer, and once a fortnight from April to the end of May and again September to October. The first cut will need to be higher than usual. Long grass looks unseemly unless in a wild garden and even if the borders and rest of the garden are trim and neat, an untidy lawn attracts the eye and spoils the effect. Edges must be trimmed too, and are often even more time-consuming. You need a place to store the equipment, which needs to be cleaned after every use. A compost bin will take care of the clippings although lawn grass alone will only make sludge, so be sure to have a good mix in the compost bin. The shape of the lawn affects the time taken to mow it. Square lawns and those with cut-out shapes such as island beds or those with raised landforms are more time-consuming than curved lawns. Edging needs to be set lower than the lawn so that the mower can skim over it. Replacing 25% of the lawned area with groundcover or shrubs will save almost double the time and energy spent on cutting the lawn. The time spent will vary on the equipment used from ride-on mower, robot mower, to hand-mower or even those die-hard gardeners who still clip their lawns with shears.
Fuel for power mowers and toxic emissions plus the large number of chemicals that lawns require are the reasons we should look for lawn alternatives. Studies from Yale University indicated that the average suburban lawn in the U.S. uses 10 times as much chemical pesticides per acre as farmland. I should think the figures are similar here in the U.K. The effects on the environment, wildlife and on our health are unsupportable. Mowers, trimmers and blowers emit more pollution than the average car. Remember quiet Sundays? Noise pollution is at an all-time high in our gardens. The U.S. Environmental Protection Agency reports that a staggering $700 is spent on maintaining the average lawn every year. Huge amounts of water are wasted, there are those who even risk a fine to keep their lawn green and flaunt the hose-ban. Where is the justification? Try corn gluten for a non-toxic way of keeping the garden free of weeds. It's time to re-think that green space. I'll go only one small step in the defence of the lawn – it does provide a habitat for many insects, but so too do alternatives to lawn.

Weeding - mostly on bare land. Borders and other planted areas are almost weed-free if they are planted with ground cover. Hoe off any weeds immediately they appear. If weeds plague the area the quick solution is to cover with weed-suppressing fabric. A slower way is to cover the area with black plastic for a season. We should be seeking alternatives to chemicals to keep our gardens weed-free. An excellent way to smother weeds is simply to use groundcover plants.

Deadheading - do you need to do it? Christopher Lloyd was not partial to deadheading. Seedheads can be pretty and useful and they can uncannily throw seedlings up in just the right place. However, if you are a very tidy person, this kind of gardening is very informal and you might have to cope with thousands of seedlings in the wrong place. If you want the attractive qualities of seedheads, usually a late season effect, then leave seed heads in place. However, know how prolific the plant seeds and act accordingly. *Papaver* (poppies) are prolific seeders. Some flowers such as *Lathyrus* (sweet peas) stop flowering if they are not deadheaded. Others like *Lunaria* (honesty) are grown primarily for their seedheads, in this case their silvery discs.

Herbaceous Plants - staking, deadheading, cutting back and dividing are all tasks associated with this group of plants. Avoid them if it all seems too much and go for easier to maintain shrubs. Look at the new perennials instead, still herbaceous, but not as time-demanding as the older style.

Hedge trimming - most hedges can be maintained in half a day, two or three times a year. Individual maintenance is given under plant descriptions.

Watering - use drip irrigation if possible but only where necessary. Never leave a sprinkler aimed high or on all day. Do not water grass - it does not go brown forever, it usually comes green again. Water is too precious to waste.

Water wisely – what does this mean? Keep a water barrel to catch rainwater. Attach a pipe to the downpipe if you can to use bathwater or to the washing machine. Early in the morning or late in the evening when evaporation is least likely is the best time to water.

Water deeply with the jet aimed directly at the roots. Try to avoid very thirsty plants unless you have moisture retentive soil. Mulching in spring conserves moisture. By watering correctly you will encourage deep root systems, doing so frequently and only wetting the surface means that roots come to the surface for water.

Trees – these are relatively maintenance free apart from a little judicious pruning. Even small gardens can have a tree but do choose carefully, taking into consideration the ultimate height and canopy of the tree. That is the secret of planting trees- to buy the right size for the given space. Some trees are suitable for containers, which can also limit their ultimate size. Try to buy burlap or balled plants instead of containerized. They can act as a windbreak and reduce noise pollution as well as bring a diverse range of wildlife into the garden.

Shrubs – all they need is a little pruning at the right time of year, which varies according to the plant. Take out deadwood and any branches that cross. Native shrubs will attract wildlife and will be suitable for your soil. Handsome, easy shrubs include *Ribes* and *Weigela*.

Perennials – the market is inundated with new plants every year. We are told to regularly douse them in chemicals for best flower production. Native plants need less maintenance and watering because they are adapted to the site. Whatever plants you choose they must be suited to your soil and aspect. Select native wildflowers and grasses and try to buy from a local nursery.

Quick Tips for Easy Maintenance

Know your soil type
Rid your garden of weeds
Water wisely
Mulch
Select easy-to-care-for plants
Remember right plant, right place
Reduce the size of the lawn
Select hedging that needs infrequent trimming
Plant in autumn
Small plants establish best
Groundcover chokes out weeds
Make a compost heap

Above: Yerba Buena Gardens; Left top: De Young Museum Garden; Below: Thames Barrier Park

Future gardens

Lessons from Urban Design

Practicality is one of the key components that render gardens useful, not just something to gaze upon. The garden has become a place to display artistic talent and creativity. So architects, artists and designers must marry the elements of the garden to one complete space that fulfils its practical object and is aesthetically pleasing at one and the same time. Integration is one lesson learned from new urban design.

Walter J. Hood Jr., is a landscape architect, Principal of Hood Design since 1993. He states that his design for the **De Young Museum** in Golden Gate Park, San Francisco is "an integration of urban and natural landscape with spaces that are an interaction between art and nature. Existing landscape features are retained. Thereby we have a double marriage, but not bigamy of urban space, the environment and art."

De Young Museum
The garden at the De Young Museum enlivens the landscape, standing in front of the futuristic rust-orange-copper structure of the museum, one is anchored back to earth by the axes of lines of palms with grasses, both lawn and ornamental at their feet, balancing the great height of the palms. There is a wonderful flow and rhythm to the planting and a great use of texture. The softness of *Stipa* is contrasted with the huge trunks of the palms. To one side a mass planting of *Scolopendrium* (fern) even rises with a set of utilitarian steps. The pond is majestic with its two bronze statues. Thought is given to contrasting materials used for the surface. Interesting plant supports are used here. The pyramidal structure is echoed by two white sphinxes. This is a very accessible public space – one that is immediately understandable with simple plants chosen for effect used in an intriguing manner. I do think it could have been more integrated with the architecture of the museum itself. I would have opted for masses of bronze plants in pyramidal shapes to link with the cantilevered sections of the museum. The attached sculpture garden is extremey small in scale, not enough space for the dynamics of the pieces exhibited. However, this is a regeneration of the Strybing, now re-named San Francisco Botanic Garden and an injection of new blood is most welcome.

Gardening has a part to play in providing open space in city centres that is safe for all. In **Lafayette**, Oakland, California, Hood transformed the last remaining downtown square troubled by homelessness and awaiting re-development. It is now a welcoming public green space.

Yerba Buena Gardens
A public park in San Francisco, where water plays an important part – falling in cascades, shooting from jets, overflowing and abundant water gives life to the gardens. Shade is provided by trees and by a large, wisteria-covered pergola covered with glass, at the highest point of this garden of many levels. Surrounded by large skyscrapers in the hub of downtown, this is a peaceful place where exotic plants such as *Canna* and *Cycas* (sago palm) mix with humble daisies, cyclamen and hydrangea. Structure is offered by clipped hedges and a large lawn as well as granite retaining walls. The greyish white granite is enhanced by the water, plants and also by large black containers handsomely planted. There are plenty of seats for enjoyment of the garden.

Thames Barrier Park, London
This really is a stunning urban garden. 22 acres are landscaped for different uses from flat expanses of lawn, benches and trees to contoured yew and maygreen hedges. Children will love to play in the fountain plaza where thirty-two dancing jets spurt water. The Green Dock was designed by Alain Cousseran and Alain Provost who selected colourful flowers, ornamental grasses and shrubs, adventurous planting inspired by the ever-changing river. It represents the former Prince Regent Dock. The plateau to either side of the dock is higher than the original. The 4.5 m high retaining walls are stabilized and irrigated to allow them to be clothed in plants, *Lonicera nitida* has been used to great effect. A micro-climate has been created where parallel herbaceous plants are balanced by green, wavy hedges and butterflies abound. Bridges cross the trench offering fantastic views. Large ornamental trees are grown in a grid pattern with wildflowers. At the end of the Green Dock there is a pavilion with irregular steel columns supporting a thin, slatted roof with clear polycarbonate and decking as a memorial to those who died in WWII from the local area, the London Borough of Newham. The Thames Path provides magnificent views of the Thames Barrier.

The park opened in 2000, described as the first riverside park in London for fifty years. The highly structured park is on a site that was for mixed industrial use including a chemical works, a dye works and an armaments factory. With the decline in industry, the site was in poor condition, the soil contaminated. During the 1980's and 1990's the London Docklands Development Corporation began to look at proposals for the site. In 1995, a competition was held for the design of the park. This is modern landscape design at its best with a sense of cohesion, a greening of the site.

Urban renovation includes calming green spaces. Well-designed parks, squares and streets give an image of civilization. What do we learn from urban development? Scale, use of open space, the relationship between buildings and objects, integration are all lessons evident in good urban design. Landscape design has much to teach us about how to garden in our backyard. Those vast admirable landscapes of Capability Brown and the way he so beautifully and seemingly effortlessly married the landscape with the house still have much to teach us, no matter what the scale of the house and garden. One cannot create a Brown landscape in a small garden, but one can marry the space with the house in another way, with a terrace. Surely we all have a yearning for a pleasant view from our home.

Deconstructivist

There is no way I could possibly conceive of this type of structure as a garden. However, it does have a place in modern society. If you have a very busy lifestyle, or are rarely at home or simply (heaven forbid) not a gardener and never will be, this method still makes use of the outdoor space as a 'room'.

This style is perhaps most suited to a person who is often away from home and does not wish to return to the nightmare of unkempt plants. More and more people will work from home and only occasionally visit their place of work. Many others, like me, are self-employed. If you are not at home with the garden, it is far more sensible to use the outdoor space than to leave it looking, untidy, neglected and useless. Use that space to create something that inspires you. For me, gardens make life worthwhile, but for you, if the deconstructivist idea appeals then create that space you feel at home in. Think of it as a useful space, a place to breathe, whether it is to draw, paint, think or just get out in the open.

Left: The Peace Gardens and the award-winning glasshouse in the Winter Gardens, Sheffield

Above: Chicago City Hall rooftop created in 2000
Below: Viking reconstruction in Labrador

Above: Life Expression Wellness Center, Sugarloaf, PA
created in 2001; Below: Turf roofs on the Faroe Islands

Below: Vancouver Library, B.C.

Below: Turf roofs.

The Living Roof

Green roofs have become a buzzword in gardening. The planet is sick and there is no cure. Urban areas have multiple problems with no immediate remedy. What can rid our cities of excess water, pollution and heat? What can re-oxygenate and provide green areas? The simple answer is plants. We need to bring greenery to the urban environment. The solution lies up on the roof. Studies have shown that a planted roof can provide enough oxygen to sustain one person for 24 hours. Smart city dwellers are going up on the roof for green space. Smart city leaders and planners are creating green roofs on Universities, libraries and corporate offices and buildings. Major cities across the world are greening up.

There are widely recognized environmental benefits. Green roofs are mainly planted with *Sedums*, contributing to sustainability. Handsome to look at, they provide insulation and also extend the life of the roof. Constant temperatures are maintained and rainfall absorbed thereby preventing storm water runoff. Air quality is improved whilst noise is reduced and wildlife attracted. The social benefits are enormous. This is the best way of turning a boring space into an environmentally sound, aesthetically pleasing, living landscape.

Flat green roofs can be extensive, which means they have a thin layer of growing material such as sedum matting or they can be intensive with a greater depth of soil which can sustain shrubs and even trees. Intensive green roofs need excellent support. Extensive green roofs are designed to be self-sustaining, requiring little more than a once-a-year feeding and fertilizing to boost growth. They can be established on a thin layer of rock wool. Amenity space is provided in what was one time considered no-zone gardening. Methods of construction are different for pitched green roofs and flat roofs.

Modern green roofing originated in Germany in the 1960's, today it is estimated that 10 per cent of roofs in Germany are greened. There are incentives in place in Chicago to encourage the use of green roofs. In 2004, 80 municipal or private green roofs were in place or planned, providing more than one million square feet of green roofs. Some of the best are **Soldier Field** (on top of the car park), **Millenium Park** and the **Chicago Center for Green Technology** (also a green building itself).

One of the largest green roofs is found at **Ford's River Rouge Plant** in Michigan, USA. An astonishing 42,000 square metres of assembly plant roofing is covered with *Sedum* and other plants. Paul Kephart of Carmel Valley's Rana Creek Restoration Ecology designed the Vancouver Convention Centre with a 6.5 acre roof garden. Kephart's vision is living architecture - 'incorporating vegetation into structural and landscape design'. The largest green roof in the USA is being created for the new **Academy of Sciences** in Golden Gate Park, San Francisco, expected to open in late 2008. Thirty-five plants were subjected to two years of testing with just five wildflowers and four herbaceous perennials making the grade. Life is tough at the top. The roof is an undulating 2.5 acres.

Of the *Sedum* type, one of my favourite projects is **The Life Expression Wellness Center** in Sugar Loaf, central Pennsylvania. The 6,000 sq ft roof was completed in 2001, an integral part of the green building proposed by Van der Ryn Architects and engineered by Roofscapes. The plants include *Allium schoenoprasm, Dianthus deltoides, and Sedums, S. acre, S. album 'Coral Carpet', S. floriferum, S. origanum, S. reflex, S. sarmentosum, S. sexangulare, S. spurium 'Fuldiglut'* and *'Tricolor'*.

Not available to public or staff at the moment, the **Vancouver Central Library** has one of the most beautiful green roofs I have seen. Designed by Cornelia Oberlander, it is almost the size of a football field. There are plans to open the garden, and all who see it will be lucky indeed. The river theme is obvious in the spectacular planting. The **European Investment Bank Building** in Luxembourg was designed by Italian architects Dr. B. Centola and Prof. M. Pozzoli. The green roof covers an area of 37,675 square feet on three levels. It won Green Roof of the Year Award in 2005. Sarnafil waterproofing membranes were used.

Today housing is no longer at one with nature. Yet, this innovation dates back hundreds of years, only now its implementation is on the increase. Early American pioneers created homes out of their environment, walls of sod, wooden roof construction covered with prairie grasses. Turf has been used for as long as people have built homes. In both Scandinavia and Iceland, there are examples of turf-roofed houses over 400 years old. Turf covered low buildings or mounds are also on the increase. Some Viking houses have been recreated in Labrador, built entirely of stone and turf.

They really are at one with nature, just emerging from the landscape. Grass roofs are a feature of many houses in the village of Bour in the Faroe Islands.

Pitched green roofs are a feature of many Scandinavian buildings. In 1914 a green roof was established at **Moos Lake** water-treatment plant, Wallishofen, Zurich, Switzerland. A meadow exists on the flat, concrete roofs of the filter tanks. In France, a large green roof of 6,500 square metres has been created at the museum **L'Historial de la Vendee** at Les Lucs Sur Boulogne.

In Egypt, soil-less agriculture is employed to grow plants on roofs, thereby eliminating the need for an insulating layer. Rooftops are being transformed into mini-kitchen gardens. At Al-Orman school in Cairo, strawberries are planted on the roof in space-saving, horizontal tubes. In Tanzania, green roofs keep buildings cool inside whilst the hottest temperatures soar outdoors.

Three bus shelters were greened in Sheffield, having their roofs planted, but although I have seen comments that this was highly successful and that the Groundwork Team who were involved in the pioneering venture are pressurizing the City Council for more, the roofs I saw were brown and looked dead just a few months after installation, they were then removed. Any surface is preferable to dead plants.

Green roofs do sometimes need maintenance as plants are growing in a much harsher environment. Plant selection is limited to low-growing, drought tolerant perennials with *Sedums* coming top of the list; grasses and herbs are suitable choices too. *Sedum* mats give ready cover but green roofs designed for biodiversity include shingle areas and grassland. Green roofs absorb up to 75% of rainfall. They improve air quality. The benefits of green gardening cannot be denied. Air-borne toxins are processed and a green roof re-oxygenates the atmosphere. It is a solution to the build up of heat in cities. Not only that but these green spaces are also therapeutic. Environmentally sound, but the green roof is more than that, it is still at the cutting edge of design, raising gardens to a new level whilst lowering power bills. In the humble back garden, it is more likely to be used to adorn the office, summerhouse or garden shed.

Above: Millenium Park, Chicago; Centre: Horniman Museum; Bottom: L'Historial de la Vendee

Future Trends

In England we may well have one foot in the present with toes gently testing the surface of the future, but we usually have the other foot firmly entrenched in the past. Most of the new ideas have an original basis, which may have come up to 40-50 years previously before being accepted. It is important to remind ourselves that garden design has changed owing to economic, environmental and ecological reasons. Over time, gardens have been created for diverse reasons with increased sophistication and individuality. Although fashion should be avoided at all times, in garden design and with regard to plants and other materials, it rears its head now and then. Far better to ignore it and create a garden reflecting your needs instead of the dictates of fashion.

Today there are much more demands on our time. Gardeners still want pretty gardens with traditional beautiful flowers such as roses, lavender, iris, peony and we are still, by and large, a nation of pastel lovers with regard to colour. The most successful show gardens are usually those with pretty flowers. Although they are popular, I would imagine it is only to gaze upon, for few want the work involved in creating such ephemeral beauty. We have already moved into an arena where foliage is now more dominant than flowers.

The basics of gardening have not changed but design is beginning to move rapidly into different areas to reflect different interests and the owner's personality. The second must-have is still scent. Somewhere along the line, scent often gets bred out of new hybrids. It has re-emerged as a desirable and popular component of gardens.

Veddw is a garden that has a sense of purpose and fits into its surroundings

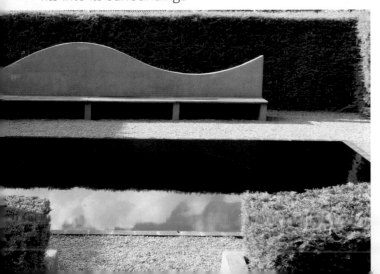

Colour remains just as important as in the days of Jekyll, but the emphasis, especially in England needs to move away from pastels. It took me 10 years to get black plants into the mainstream, and some of those plants have been around since the 1600's. Black has now taken its rightful place alongside other colours; it is no longer an outcast. It can be used in any situation, dry scheme or moisture-retentive soil; in any style from herbaceous to Japanese garden. My book, 'Black Magic and Purple Passion' has provided inspiration to thousands of gardeners across the world. For me plants are just as important as colour, each a part of a whole. Some separate the two, giving one more dominance. This must surely stem from the days of the Victorians when plants were considered trophies, understandable perhaps at the time, with so many new plants introduced at a great cost, and not only in financial terms but also in lives. Yet, each new hybrid today is launched with a fanfare hardly appropriate.

In the future plants, colour and texture will be increasingly used for effect, to stimulate and create an atmosphere. Their emotional and sculptural impact used dramatically, to communicate a purpose. Plant usage will change from the cluttered, crammed-in style to accent that enhances their sculptural qualities; softening and enriching the hardscape and structure of the garden. The number of different plants will decline. There will be more demands upon plants to cope with the changes in climate and needs of gardeners than any other element in the garden. Many of the natural, environmental styles from the end of the last century will continue to develop and predominate.

The concept of garden design has shifted too from an aesthetically pleasing design that suited the site to greater consideration for the personality of the garden owner and a greater understanding of habitat. Gardens have often been divorced from their surroundings, introspective and plant-led. Today's garden is more likely to be used for a purpose than to be merely admired; it is more personal in style. The manipulated 18th century English landscape garden linked to its surroundings but today's gardens attempt to be far more natural. Good modern design successfully demonstrates a sense of place. However, we must take note of elements outside our control that will affect the future of gardens the world over.

Climate Change

In their natural state, gardens help clean the air. They contribute to the oxygen supply. Plants can help prevent soil erosion. Tending a garden can help you health wise, it is a beneficial hobby that can provide you with flowers or food. However, we have to be careful what we put in the garden or it can be transformed into a cocktail of chemicals polluting the air. Climate change affects gardens the world over; in England possibly leading to longer growing seasons. Warmer winters with fewer frosts and less snow, will mean we can grow a wider range of plants. Hotter, drier summers will mean less water and we may have to cope with wetter winters. Gardeners will need to improve drainage in winter and improve irrigation in summer. Collection of rainwater, mulching and growing the right plants will become even more important.

In England hotter, drier summers will probably see a rise in the number of plants from arid climates. Although plants from southern and eastern Europe, South Africa and Australia are adapted to growing in arid climates and do not need so much water, they are not British natives. **Hyde Hall** in Essex, one of the RHS gardens, is situated in one of the driest areas of England. Some years it actually has a lower rainfall than Beirut, but of course, not the intense heat. **Beth Chatto's garden** is also in a dry area of Essex, near Colchester. Both have dry gardens demonstrating many plants that once established, will survive without artificial irrigation. Chatto's gravel garden has become one of the best known in England, demonstrating ecologically sound principles of planting. Climate change will have an effect on the plants we grow. Herbaceous borders, already considered the most time-consuming will face problems as many of the plants require deeply-cultivated, moisture-retentive, fertile soil. Plants such as *Asters, Delphiniums, Lupins* and *Phlox* may lose popularity. That icon of the English Garden – the lawn – the time-consuming, chemical-laden, water-gulping green square may disappear as we know it. The future might well see traditional lawns requiring year-round maintenance. Many will choose to go without it, others will adapt to slower-growing, coarser grasses. Southern counties may no longer be able to grow plants that require a winter chill to stimulate flower buds such as cherries. Bulbs such as snowdrops, crocus, bluebells and daffodils are not tolerant of mild winters.

Tulips, iris and cyclamen are tolerant of mild winters but not of winter wet. Likewise, plants that love cool summers such as Rhododendron, primulas, alpines and many conifers will struggle with higher summer temperatures. Beech and willow are exceptionally susceptible to drought and it is envisaged that prolonged summers will affect our native woodlands. Warmer, wetter winters will also see an increase of susceptibility to diseases with Yew, box and holly expected to suffer. This would affect the formal hedging in many heritage gardens.

Plants such as Asters and the time-consuming herbaceous border might be less popular in the future

Make Your Garden Greener

It is easier than you think. Natural alternatives to many nasties are available. We need to address the environmental issues and get closer to nature. A garden is an ecosystem. I believe many more gardeners will return to or begin growing their own vegetables organically as a way to ensure natural health and safe food. We will garden in tune with nature and stop trying to work against her. Naturalistic gardening will increase in popularity alongside native plants. Meadows will be a prominent feature. Gardens will be full of colourful plants whilst at the same time be low maintenance and also low on water requirements yet attractive to wildlife and organic. We will have to face climate change and adapt. We need to acknowledge that if we all do our own little bit, it adds up to a lot. There has been an alarming increase in the use of concrete and patio heaters in gardens in recent years. We need to think of the effect of what we use.

Avoid outdoor electrical goods – purchase goods that use solar energy instead. Avoid planting thirsty plants in dry borders – plant to suit your soil. Ensure you store rainwater by using a water butt. With a new build house, look into a rainwater harvesting system. Try to use appropriate materials in the garden – sustainable and locally-sourced are the best. Wood from renewable sources is a must. Peat sources have become depleted so look at coir as an alternative for growing plants. Recycled materials include reclaimed bricks, railway sleepers or reclaimed steel. We need to avoid using cement and concrete wherever possible. Cement the active ingredient in concrete uses a lot of energy and emits CO_2 in the process. Cement bulked out with large aggregates is being used to build greener houses. There are also recycled aggregates such as crushed waste concrete which can be used. Concrete is still cheaper than some alternatives, but the ultimate cost to the planet is far greater.

We really need to garden for the good of the earth. Be conscious of the planet and the damage we do in our everyday lives. We need to be environmentally aware.

Try out all the ideas here, and those under Xeriscaping for water conservation and native plants. See also the section on growing your own food - not only can you do this chemical free, but it also saves fuel costs on transport.

Peat

Peat bogs are precious wildlife sites and some help to control flooding, yet many have been depleted almost completely. Peat-free alternatives have been available for many years.

Avoid Garden Chemicals

The garden often uses chemicals harmful to humans, wildlife and the environment. Pesticides and wood treatments are some of the worst offenders. Garden organically, encourage wildlife and opt for low-toxicity timber treatments.

Avoid Creating Carbon Dioxide

Out in the garden in all temperatures? Consider a garden building or conservatory or simply wear thermals and extra clothing. Avoid using patio heaters, burning rubbish and bonfires. Compost and recycle instead.

Timber

Unsustainable timber products destroy forests around the world. This in turn affects the local environment and wildlife of each region. Look out for the FSC logo (Forest Stewardship Council), which ensures that timber is from sustainable sources. Do not accept other logos which might be fraudulent. You could also buy reclaimed timber products and recycle paper.

Plastics

Look for recycled plastics. The American Plastics Council's resource guide lists over 1200 products with recycled content. For the garden, they include hose pipes, flower pots, lawn edging, paving materials, tiles, tools, tree root barriers, bird feeders and tables.

Christmas

If you buy a tree, buy one with roots. When you have finished with it, either plant it in the garden or get it shredded. Many DIY centres now have facilities for shredding. Do not buy trees that have no roots. A live tree with its roots intact is far more environmentally friendly than plastic trees.

Composting

Composting reduces the amount of waste for collection and puts something back into the soil. It reduces the amount of landfill. If you do not have a compost bin, most local councils will collect garden waste for composting. Compost can also produce liquid fertilizer to feed your plants. Recycled plastic bins are available, but I prefer the wooden compost bins which are also relatively easy to make. Choose a bin with good air circulation. To make good compost you need alternate layers of waste. Grass, flower cuttings, dead leaves and weeds can all go into the compost bin. You can also add egg shells, vegetables and fruit, tea leaves, coffee grounds, straw and even paper bags and cardboard including egg boxes. Keep it moist but not wet. In Australia, community gardens make compost. In England, many local councils offer compost bins at a reduced rate. Use compost as a soil conditioner. You might also like to consider a wormery for use under the kitchen sink, They are odourless. The **Techniquest Science Discovery Centre** in Cardiff Bay, Wales has a walk-in wormery.

What to avoid when composting is the key to making good compost. Too much grass makes slime. Achieve a balance between grass and soft cuttings, food and woody material, shredding the latter first. Avoid fish, meat, cooked food, newspapers, glossy magazines and colour print, really persistent weeds, sawdust, wood shavings and timber treated with preservative.

Add at least 30cm (12") of composting material at a time. Weed the garden, mow the lawn, trim the hedge, dead-head the flowers, empty the kitchen bin and add those paper bags and egg boxes. The ideal layer is a few woody plant materials on the bottom, especially if you are using a recycled plastic bin. Alternate soft and tough items across the whole surface, firming down gently. Water well every 30-60cm (12-24"). Water when dry, or if too wet add some more dry material. It is often best to turn the heap when it begins to cool down. Compost can take from six weeks to one year to make. It is usable when it is brown and earthy-smelling.

Leaf mould is another option. It is best made in an open frame, such as a wire frame. Simply collect leaves and leave them for two years, turning at intervals and it makes wonderful rich loamy soil. Wet leaves can also be loosely tied in black plastic sacks. A small quantity of grass mowings can be incorporated.

Recycling

The garden is the ultimate recycling centre. Creating a new garden can mean re-using existing hard landscaping, even if it is dismantled and rebuilt in another area. Recycled materials are worn and used. They render the garden less formal and more appealing than when everything is brand spanking new. They are of great use in informal situations. Many gardeners make their own compost, a recycling feat. Others bury newspapers to improve soil, manure and so on. Many make pots from newspapers or old plastic yogurt pots or margarine tubs. Imagine making a whole garden from reclaimed artefacts. Think out of the box. Whilst many will know of railway sleepers which can make superb steps or even raised beds; objects can be as obscure as industrial cogs. Timber is the most obvious recyclable material, worn-in timber is always more appealing than when new imparting an established aura to the garden.

There is a wonderful Reclaim garden at Barnsdale that includes a distinctive water feature, the copper rose fountain amongst other recycled items. It was originally built for the Daily Express at the 1996 BBC Gardeners' World Exhibition. The garden includes an ornamental area and areas to grow fruit and vegetables.

I believe the health side of gardening will become more attractive and a lot more people will see the benefit of gardening and being in the fresh air. It beats the gym. You can grow healthy food and save a lot of money by doing so, but you can also tackle keeping trim and slim at the same time. If you don't have room to grow vegetables in your own garden, or you are garden-less, then try an allotment. Large plots of land are available from most local authorities for a very small annual fee.

By recycling waste, making compost and collecting rainwater, gardeners can do their bit for the environment. We can also help to protect wildlife habitats by not using chemicals and by growing plants that encourage wildlife. Gardening can be at the forefront of the lifestyle changes we need to make to adapt to climate change. We have to go without some of the things we regard as comfort. The industry has recently made this move into outdoor gardening as an entertaining space in a big way. It has encouraged use of materials and objects that might make life comfortable but at the same time harm the planet. The time to help conserve resources and protect the planet is now. The climate is dictating what we grow.

The Changing Face of the Garden Centre

The modern-day garden centre is rapidly changing from a dull place you went when you were 60 and thinking of retirement, to a trendier zone altogether. It's finally hip to garden. Younger people have decided to use their garden space but they don't want to know how to prune roses or graft a *Cercis*. In the emerging new garden centre, you are more likely to find ready-planted pots, so you don't even have to think about it. It's like the magic of Blue Peter - and here is one I made earlier. Great, you might think! This however, has a downside, a huge downside that all gardens will look the same. For me, individuality has always been top of my list of must-haves. The garden is a space upon which it is relatively easy to imprint your own creativity. It is a reflection of your personality. Although gardens can be very costly to create, especially if the space is large and you opt for expensive materials, it is easy to create a garden on a small budget, if you are prepared to do the work yourself. Nowadays we can shop for plants like we shop for food, it's all ready-made. The downer of ready-made gardens and plants in pots to go is that it takes away much of the skill. How many of those potted plants die within a week or two? However quick we want it, usually yesterday, it's best to learn a few basics. Dead plants put people off gardening; thereby the ready-made, instant gardening market is quickly lost. Beginners, who kill plants, soon believe that they just cannot garden. Potted up containers also demand a premium price. Garden centres are still far too full of environmentally unfriendly products such as gas-guzzling patio heaters that people buy without thinking just because the products are easily available and appear to offer a solution. Want to stay warm? Find an alternative to the patio heater. Garden centre owners and manufacturers need to re-think their product lines and supply environmentally-friendly goods. Peat, pesticides, patio heaters, plastics and unsustainable timber are still found in vast quantities in garden centres.
The image has changed for the better, but garden centres still have a long way to go yet. What we need is products that protect the environment, products for a greener garden. With the right plants, you do not need a zillion gadgets. Think sustainable.

Fabulous colour schemes and interesting plants are in fashion thanks to designers like Tom Stuart Smith who created this design for Laurent-Perrier at Chelsea

The New Gardener

The image of the gardener has changed too. It's no longer the archetypal Percy Thrower, cap in hand. The old man in the shed, is passé. The garden is no longer the haunt of the man either. Women often select plants and colour whilst men choose the hardscaping and if you are lucky do the work.

These days we are more conscious of the garden image. Designers have fuelled a revolution in colour, plants and gardens. Many gardeners are more plant conscious and savvy. Bedding is fast disappearing from all but public parks. Perennials and grasses are hip. Fashions come and go, but one thing is certain - a garden is not a garden without plants.

Outdoor Living

The garden has fast become the place to relax and as such, hot tubs have invaded the patio and even outdoor sauna rooms. The ultimate in luxury still has to be the swimming pool, relaxing yet healthy. Hammocks are a very popular feature in the garden. You no longer need two trees as most hammocks come with a stand. Perfect! All you have to master is how to get in and out without breaking any bones.

To sit in the garden is to view it at eye level but to have somewhere to look down adds a beautiful dimension. Hence the tower at Sissinghurst, the platform at Ness botanic garden. Alternatively this can be the means to view a borrowed landscape, such is the purpose of the podium in the garden in the film 'Ladies in Lavender', offering a supreme view of the sea. Similarly at **Plas Newydd**, Anglesey, the seats are set into recesses down a slope where one can contemplate the magnificent view over to Snowdonia.

The more time we spend outdoors in a climate like Great Britain, we need to consider ways of keeping warm so that the garden can be used when the weather is too cool to brave the outdoors. If you have room you can encompass various ideas to shelter from the storm. An open shelter is useful for respite from hot, blazing sun or from summer showers. Something more permanent is needed for the British climate to extend the period when the garden can be used as an outdoor room. Offices can be used in the garden to make a striking and useful feature. Estate agents (realtors) claim that these add up to triple their initial cost to the value of a home.

One of the most valuable design aspects of the garden is an outdoor room. Only limited by your imagination and pocket, there are endless possibilities here in this real growth area of the horticultural industry. Existing buildings are not too difficult to transform. Whatever structure you choose, give thought to maintenance of the chosen materials and also to the environment with regard to what you have in your outdoor room. A living roof would go a long way to creating a greener space.

Outdoor living is on the increase with entertaining or a quiet tête à tête later into the evening a must on the list of many working couples. Decking has risen dramatically in popularity and so too heaters. I used to laugh at the braziers used in Spain indoors under the table, as I always had visions of the whole table setting on fire. Think about the environment and make a sensible choice since the patio heaters that are rising alarmingly in popularity are also emitting greenhouse gases.

Furniture needs to fit in with the style of the garden. Comfort is top of the agenda. Seating can fit into the surrounding walls of raised beds if space is tight, or you can allow space for seating and dining area. For formal gardens, simple lines and geometric shapes work best. Style can sometimes look sculptural but some modern pieces are not made to sit in comfortably. Make sure there is room to push back the chairs from the table on any raised area or patio. You usually need one metre on all sides. For planted areas, make sure you can get to the plants. Containers too need to fit in with the design and be planted sympathetically. Large urns look good in borders even when empty.

A garden at Hampton Court Flower Show showing the pleasures of the outdoor life

Going greener - changes to make
Buy peat-free composts or better still make your own
Buy timber from sustainable sources only
Mulch to conserve water
Don't buy patio heaters or barbecues that use bottled gas
Don't tarmac or concrete over gardens
Use solar power for lighting
Use recycled products
Use water wisely
Use your garden to reduce carbon dioxide emissions from your house
Encourage deep roots
Plant a tree
Create a log pile in a shady corner
Create a sink, tub or pond
Don't use chemicals in the garden
Don't use pesticides
Don't use creosote or creosote-treated timber
Use natural products instead of plastic
Use a water barrel
Encourage wildlife into the garden
Garden with your environment
Green roofs and walls
Grow your own food
Recycle

Above: A living wall
Below: Beth Chatto's Garden, Essex

Make a rain garden
The emergence of rain gardens will gain momentum. Water is diverted from roofs and runs into a shallow depression in the garden planted with native plants. Rain soaks into the earth. The depression needs to be 10-15cm (4-6") deep, shallower for clay, and is best over an area of 150-300 square feet or for small gardens use the guideline of 30% of the roof area on clay soil and just 20% of the roof area on sandy soil. A rain garden needs a flat bottom; the dug-out soil can be used at the edges. Aim a down pipe at the depression. A steeply sloped site should not need a depression. Create one at least 3m away from the house and stay clear of retaining walls. Try to select natives, avoiding cultivars and tall plants. Mulch, water and weed until plants are established.

Innovation

Gardening can and should break new ground, but one has to be grounded. Can you live with it? That's the ultimate measure of the success of a garden design. Gardeners have a traditional streak. We can and should learn from what has gone before, but we need to look to the future and push the boundaries. We cannot rigidly stick to the past but by the same token we must never forget the purpose of the garden.

I believe what is new and just released in ornamental horticulture will largely lose its hold on many, who will see through the 'new introductions craze' when plants are only marginally different from what has gone before. So often they are the same plants with a different name tag. The appeal of highly hybridized plants will falter and lose its grip on modern horticulture. The trade needs to understand that if it supplies what gardeners need, it will survive and prosper. For 14 years now, as a consultant, I have been advocating the need for a change in the way plants are displayed and sold, the need for greater information. I know that consumers want the changes I am proposing. The industry seems to lack the impetus to make the change and so we see a fall off in sales and many companies falling by the wayside because they resist the inevitable change.

New is a difficult word. Everyone likes to think they are doing something new. We all borrow from what has been and hope that we can put a new slant on it. This is not a history lesson, but much of what we see has gone before. History repeats itself. By 1910 Frank Lloyd Wright showed that the modern lines of Robie House in Chicago could be extended to the outdoor space. Le Corbusier linked architecture to green space. In breaking new ground, perhaps that's where we need to look, or at least understand art and architecture and its place in the realm of the garden. Christopher Bradley-Hole trained as an architect. His design at the Chelsea Flower Show in 1997, the Virgil Garden offered a clean geometric structure of stark, almost white walls softened by perennial plants. So the art of the garden comes to the ordinary man and woman in the street ten years on. This new slant on modernism is predominant and will continue to be so.

Books on the modern garden talk about the turn of the 20th century, the 1930's and up to the 1980's. Artists such as Mondrian, architects like Le Corbusier and we can all see the cause and effect. Few talk about the future. Where is gardening going? Who will supply the innovation? Modern means the last century and radical often means impractical. We need a big push to get gardening into the 21st century. A time for renewal. Horticulture is coming back to its roots – a partnership with the natural world.

Thought needs to be given to the garden space. Even the fashion conscious cannot change their garden style as often as the indoor decoration in their home. Plants take time to grow so gardens take time to evolve.

Some striking new ideas I have seen include the facade of the **Musee de Quai Branly**, designed by Patrick Blanc, which opened in Paris in June 2006. The facade is a living sculpture of 800m^2, made with 15,000 plants from 150 species. Blanc, a botanist with the National Centre for Scientific Research has brought life to public buildings from Paris to Bangkok. Blanc, now creating a vertical garden 200m (600ft) high for a hotel in Kuala Lumpur, prefers to call his 'off the wall' creations, vegetation walls. It's one solution, and a very good one, to blank concrete. First exposed at the celebrated gardening festival of Chaumont-sur-Loire in 1995, his innovation is now trademarked. Blanc has received commissions from many private and public clients in France, U.S. and European cities. His next step is to go underground, to create vertical gardens in the Metro, parking lots or train stations, where one does not expect to see living plants. The key for vertical walls, as with green roofs, is selection of plants. The vertical walls by Blanc use tropicals. Plants can grow on a light, supporting system such as a specially built trellis that can withstand surface winds and drain readily. Blanc uses PVC boards with felt layers with punctured hose pipes for drip irrigation. Such plantings offer an alternative to cities clogged with poisonous fumes and lack of oxygen. Psychologically, the benefits are enormous - plants lift the spirits. The greening of our cities has never been more important and these ideas can be adapted.

The Green, Green Screen is brainchild of Astrid Klein and Mark Dytham and was seen at Omotesando in Tokyo for 3 years from 2003. The 275 metre long screen combined live plants and advertising panels to hide construction.

On a smaller scale, Rana Creek in the USA make living wall panels from metal. Open slots allow you to pop in succulents that appear to grow from the wall. Towering walls of plant life defy gravitation.

One of the concepts I am working on is to take the garden to higher levels. We all know and understand the vertical element but so far it has been limited to climbing plants, trellises and pergolas and the like. I am exploring innovative ways to take this further as a solution to those amongst us, me included, who complain about a lack of garden space.

Innovation is one way forward, but we must bear in mind function and practicality. The garden, especially the city garden has become the theatre for new techniques, materials and the imagination. Gardens have become much more individual like the inside of homes. Easily managed gardens are a necessity for the majority of gardeners. Simplicity is still the byword. Materials are readily available and many will opt to create a small haven in their outdoor space. Leisure time will be spent relaxing or entertaining and this will shape the gardens of the future. Gone are the days when most will choose to slave away to keep the lawn or borders pristine. Low maintenance plants will be in their supremacy. This does not mean a lack of plants or boring landscapes, but an exciting new look. If you are still mowing the lawn every week, feeding plants, watering containers twice a day in summer - you are wasting valuable resources. Garden with nature and in tune with your lifestyle.

Another aspect is working with the environment and education. More public gardens should educate, demonstrating sound principles. Beth Chatto's garden is a place to see plants growing in dry conditions; the Eden Project has underlying educational tones with plants useful to man being grown. It has more visitors than any other garden-related attraction but in many respects, it is more theme park than garden. However, its biomes were both innovative and practical. Botanic gardens with order beds show plants in families and plants are usually clearly labelled but in many eyes are too passe to visit. Botanic gardens need an injection of new ideas that appeal to the younger gardener. Teach your children to garden and instil a love of plants. Children are the future gardeners. Show them what fun gardening is. More public gardens and possibly private gardens will take on an educational role.

In a small setting, perhaps no-one has quite married the garden to its surroundings quite like Derek Jarman, the filmmaker. In his final years, Jarman wrote an evocative book about his home, **Prospect Cottage**, under the shadow of Dungeness nuclear power station. The bleak landscape is matched by the creativity of Jarman's garden. Faced with the challenging conditions, he produced a garden from 1987 until his untimely death with items borrowed from the sea and beach using plants adapted to survive in such harsh conditions. Pebbles, driftwood and stones intermingle with native plants in a garden that blends into the bleak landscape. His influence can be seen in many coastal gardens around the world.

Employing a clear design concept that links different parts of the garden together will bring the garden alive. Selecting plants ecologically ensures a link with the surroundings. Thinking about maintenance means that you end up with a garden that is easier to cope with. Giving consideration to the environment will improve not only our own lives but benefit the planet. Our gardens need to be green in more ways than one.

Below: Derek Jarman's Prospect Cottage At Dungeness

Suppliers

Slate
www.amslate.com
www.burlingtonslate.co.uk
www.welshslate.com
Australia
www.bellstone.com.au
www.slatestone.com.au
Germany
www.cns-naturschiefer.de
U.S.
www.americanslate.com
www.americanslategroup.com
www.universalslate.com

Aggregates
www.aggregain.org.uk
www.brett.co.uk
www.aggregate.com

Coloured asphalt
www.cornishlime.co.uk
www.Dandys.org
www.onlinegravel.co.uk
Australia
www.decorpebble.com.au
U.S.
www.aggregatesamerica.com

Stone
www.butterfieldnatstone.co.uk
www.longrakespar.co.uk
www.rock-unique.com
Australia
www.graniteworks.com.au
www.stonemerchants.com.au
www.yarrabee.com.au
U.S.
www.cambridgepavers.com
www.flooringwebsite.com
www.hawkbros.com

Granite
www.xhlstone.com
www.stonepaveuk.com
www.solopark.co.uk
Australia
www.graniteworks.com.au
U.S.
www.in-vermont.com
www.swensongranite.com

Astroturf
www.artificiallawn.co.uk
www.asgoodasgrass.co.uk
U.S.
www.astroturf.com
www.synlawn.com

Synthetic Materials
www.bayplastics.co.uk
www.gcip.co.uk
www.jaymart.net
U.S.
www.armorpoxy.com
www.smooth-on.com
www.polytek.com

Topsoil
www.norfolktopsoil.co.uk
www.rolawndirect.co.uk
www.turfonline.co.uk

Metal
www.expandedmetalcompany.co.uk
www.decorativemesh.co.uk
www.luxtrade.co.uk
www.victorian-lace.co.uk
Australia
www.wiremesh.com.au
U.S.
www.kentuckymetal.com
www.mcnichols.com
www.mechanicalmetals.com

Fencing and Trellis
www.ashleytimber.com
www.forestgarden.co.uk
Germany
www.dura-garden.de

Sculpture
www.brian-alabaster.com
www.craigclarke.com
www.davidharbersundials.co.uk

www.designs-in-stainless.co.uk
www.mark-stoddart.com
www.peterrandall-page.com
Australia
www.roberthague.com
www.studiomauriks.com
Europe
www.dorothee-wenz.de
www.uniquesteelart.com
www.vandansik.com
U.S.
//aftenie.com
www.negardenornaments.com
www.russelljacques.com

Ironwork
www.makingmetalwork.com
www.wessexforge.co.uk
New Zealand
www.treillage.co.nz
U.S.
www.ironwork.com
www.obrienironworks.com

Recycled glass
www.longrakespar.co.uk

Glass artists
www.amandalawrenceglass.com
www.artglass-uk.com
www.peterlaytonglass.co.uk
www.sandles-glass.co.uk
www.stainedglassartshop.co.uk

Glass blocks
www.luxcrete.co.uk
www.shackerley.com

Glass sheet
www.fusion-glass.co.uk

Solar Domes
www.solardome.co.uk

Wood (Australia)
www.hyne.com.au
www.pine.com.au
www.thatch.co.uk

Sleepers
www.hurdle.co.uk
www.londondecking.co.uk
www.fencestore.co.uk

Flooring Tiles
www.aldershaw.co.uk
www.hathernware.com
www.yorkhandmade.co.uk

Pots and Planters
www.exterior-interior.com
www.whichfordpottery.com
U.S.
www.counterbalancesculpture.com
www.seibert-rice.com
Canada
www.listoproducts.com

Garden Buildings
www.ardisdesign.co.uk
www.willowpool.co.uk
www.yurtshop.com
U.S.
www.daltonpavilions.com
www.rusticgardenstructures.com
www.summerwood.com

Outdoor Kitchen
www.fire-magic.co.uk
www.grovelands.com
U.S.
www.outdoorkitchen.com
Australia
www.outdoorkitchensolutions.com.au

Conservatories/Greenhouses
www.altongreenhouses.co.uk
www.robinsonsgreenhouses.co.uk
U.S.
www.renaissanceconservatories.com
www.private-garden.com
www.sbgreenhouse.com

Green Roofs
www.evergreenroofgardens.co.uk
www.greenroof.co.uk

U.S.
www.greenroofplants.com
www.greenroofs.com
www.greenroofs.org

Brick
www.flb.uk.com
www.baggeridge.co.uk
www.chelmervalley.co.uk

Reclaimed materials
www.mallgladeantiques.com
www.reclaimedbricks.com
www.reclaimed.co.uk
Australia
www.shivermetimbers.com.au

Paving
www.brett.co.uk
www.marshalls.co.uk
Australia
www.texipave.com.au

Decking
www.hld.co.uk
Canada
www.builddirect.com

Furniture
www.graniteplanet.co.uk
www.jakephipps.com
www.karenplatt.co.uk
www.moderngarden.co.uk
Australia
www.jensenjarrah.com
U.S.
www.agio-usa.com
www.cedarstore.com
www.centuryfurniture.com
www.dwr.com
www.gloster.com
www.kingsleybate.com
www.michaeltaylordesigns.com
www.munder-skiles.com

Electric Outdoor Lighting
www.johncullenlighting.co.uk
www.lightprojects.co.uk

Parasols and Umbrellas
www.shademakers.co.uk

Willow
www.bramptonwillows.co.uk
www.greatbritishhurdles.co.uk

Water
www.aquatics-direct.co.uk
www.bradshawsdirect.co.uk
www.croftstudios.co.uk
www.fountains-direct.co.uk
www.hozelock.com
www.williampye.com
U.S.
www.kineticfountains.com
Swimming Pools
www.goldenc.com

General
www.touchofmagic.co.uk
U.S.
www.charlestongardens.com
www.horchow.com
www.velocityartanddesign.com
www.walpolewoodworkers.com

Plants
Colour
www.blackplants.co.uk
www.karenplatt.co.uk
Topiary
www.topiaryshop.co.uk
www.entirelytopiary.co.uk
www.hedgingandtopiary.co.uk
www.seagravenurseries.co.uk

Hedging
www.bucknur.com
Lawns
USA
www.eartheasy.com

Gardens to visit
In order from main sections

Japanese Gardens
Kew RBG
Kew, Richmond
Surrey TW9 3AB

Kyoto Garden, Holland Park, London

Pine Lodge
Holmbush, St Austell, Cornwall

Japanese Garden Bonsai Nursery
St.Mawgan, Nr Newquay,
Cornwall TR8 4ET

Tatton Park
Knutsford, Chesire, WA16 6QN

Japanese Friendship Garden of San Diego
2215 Pan American Road San Diego, CA 92101, USA

Japanese Garden,
Butchart Gardens
800 Benvenuto Ave, Brentwood Bay, BC. V8M 1J8, Canada

Japanese Garden,
611 S.W. Kingston Ave. Portland, Oregon 97205, USA

Yao Japanese Garden
Bellevue Botanic Garden
12001 Main Street Bellevue,
WA 98005, USA

Japanese Tea Garden
Golden Gate Park
San Francisco CA 94118, USA

Museums
Geffrye Museum
136 Kingsland Road
Shoreditch London E2

Weald and Downland Museum
Singleton Chichester West Sussex PO 18 0EU

Several Styles
Mapperton
Beaminster Dorset DT8 3NR

Medieval Gardens
Bede's World
Church Bank
Jarrow Tyne & Wear NE32 3DY

Dean's Court
Wimborne Minster
Dorset BH21 1EE

Norton Priory Museum & Gardens,
Tudor Road, Manor Park,
Runcorn, Cheshire WA7 1SX.

Prebendal Manor House
Nassington Nr Peterborough
PE8 6QG

Queen Eleanor's Garden
The Great Hall, Winchester,
Hampshire SO23 8PJ

Tudor Gardens
Buckland Abbey. Yelverton,
Devon PL20 6EY

Cawdor Castle
Nairn Scotland IV12 5RD
Helmingham Hall Gardens
Helmingham Stowmarket
Suffolk IP14 6EF

Holdenby House
Northampton, NN6 8DJ

Little Moreton Hall
Congleton, Cheshire CW12 4SD

Lytes Cary Manor
nr Charlton Mackrell,
Somerton, Somerset TA11 7HU

Lyveden New Bield
nr Oundle,
Peterborough, Northamptonshire
PE8 5AT

Montacute House
Montacute, Somerset TA15 6XP

Owlpen Manor
Near Uley Gloucestershire
GL11 5BZ

Packwood
Lapworth, Solihull,
Warwickshire B94 6AT

Pitmedden
Ellon, Aberdeenshire, AB41 7PD

Plas Mawr
High Street, Conwy,
Caernarfonshire), North Wales

Red Lodge
Park Row Bristol BS1 5LJ

Tudor House Museum
Bugle Street
Southampton SO14 2AD
Hampshire

Renaissance & Restoration
Aberglasney Gardens
Llangathen Carmarthenshire
SA32 8QH

Boscobel House
Shropshire - ST19 9AR

Bramham Park
Wetherby,
West Yorkshire LS23 6ND

Castle Bromwich Hall Gardens
Chester Road,
Castle Bromwich. Birmingham,
B36 9BT

Grimsthorpe Castle
Bourne PE10 0LY

Cranborne Manor House
Cranborne Dorset, BH21 5PS

Haddon Hall
Bakewell
Derbyshire DE45 1LA

Ham House
Ham Street, Ham,
Richmond-upon-Thames
Surrey TW10 7RS

Hampton Court Palace
East Molesey Surrey KT8 9AU

Hatfield House
Hatfield Hertfordshire AL9 5NQ

Kenilworth Castle
Castle Green
Kenilworth
Warks CV8 1NE

Levens Hall
Kendal Cumbria LA8 0PD

Moseley Old Hall
Moseley Old Hall Lane,
Fordhouses, Wolverhampton,
Staffordshire WV10 7HY

Museum of Garden History
Lambeth Palace Road,
London,
SE1 7LB

Pimedden
nr ellon
Aberdeenshire
Scotland

Powis Castle
Welshpool, Powys SY21 8RF

Queen's Garden, see Kew

Westbury Court Gardens
Westbury-on-Severn,
Gloucestershire GL 14 1PD

Georgian and Regency Gardens
Georgian Garden
4 The Circus, Gravel Walk, Bath

English Landscape Movement
Adlington Hall
Mill lane, Adlington, Macclesfield,
Cheshire SK 10 4LF

Blenheim Palace
Woodstock Oxfordshire OX20 1PX

Castle Howard
York, North Yorkshire
YO60 7DA

Chiswick House
Burlington Lane, W4 2RP

Claremont Landscape Garden
Portsmouth Road, Esher,
Surrey KT 10 9JG

Duncombe Park
Helmsley York
North Yorkshire YO62 5EB

Euston Hall
Estate Office, Euston,
Thetford, Norfolk, IP24 2QP

Farnborough Hall
Farnborough, Banbury,
Warwickshire OX 17 1DU

Goldney Hall
Lower Clifton Hill, Bristol,
BS8 1BH

Kensington Gardens
Magazine Gate, Kensington
Gardens, London W2 2UH

Mount Edgcumbe House
Cremyll Torpoint Cornwall
PL 10 1HZ

Painshill Park
Portsmouth Road, Cobham,
Surrey, KT 11 1JE

Painswick Rococo Garden
Painswick Glos GL6 6TH

Petworth House
Petworth, W.Sussex. GU28 0AE

Plas Newydd
Llanfairpwll, Anglesey LL61 6DQ

Prior Park Landscape Garden
Ralph Allen Drive,
Bath, BA2 5AH

Raby Castle
Staindrop, Darlington,
Co. Durham, DL2 3AH

Rousham House
nr Steeple Aston
Bicester Oxfordshire OX25 4QX

Stourhead
Stourton, Warminster, Wiltshire
BA 12 6QD

Stowe Landscape Gardens
Buckingham, Buckinghamshire
MK 18 5EH

Studley Royal Water Garden
Ripon Nr Harrogate
North Yorkshire HG4 3DY

West Wycombe Park
West Wycombe,
Buckinghamshire HP 14 3AJ

Wrest Park Gardens
Silsoe
Bedfordshire - MK45 4HS

Victorian Gardens
Arley Hall
Northwich, Cheshire. CW9 6NA

Ascog Hall
Ascog
Isle Of Bute
PA20 9EU Scotland

Biddulph Grange
Grange Road, Biddulph,
Staffordshire ST8 7SD

Brodsworth Hall
Brodsworth
South Yorkshire - DN5 7XJ

Cragside
Rothbury. Morpeth
Northumberland
NE65 7PX

Drummond Castle
Muthill, Crieff, PH5 2AA

Erddig
Wrexham LL 13 0YT

Glendurgan
Mawnan Smith, nr Falmouth
Cornwall TR 11 5JZ

Gwydir Castle
Llanrwst North Wales LL26 0PN

Harlow Carr
Crag Lane, Harrogate,
N. Yorkshire HG3 1QB

Larmer Tree Gardens
Tollard Royal
Salisbury Wiltshire SP5 5PT

Osborne House
Isle of Wight
PO32 6JY

Sheffield Botanic Gardens
Clarkehouse Road,
Sheffield, S 10 2LN

Shugborough Hall
Shugborough Estate, Milford,
Near Stafford, ST 17 0XB

Spetchley Park
Worcester, Worcs, WR5 1RS

Waddesdon Manor
Waddesdon Nr Aylesbury
Buckinghamshire HP 18 0JH

Cottage Gardens
Alfriston Clergy House
The Tye, Alfriston, Polegate,
East Sussex BN26 5TL

Barnsdale Garden
The Avenue, Exton,
Oakham, Rutland LE 15 8AH

Chiffchaffs
Chaffeymoor.
W end of Bourton village,
nr Wincanton, Somerset

Dorneywood Garden
Dorneywood, Burnham,
Buckinghamshire SL 1 8PY

East Lambrook Manor
South Petherton,
Somerset, TA 13 5HH

Gant's Mill
Bruton, Somerset, BA 10 0DB

Lower Severalls
Crewkerne Somerset TA 18 7NX

RHS Rosemoor
Rosemoor, Great Torrington,
North Devon EX38 8PH

Arts and Crafts Gardens
Barrington Court
Barrington, nr Ilminster,
Somerset TA 19 0NQ

Bodnant Gardens
Tal-y-Cafn Nr
Colwyn Bay, Conwy LL28 5RE

Cothay Manor Gardens
Greenham,
Nr Wellington Somerset TA21 0JR

Eaton Hall Gardens
Eccleston
Chester
CH4 9ET

Great Dixter
Northiam Rye East Sussex
TN31 6PH

Great Fosters
Stroude Road, Egham, Surrey
TW20 9UR

Hestercombe Gardens
Cheddon Fitzpaine, Taunton
Somerset TA2 8LG

Hidcote Manor Garden
Hidcote Bartrim, nr Chipping
Campden, Gloucestershire
GL55 6LR

Munstead Wood
Heath Lane, Busbridge,
Godalming, Surrey, England

Rodmarton Manor
Cirencester,
Gloucestershire, GL7 6PF

Sissinghurst Castle Garden
Sissinghurst, nr Cranbrook, Kent
TN 17 2AB

Tintinhull
Farm Street, Tintinhull, Yeovil,
Somerset BA22 8PZ

20th century gardens
An cala
Isle of Seil Argyll PA34 4RF

Festival of Britain, Battersea Park
Prince of Wales Drive, Battersea,
London SW3

The Peto Garden
Iford Manor Bradford on Avon,
Wiltshire

Portmeirion
Gwynedd,
LL48 6ET, Cymru/Wales.

Renishaw Hall
Renishaw, Sheffield. S21 3WB

Trentham Leisure
Stone Road, Trentham,
Stoke on Trent ST4 8AX

Homewood
Portsmouth Road, Esher
Surrey KT 10 9JL

Denmans
Denmans Lane, Fontwell,
West Sussex, BN 18 0SU

Veddw House
Devauden, Monmouthshire,
NP 16 6PH

Sculpture Gardens
Barbara Hepworth Garden
Barnoon Hill
St Ives Cornwall TR26 1AD

Cass Sculpture Foundation
Sculpture
Estate Goodwood Chichester
West Sussex PO 18 0QP

Chatsworth House and Gardens
Chatsworth Bakewell Derbyshire
DE45 1PP

Gibberd Garden
Marsh Lane, Gilden Way
Harlow, Essex. CM 17 0NA
Newby Hall
Estate Office, Newby Hall, Ripon,
North Yorkshire, HG4 5AE.

Yorkshire Sculpture Park
West Bretton Wakefield WF4 4LG

AUSTRALIA
Australian Garden
RBG Cranbourne
Cnr Ballarto Road and Botanic
Drive Cranbourne (off South
Gippsland H'way)

Buda Historic Garden
42 Hunter St
Castlemaine 3450

Chinese Garden of Friendship
Southern End
Darling Harbour. Sydney

Everglades
37 Everglades Avenue
Leura NSW

Fernbrook Garden
2 Queen Street, Kurrajong
Heights, NSW 2758

Heronswood
105 Latrobe Pde Dromana, 3936
Victoria

Hopweood Estate
Centennial Road, Bowral NSW
2756

Katandra Gardens
49 Hunter Road, Wandin, Victoria

Karkalla
Sorrento
Victoria (Check the AOAG)

Queen Victoria Gardens
Domain Parklands
St. Kilda Road. Melbourne

Sydney Botanic Garden
Mrs Macquaries Road Sydney
NSW 2000, Australia Phone: 02-
9231 8111

Vaucluse House
Wentworth Road, Vaucluse
Telephone: +61 2 9388 7922

Jim Fogarty Design Pty Ltd
Ground Floor, 61 Station
Street Malvern, Victoria, 3144
Australia
www.jimfogartydesign.com.au

BELGIUM
Freyr Castle and Gardens
B 5540 HASTIERE, BELGIUM

Royal Greenhouses
Avenue du Parc Royal
Domaine Royal de Laeken 1020
Laeken

BRAZIL
Sitio Roberto Burle Marx
Estrada de Guaratiba, 2019 Rio de
Janeiro 23020-240 Brazil

CANADA
Annapolis Royal Historic Gardens
441 St. George Street Annapolis
Royal, NS B0S 1A0

Butchart Gardens
800 Benvenuto Avenue
Brentwood Bay
BC V8M 1J8

FRANCE

Vaux-le-Vicomte
77950 Maincy, Ile-de-France

Versailles
Ile de France

Villandry
37510 Villandry

Le labyrinthe
Jardin des Cinq Sens
Rue du Lac F-74140 Yvoire

Fontainebleau
S. of Paris

Luxembourg Gardens
Paris

Tuileries
Adjacent to Louvre
Paris

Monet's Garden
Rue Claude Monet, 27620
Giverny

Parc Andre Citroen
Quai André-Citroën 75015 –
PARIS

Musee Zadkine
100 Rue d'Assas
Montparnasse, Paris

GERMANY

Herrenhausen Gardens
Hannover, Niedersachsen,

Schleissheim New Palace
Schloss- und Gartenverwaltung
Schleißheim Max-Emanuel-Platz
1 85764 Oberschleißheim

Schwetzingen
Heidelberg

HOLLAND

Hortus Botanicus
Plantage Middenlaan 2a
Amsterdam

Hortus Botanicus
Rapenburg 73
Leiden

Hortus Bulborum
Zuidkerkenlaan 23A
NL-1906 AC
Limmen

Keukenhof
Stationsweg 166a 2161 AM Lisse

Palais Het Loo
Koninklijk   Park   1 7315   JA
Apeldoorn

Mien Ruys Tuinen
Dedemsvaart

Piet Oudolf
Broekstraat 17
6999 dE Hummelo

ITALY

Villa Lante
Via J Barrozzi, 71
01031 Bagnaio (Viterbo)

Villa d'Este
Piazza Trento, 1
00019 Tivoli (Rome)

Villa Rotunda
Vicenza, Veneto 30030

Villa Gamberaia
Via del Rossellino, 72
50135 Florence

Villa Garzoni
Via di Castello
51014 Collodi (PT)

MOROCCO

Majorelle Gardens, Marrakesh

RUSSIA

The   Peterhof   State-Museum
Reserve 198516, St. Petersburg,
ul.Razvodnaya, 2 Russia

SPAIN

The Alhambra
Calle   Real   de   la
Alhambra, s/n 18009 Granada

Alcazar
Plaza del Triunfo. Sevilla

Casa de los Pilatos
Plaza de Pilatos. Sevilla

Parque Maria Luisa
Plaza de Espana. Sevilla

The Great Mosque
Calle Cardinal Herrero
Cordoba

Parc Guell
Calle Olot, 7 08024 Barcelona

USA

Dumbarton Oaks
R and 32nd Street,
Georgetown
Washington DC

Robie House
5757 S. Woodlawn Avenue,
University of Chicago campus,
Chicago, IL

Fallingwater
Rural Route 1
Mill Run. PA

Lakewold Gardens
12317 Gravelly Lake Drive
Lakewood, WA 98499

Bloedel Reserve
7571 NE Dolphin Drive, Bainbridge
Island, WA 98110

Chicago Botanic Garden
1000 Lake Cook Road, Glencoe, IL
60022

Center for Medieval Studies
mail: S409 Burrowes Building
Pennsylvania   State   University
University Park, PA 16802

Agecroft Hall
4305 Sulgrave Road, Richmond,
Virginia 23221

Glebe House Museum
Hollow Road P.O.
Box 245 Woodbury, CT 06798

Heart Castle
750 Hearst Castle Road,
San Simeon, CA 93452-9741

Lloyd Border
Whiteflower farm
P.O. Box 50, Route 63 ~ Litchfield,
Connecticut 06759

Tryon Palace Historic Sites &
Gardens 610 Pollock Street, P.O.
Box 1007 New Bern, NC 28563

Fort Worth Water Gardens
Fort Worth
Texas

Dan Weedon
DW/LA   Landscape   Architects
Venice CA 90291

Future Gardens
De Young Museum
50 Tea Garden Dr. San Francisco,
CA, 94118

Yerba Buena Gardens
760 Howard St. San Francisco,
CA 94103

Beth Chatto
Elmstead Market
Essex

Eden Project
Bodelva, St Austell,
Cornwall, PL24 2SG

Thames Barrier Park
North Woolwich Road
London E 16 2HP

Japanese Tea Garden, San Francisco

Photo Credits

All photos and watercolors P. 131-2 © Karen Platt unless noted below.
Front cover and P.13 © Hadrian Garden Design, hadriangardendesign.com; P.14, 223 © Charles Hawes, veddw.co.uk; P.31 © Prebendal Manor; P.85 © Steven Wooster, garden design and photo; P.88 © Lizzie Taylor/Dawn Isaac, designing-gardens.co.uk; P. 95, 99 © Jim Fogarty design; P.126 © Clifford Public Relations; P.137, 164 © Brian Makin, counterbalancesculpture.com; P.157 © Rooftop Garden. Richard Marti Garden Architecture, rmgardendesign.com; P.163: EcoHouse © The Garden Escape, thegardenescape.co.uk; P.169 bl , br © moderngardencompany.com; P.179 photo courtesy of David Kaye; P.217 © Joshua Coventry; P220 Chicago City Hall and Lewc, © Roofscapes Inc., roofmeadow.com;
P220 Vancouver, American Hydrotech, Inc., hydrotechusa.com

Public Domain:
Levens Hall in 1880 from Morris' Country Seats, p.42
Blenheim Palace, Boddah, P.58
The Palladian Bridge, Stowe Gardens, Peter Dean, P.58

Creative Commons:
Sissinghurst Castle, by Eric, P.16, Labyrinth at Garfield Conservatory, USA, Tammy Green, P.35; The Elizabethan Garden, Kenilworth Castle, P.39: Maze, Getty gardens, USA, Emily, P.39; Haddon Hall, Astrowoosie, P.41; Studley Royal Water Garden and gothic folly, by Rachel and Ben Dearlove, July 2004, P.50; Waddesdon Manor, Foshie, P.65; Great Dixter Meadow, Miles Berry, P.91; Ecohouse, John Bointon, P.94; Red Sand Garden and Ephemeral Lake Sculpture, Australian Garden, RBG Cranbourne, Victoria, Australia by John O'Neill. P.96

Royal Greenhouse, Belgium by Jean-Pol Grandmont, P.100; Schwetzingen, Beketchai, P. 11; Villa Rotunda, by Philip Shafer, P. 116; Villa d'Este, Italy Gargoyle Fountain, Sue Hutton, P.117 Villa Garzoni, Aloa, P.117; Villa Lante Zac mc P.117Majorelle, by Luc Viatour P 18; Alhambra, Spain by Philip Capper P.121; Alcazar, Sevilla, Ruth Lozano, P.121; Generalife, Granada, Janex, P.121; Alcazar, Cordoba Ulybug , P.121; Guell Park, by Deror, P.122; Dumbarton Oaks, John Weiss, P.125, Imperial Palace East Garden, Tokyo, John Weiss P.2; Hearst Castle, by Michael Darter, P.125; Frank LLoyd Wright's Taliesin West, Arizona, Lumierefl, P.125 P.220 Faroe Islands, Erik Christensen; Viking recreation, Dylan Kereluk; Ósvör Fishing Museum at Bolungarvik, Iceland, Herbert Ortner, Vienna, Austria; P.222 Chicago Millenium Park, Sookie; Horniman Museum roof; Robert BrookVendee, Le lucs, by Simon Garbutt; P.229 Living Wall, Toby Oxborrow; Beth Chatto Garden, King Coyote; P.231 Derek Jarman's Prospect Cottage, Tim Brighton

Wikipedia, GNU Free Documentation Licence
Stourhead, Daderot , P.58, Hidcote Manor, by Vashi Donsk, P.78; Van Dusen Botanic Garden, Vancouver, by Stan Shebs, P.101 French Parterre, Loire by Daderot, P.106: Peterhof, by Marti Mustonen and Peterhof, by Togukawapants P. 19 Guell Park Dragon, by Fiachs, Guell Park, entrance, by Marc Desbordes, Guell Park Bird's Nest Walk, by Gottfried Hufnagel P. 122

Acknowledgements:

In gratitude to all who open their gardens to the public.
With immense thanks for my son's technical ability at all hours, without whom typography, photos and the appearance of the book would not be the same